D0478104

New Ways in English for Specific Purposes

Peter Master and Donna M. Brinton, Editors

WITHDRAWN
UTSA LIBRARIES

New Ways in TESOL Series II

Innovative Classroom Techniques

Jack C. Richards, Series Editor

TESOL

Founded 1966

Teachers of English to Speakers of Other Languages, Inc.

Library
University of Texas
at San Antonio

Typeset in Garamond Book and Tiffany Demi
by Capitol Communication Systems, Inc., Crofton, Maryland USA
and printed by
Pantagraph Printing, Bloomington, Illinois USA

Teachers of English to Speakers of Other Languages, Inc. (TESOL)
1600 Cameron Street, Suite 300
Alexandria, VA 22314 USA
Tel 703-836-0774 • Fax 703-836-7864 • e-mail: publ@tesol.edu • http://www.tesol.edu

Director of Communications and Marketing: Helen Kornblum
Managing Editor: Marilyn Kupetz
Copy Editor: Ellen F. Garshick
Cover Design: Ann Kammerer

Copyright © 1998 by Teachers of English to Speakers of Other Languages, Inc.

Part title images copyright © 1997 by Photodisc, Inc.

All rights reserved. No part of this publication may be reproduced or transmitted in any form or by any means, electronic or mechanical, including photocopy, or any informational storage or retrieval system, without permission from the publisher.

Every effort has been made to contact the copyright holders for permission to reprint borrowed material. We regret any oversights that may have occurred and will rectify them in future printings of this work.

ISBN 0-939791-49-8
Library of Congress Catalogue No. 98-060381

Library
University of Texas
at San Antonio

Contents

Acknowledgments

This is the second volume in TESOL's New Ways series that we have coedited. Compiling such a volume is a rewarding task due to the new professional friendships that result and the many stimulating interactions that one has with the contributors and the editorial staff. It is also quite a challenging task: Contributions arrive in a wide variety of word-processing formats via fax, e-mail, Express Mail, and snail mail from all corners of the globe and must be translated into readable form; there are also countless details to attend to, such as clarifying the author's intent and tracking missing references or permissions. The project has had a long "birthing" process due to these complications. We hope that the contributors can forgive the lengthy production time and that they and the volume's readers will enjoy the final product.

This project would not have seen completion without assistance and encouragement from a number of individuals. We would especially like to single out the following: Jack Richards, the New Ways II Series Editor, who conceived of the volume and convinced us to coedit the volume; Marilyn Kupetz, TESOL's Managing Editor, who gave much-needed expert guidance at every stage of the project; Ellen Garshick, who patiently, painstakingly, and professionally copy edited the manuscript; and, perhaps most importantly, our many colleagues around the world who so generously shared their ideas and expertise to co-construct this volume.

Sincere thanks are due to our home departments (the Department of Applied Linguistics & TESL at the University of California, Los Angeles, and the Department of Linguistics and Language Development at San José State University), which provided financial support for outgoing mail, e-mail, faxes, and telephone calls.

Introduction

English for specific purposes (ESP) arose in the early 1960s in response to the need for improved communication between the developed and developing countries of the world (Hitchcock, 1978). It led the English language teaching (ELT) profession to realize that the English language was desired "not for the purpose of spreading British or American social and cultural values but as a natural link within multi-cultural, multi-lingual societies as a vehicle for international communication, as a global carrier-wave for news, information, entertainment and administration, and as the language in which has taken place the genesis of the second industrial and scientific revolution" (Strevens, 1977, p. 89). This global state of affairs, in conjunction with the increasing recognition of the need for relevance in ELT and the work of William Labov, Dell Hymes, and John Gumperz on language in social contexts, all came together under the rubric *ESP*, English for special (now specific) purposes (Master, 1985).

As the coeditors of *New Ways in Content-Based Instruction*, we agreed to oversee this volume largely because we did not want to give the impression that ESP was subsumed by content-based instruction (CBI). We had also received a few submissions to the CBI volume that we thought were clearly oriented more toward ESP than toward CBI, and we wanted to be able to divide the submissions accordingly. This raised the question of what the boundary is between CBI and ESP.

In our view, CBI is a type of syllabus, the organizing principle on which a curriculum is based. It joins the other types of syllabi recognized in the field, namely, the grammatical, the notional-functional, the rhetorical, and the task-based syllabus. The organizing principle is the content or subject matter on which any implementation of CBI (i.e., adjunct, sheltered, and thematic courses) is based. ESP, on the other hand, is a division of ELT that has only one other member, namely, English for general purposes (EGP). ESP makes extensive use of the content-based and the task-based, and varying use of the grammatical, notional-functional, and rhetorical syllabi.

In other words, there is no "boundary" between ESP and CBI; instead, they operate independently because both ESP and EGP may make use of any of the syllabi (Master, 1997/1998).

The division of contributions into ESP and CBI thus became a rather arbitrary one, and we had to determine our own principle for making the choice. Our solution was to include in the ESP volume those submissions that were specifically linked to an acknowledged subdivision of ESP, such as English for academic purposes (EAP), English for science and technology (EST), and English for vocational purposes (EVP), and to put all others (many of which were EAP related) into the CBI volume, where the submissions were classified by task (i.e., information management, critical thinking, hands-on activities, data gathering, and text analysis and construction).

The contributions in this volume come from 14 countries representing every continent on the globe (Argentina, Australia, Brazil, Finland, France, Hong Kong, Japan, Korea, Slovenia, Malaysia, Spain, the United Kingdom, the United States, and Zimbabwe). They are divided into the following specific subdivisions of ESP:

- Part I, General English for Specific Purposes: English taught in a variety of ESP settings with no specific focus, including preparing for professional meetings, using the Internet, using specific elements of grammar, and so on
- Part II, English for Academic Purposes: English taught within an academic setting, often concerned with academic reading and writing, study skills, test-taking strategies, listening and note-taking techniques, and cognitive mapping for content/lecture comprehension
- Part III, English for Art and Design: English taught within an art school, school of design, or department of art or design, usually concerned with art history and the language of the studio
- Part IV, English for Business and Economics: English taught within a company, business school, or professional/corporate setting, usually concerned with effective communication and negotiation in meetings, technical and business writing, workplace idioms and vocabulary, and business customs and culture

- Part V, English for Legal Purposes: English taught within a law school, law office, or other legal setting, usually concerned with written cases and judgments, lawyer-client consultation, legislation, contracts, and agreements (Bhatia, 1993)
- Part VI, English for Science and Technology: English taught within an academic science or engineering department, a laboratory, a scientific or technological company, or any other scientific or technical setting, usually concerned with reading and writing technical reports (particularly research reports, proposals, feasibility studies, and lab reports), with technical oral communication, and with the understanding and use of subtechnical and some technical vocabulary
- Part VII, English for Vocational Purposes: English taught within the workplace, factory, adult school, or other vocational setting, usually concerned with the finding and keeping of a job, training procedures, tools and equipment, quality control, safety and health concerns, worker's rights, advancement, and relationships with coworkers, employers, and customers (West, 1984)

Another important subdivision of ESP is English for medical purposes. Because we received only two submissions in this area, they are included in Part I and Part VII.

Each contribution follows a standard, easy-to-follow format. In the scholar's margin is information pertaining to the level of student for whom the activity is designed, its instructional goals or aims, the estimated preparation and class time needed, and the resources required. This information is followed by a summary of the activity and step-by-step procedures for the teacher to follow. Any additional suggestions or tips that the contributor wishes to pass on to users are contained in Caveats and Options, and the References and Further Reading section contains useful sources for follow-up. The Appendixes generally contain classroom handouts demonstrating how the suggested activity was applied to a specific classroom with a given set of learners. These materials are samples only and should be adapted as necessary for a particular classroom. Finally, the Contributors section provides brief biographical information on the author(s).

None of the activities included in this volume is a recipe to follow exactly. We encourage readers to experiment, like good cooks, by adding their own ingredients to spice up an activity and adapt it to suit the needs and interests of their learner population.

References

Bhatia, V. K. (1993). *Analyzing genre: Language use in professional settings*. London: Longman.

Hitchcock, J. (1978). Reading and scientific English: Prospects, problems, and programs in Iran. In M. T. Trimble, L. Trimble, & K. Drobnic (Eds.), *English for specific purposes: Science and technology* (pp. 9–52). Corvallis: Oregon State University.

Master, P. (1985). The development of ESP. *CATESOL News, 17*(2), 15, 19; *17*(3), 12, 15.

Master, P. (1997/1998, December/January). Content-based instruction vs. ESP. *TESOL Matters,* p. 10.

Strevens, P. (1977). *New orientations in the teaching of English*. Oxford: Oxford University Press.

West, L. (1984). Needs assessment in occupation-specific VESL, or how to decide what I teach. *English for Specific Purposes, 3*, 143–152.

Users' Guide to Activities

Outline

I. Subject
  A. General English for specific purposes
  B. English for academic purposes
  C. English for art and design
  D. English for business and economics
  E. English for legal purposes
  F. English for science and technology
  G. English for vocational purposes

II. Form of Communication
  A. Academic text
  B. Advertisement
  C. Annual report
  D. Case study
  E. Catalogue
  F. Graphic organizers
  G. Internet communications
  H. Interview
  I. Lecture
  J. Legal case
  K. Magazine, newsletter, newspaper
  L. Meeting
  M. Presentation
  N. Proposal
  O. Research report
  P. Technical and scientific prose
  Q. Vocational manual

Subject

General English for Specific Purposes

English for Academic Purposes

English for Legal Purposes

English for Science and Technology

English for Vocational Purposes

Form of Communication

Academic Text

Advertisement

Annual Report

Case Study

Catalogue

Graphic Organizers

Internet Communications

Interview

Lecture

Legal Case

Magazine, Newsletter, Newspaper

Out-of-Class Activity

Paraphrase and Summary

Vocabulary/Lexis

Part I: General English for Specific Purposes

Editors' Note

The activities in Part I teach and practice general English for specific purposes (ESP), a catch-all category for English taught in a variety of ESP settings with no specific focus. Skills taught and practiced in general ESP include preparing for professional conferences, using the Internet, and understanding specific elements of grammar.

What Does the *Writer* Think?

Levels
Low advanced

Aims
Learn semantic and
rhetorical implications
of reporting expressions
Read texts in light of
the rhetorical
perspective suggested
by reporting
expressions

Class Time
1½ hours

Preparation Time
1-2 hours

Resources
List of common
reporting verbs
Short, relevant article,
review, or text extract

In the process of writing a short review of an author's argument in an article (or book review), the students are encouraged to identify and respond to the author's rhetorical strategies (e.g., how the author emphasizes a point in, cites, agrees with, or dismisses the work of other authors). A comparison of reviews enhances the students' awareness of the subjectivity of their own and others' written responses to academic texts and highlights the reasons for which they, as authors, may choose to draw on a range of reporting expressions.

Procedure

1. Write a few sentences using common reporting verbs (e.g., *argue, state, mention*) on the black- or whiteboard, underlining the verbs. Ask the students to describe the differences in meaning they discern. Elicit other reporting verbs from the students, and ask the students to categorize them as *evaluative—positive or negative* and *descriptive—neutral*. (Some verbs may clearly be both.)
2. Highlight the typical grammatical complements of reporting verbs: a clause beginning with *that* (which may be omitted) or a noun phrase.
3. Distribute copies of a short article, review, or extract (no more than two pages) on a relevant English for academic purposes (for non-discipline-specific classes) or ESP subject. If you wish, highlight sections for particular attention.
4. Ask the students to read the article and then examine the classification of reporting verbs and functions in the Appendix.
5. Have the students work in pairs to write a short review of the article (in a paragraph or so), drawing on reporting verbs from a variety of classifications.

6. When the students have finished, ask the pairs to separate and join other students to compare reviews of the same article.

Caveats and Options

1. The classification of reporting verbs in the Appendix covers only a very small subset of reporting expressions. Thompson and Ye (1991) list more than 400 such expressions and note that the list of potential reporting expressions is in fact unlimited.

2. Ask students in an advanced, discipline-specific class to construct their own discipline-specific classification based on the frequency of occurrence and functions of particular reporting verbs or expressions:

   - Have pairs of students each examine a different article relevant to their discipline and compile a list of reporting expressions, together with their immediate context of use (a single sentence or a paragraph).
   - Hold a pyramid discussion, in which pairs of students together compile a classification.
   - In the final stage, have the whole class produce and discuss the complete classification (and possibly compare it with the sample classification given in the Appendix).

References and Further Reading

Pickard, V. (1995). Citing previous writers: What can we say instead of "say"? *Hong Kong Papers in Linguistics and Language Teaching, 18,* 89-102. (ERIC Database ISSN 1015-2059)

Thompson, G., & Ye, Y. (1991). Evaluation in the reporting verbs used in academic papers. *Applied Linguistics, 12,* 365-382.

Appendix: A Classification of Reporting Verbs

Group 1: Author's Argument

argue	claim	propose
contend	hold the view	recommend
	maintain	suggest

Function: The author of the book or article you have read presents a particular opinion or perspective. You wish to discuss that opinion and possibly challenge (disagree with) it. You report the author's argument using one of the expressions above or a similar expression.

Group 2: Author's Definition

state	define

Function: The author presents a definition as background to his or her argument. You wish to use this definition as background to your own argument. You attribute it to the author using a verb such as *state* or *define.*

Group 3: Author's Emphasis

draw attention to	emphasize
mention	focus on
note	insist
observe	reiterate
point out	remind
remark	stress
	underline

Function: The author draws your attention to an interesting example or illustration, or returns repeatedly to a point that is important, and possibly essential, to his or her argument.

You might wish to report the author's emphasis because
1. you want to use the author's illustration or example to support your own argument (*draw attention to, mention, note, observe, point out, remark*), or
2. you are emphasizing a particular point or perspective in your own argument, and you want to show that others agree with your chosen emphasis (*emphasize, focus on, insist, reiterate, remind, stress, underline*), or
3. you believe the author's emphasis is incorrect or too narrow, and you want to compare it with your own chosen emphasis (*emphasize, focus on, insist, stress*).

Group 4: Author's Omission

```
assume
imply
take for granted
```

Function: An *implication* is an idea or conclusion that can be drawn from an author's work without being openly stated; an *assumption* is an idea the author thinks is true (i.e., a fact on which to base an argument). When you evaluate an author's argument, you may need to discuss what such a view *implies*. For example, if an author is arguing the benefits of a particular management system from a manager's point of view, you might ask yourself what the *implications* of the system would be for the workers.

Sometimes an author's argument depends on a particular idea that he or she thinks is true, but this idea is not mentioned or stated clearly in the book or article; if it were stated clearly, some people might not agree with it. For example, an author might assume that mental illness is caused by a chemical imbalance in the brain; however, you know that other studies, not mentioned by the author, have suggested social pressures as the cause of mental illness. In this case, you may criticize the author's omission by indicating what he or she *assumes* or *takes for granted*.

Often, however, authors will state their assumptions clearly; this is good academic practice. When you describe the work of an author, you may need to refer to the assumptions he or she makes.

Group 5: Author's Admission

```
acknowledge
admit
recognize
```

Function: The author recognizes that there is something incomplete or limited in his or her present study or past work or discipline as a whole. You might report the author's admission because (a) the limitations on your own study are the same, and you want to show that these limitations are general in the discipline and not specific to your own study; or (b) you want to show where work in your field of study remains to be done (perhaps the work that your study will do).

Group 6: Author's References to Other Authors

cite	accept	challenge
consider	affirm	dispute
discuss		question
refer to		reject

Function: In the book or article you are reading, the author refers to the work of other authors. Whom does the author agree with? What ideas does the author reject or challenge? What does this suggest about the author's own position? You can use what the author says about other authors to help you interpret and describe the author's position. Why does the author accept X's theory, but reject Y's? Or you can refer to the author's article to support your own views of the other authors' work.

Group 7: Author's Success, Writer's Background Information

account for	overcome	discover
demonstrate	solve	find
establish		
explain		
prove		
reveal		
show		

Function: You believe the author has successfully established a fact or theory, or solved a problem. You may wish to refer to the author's finding as background information to your own question, as support for your argument, or as a way to determine what work remains to be done.

Group 8: Writer's Support

> exemplify
> illustrate
> support

Function: The author gives an example or a point of view that you want to use to support your own argument. You want to make clear to the reader that you are using the author's point to support your argument.

Group 9: Writer's Comparison of Authors' Ideas

> anticipate   contrast with
> be in accord with
> correspond to

Function: In reviewing literature, you construct a "map" of the ideas and arguments in the field relevant to your paper. Which authors agree with your position? Which authors agree with each other? Which authors disagree? How does your work differ from what has already been done? You may need to show the reader how your work contributes to the work done in the field so far. You can use this group of verbs to show how the work of various authors is related and how it relates to your own.

Contributor

Judith Bishop works in the Language and Learning Unit at Monash University, in Victoria, Australia.

Mark Your Move

Levels
Intermediate +

Aims
Understand the role of
notation in science
Learn to create notation

Class Time
9-square chess: 1 hour
16-square chess: Variable

Preparation Time
30 minutes

Resources
Overhead projector and
pen
9-square game board
and transparency
16-square game board
Two types of coins

Nonlanguage games are an endless source for teaching ESL skills in general and ESP skills in particular. The trick is making the connection between the game and the skill. This activity matches the game to the skill and then teaches the process.

Procedure

1. Make one photocopy of the empty 9-square game board (see the Appendix) for each pair of students in your class.
2. Divide the class into pairs, trying to match partners evenly (e.g., both intermediate, both advanced, or both non–chess players). Have the partners sit across from each other.
3. Distribute a board plus three coins of two different types (e.g., three pennies and three nickels) to each pair.
4. Have the students lay out their pieces (pennies for one partner, nickels for the other) in the row nearest them according to the layout in the Appendix.
5. Explain that the pieces are pawns and that they move the way pawns do in chess, except that a piece does not have to take another piece. Have a knowledgeable student explain how a pawn moves and takes a piece. If nobody knows, explain it yourself:
   - A pawn can move only one square forward at a time.
   - It can capture another piece only by moving into its space diagonally and taking it off the board.
6. Explain that the winner is either (a) the first person to get a pawn to the opposite end of the board or (b) the last person to move. You may want to demonstrate this on the overhead transparency of the board (see the winning moves in the Appendix).

7. Have the students work out what kinds of notation they need to describe the moves of the game. Some suggestions are (a) designations for the squares (e.g., 1a, 1c;), (b) designations for the pieces (e.g., BL1, BL2, W1), (c) designations for the moves (e.g., fi for move; **X** or fl for capture; >, !, or * for win; see the Appendix). For example, *W1* fi *1b* means that White Piece 1 moves to Square 1b, and *BL2* fl *W3* means that Black Piece 2 captures White Piece 3.
8. Have the students discuss their choices and agree on a common set of notation to use.
9. Have the pairs play the game, and have each person record the moves of both sides.
10. As each pair finishes, have the partners compare their notations.
11. When all the pairs are finished, have a person in each describe that pair's notation to the class. Follow up with a class discussion.

Caveats and Options

1. The game is very simple and lasts no more than three or four moves, but certain strategies can improve one's chances to win. If you have the students play the game several times, they will begin to discover these strategies.
2. If the session goes well, ask one pair to replay its game by laying out the pieces on the overhead transparency, having someone else read the moves, and having the two original players move their pieces as indicated.
3. If they are able, have the students play the game on a 16-square instead of a 9-square board. This makes the game far more challenging.

References and Further Reading

This activity evolved from the following volume, which is filled with many stimulating suggestions:

Kohl, H. R. (1974). *Math, writing, and games in the open classroom.* New York: New York Review.

Appendix

Layout for 9-Square Chessboard

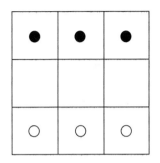

Winning Moves

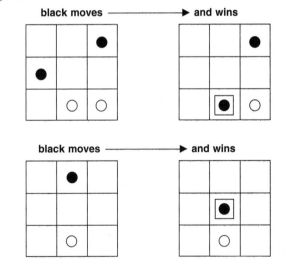

Contributor

Steven Darian chairs the Education Department and directs the TESL Certification Program at Rutgers University, Camden, New Jersey, in the United States. He previously served as the coeditor of ESP News *(the newsletter of TESOL's ESP Interest Section).*

Putting Humpty-Dumpty Together

Levels
Intermediate +

Aims
Learn to follow and
write instructions

Class Time
Two sessions, about
1 hour each

Preparation Time
20 minutes

Resources
Tinkertoy set
Parts list
4-in. × 6-in. index cards
(optional)

Instructions are an important and nicely delimitable element in many areas of ESP. One of many involving ways of teaching instructions is with Tinkertoys or a similar set of construction toys. Teachers can probably create 10–15 different instruction activities with a set. Here are a few for openers.

Procedure

1. Before class, use the Tinkertoys to build one finished structure for each group of three to five students in your class. For each group, make two to three copies of the parts list that comes with the Tinkertoy set.
2. In class, divide the students into groups of three to five.
3. Give each group an assembled structure and two to three copies of the parts list.
4. Have each group use the words from the parts list to write out instructions on how to assemble the structure.
5. Collect and disassemble the structures, and store each one in a separate bag.
6. Have one student type up the group's instructions at home and make two extra copies.
7. In the next class, have the groups exchange structures and instructions and assemble their new structure, following the instructions written by the other group.

Caveats and Options

1. If Tinkertoys are not available, use a different set of construction toys. Be sure the toys have a printed parts list containing the names and pictures of the parts.

2. Paste a picture of each assembled structure on a separate 4-in. × 6-in. index card. Give the cards to the groups in Step 7 after the students have finished so they can see whether they have followed the instructions correctly in assembling the structure.
3. Repeat the activity several times. The first time, be sure to match the level of complexity (e.g., the number of parts in a given structure) to the ability of the students. Then increase the complexity each time the students do the activity.
4. I have used this activity successfully with everyone from high school dropouts to students pursuing master's degrees in business administration.

Contributor

Steven Darian chairs the Education Department and directs the TESL Certification Program at Rutgers University, Camden, New Jersey, in the United States. He previously served as the coeditor of ESP News *(the newsletter of TESOL's ESP Interest Section).*

Defining the Everyday

Levels
Intermediate +

Aims
Practice writing
definitions

Class Time
Four or more 30-minute
sessions

Preparation Time
30 minutes/session

Resources
Text(s)
Definition cards

Making to-the-point definitions of well-known objects or concepts is a hard task in any language, including one's native tongue. When a concept is well known (e.g., *table*), students tend to forget its basic elements and get lost in secondary details. The following activities help students learn to write definitions, either in their own field of expertise or in fields of a more general interest.

Procedure

Part 1

1. Find a text containing everyday vocabulary, especially words from the textbook. Short poems (see Appendix A) work well for this exercise: The students can see that the task is limited in scope. Highlight the target words (e.g., with boldface type).
2. Tell the students to pretend that they are aliens from another planet. Although their civilization is very advanced technologically, they have heard certain words on earth whose meaning they do not understand. Tell the students you have made a list of such words and that they will have to explain them.
3. Model the activity by defining words for common items (e.g., *tea, toothbrush, petrol*) and then move to more abstract terms (e.g., *pollution, hunger, obedience*). The abstract elements may prove easier to define than the concrete ones.
4. Distribute the text. Write on the blackboard the various elements needed to define a word or concept: size, shape, color, weight, material, use. Ask the students to work together to define the highlighted words in the text.

5. Continue with the activity until the students can do it reasonably well. Lower level students may need more guidance at the beginning of the task.

Part 2

1. Compile a list of words commonly used in the specialized field of your students.
2. Divide the class into teams of three or four students, and give each team a few words to define. Help with the phrasing as they work.
3. Have the teams quiz one another on the definitions of the words, and award points to each team.

Part 3

(for students who are advanced in their specialized field or in various fields of specialization)

1. Either write some definitions of terms from the students' fields or, if suitable, use the definitions from Appendix B, which describe natural phenomena and basic concepts from various branches of science.
2. Give each student a definition. Have each student rephrase it in simpler language.
3. Have the students guess the word corresponding to their classmates' definitions. Award points to the students who give the correct word first.

Part 4

1. Have the students make up their own definitions for a term in their specialized field or a general one. Encourage the students to choose not only concrete objects (e.g., tools, materials) but also more abstract ones (e.g., processes, phenomena, laws).
2. Have the students quiz one another as in Part 3.

References and Further Reading

Poems with everyday words:

Evans, M. (1970). And the hotel room held only him. In *I am a black woman* (pp. 37-38). New York: Morrow.

Joseph, J. (1974). Warning. In *Rose in the afternoon*. London: Dent.

Lists of words with their definitions:

The English idiom. (1990, April). *English Teaching Forum, 28*, 51. (on recently coined words)

The English idiom. (1992, April). *English Teaching Forum, 30*, 52. (on computers)

Martin, A. (1993, June 13). Are you scientifically literate? *The Observer Magazine,* 82. (on science)

So you think you're science literate? (1990, April 9). *Newsweek,* 52-53.

Appendix A

The Pessimist[1]

Nothing to do but **work**,
   Nothing to **eat** but **food**,
Nothing to **wear** but **clothes**,
   To keep one from going **nude**.

Nothing to **breathe** but **air**,
   Quick as a flash 'tis gone;
Nowhere to fall but off,
   Nowhere to stand but on.

Nothing to **comb** but **hair**,
   Nowhere to **sleep** but in **bed**,
Nothing to **weep** but **tears**,
   Nothing to **bury** but **dead**.

[1]From *The Penguin Book of Comic and Curious Verse* (p. 177), by J. M. Cohen, Ed., 1952, Harmondsworth, England: Penguin Books. Copyright untraced. Reprinted with permission.

Nothing to sing but **songs**,
Ah, well, alas! alack!
Nowhere to go but out,
Nowhere to come but back.

Nothing to see but sights,
Nothing to quench but **thirst**,
Nothing to have but what we've got.
Thus through life we are cursed.

Nothing to strike but a gait;
Everything moves that goes.
Nothing at all but common sense
Can ever withstand these woes.

—B. J. King

Appendix B: Definitions

antibody: naturally produced protein formed by the blood in response to an invading antigen, such as a bacterium. After such exposure, the body has acquired immunity to this particular pathogen.

astrology: the study that professes to interpret the influence of the heavenly bodies on human affairs.

astronomy: the science that deals with the material universe beyond the earth's atmosphere.

atom: the smallest unit of matter that can take part in a chemical reaction; consists of a *nucleus*, which in turn is composed of one or more *protons* and *neutrons* orbited by one or more electrons.

bacteria: microscopic organisms larger than viruses that replicate by splitting or forming spores and, unlike viruses, are vulnerable to antibiotics.

big-bang theory: the theory that the universe was created from the explosion of a mass of hydrogen atoms, is still expanding, and will eventually contract into one mass to explode again to complete the cycle; the whole cycle should take 80 billion years.

byte: a unit of information consisting of a fixed number of *bits* sufficient to represent a functional piece of information.

cell: the basic unit of life. Within cells, *DNA*, the molecule that encodes heredity, contains the blueprint for producing proteins, which fuel biochemical reactions and comprise the structural components of the organism.

centigrade: temperature scale, also known as *Celsius*, in which water boils at 100 degrees and freezes at zero.

cholesterol: fatty substance present in the body, as well as in all animal fats, blood, nervous tissue, and bile; strongly linked to hardening of the arteries.

chromosome: a stringlike body, usually in a cell nucleus. Along it are strung *genes* that govern heredity.

comet: a ball of frozen gas and dust that follows a very stretched-out orbit around the Sun.

conductor: any material that transmits heat, light, or other energy.

dinosaur: a creature that lived from about 220 million to 65 million years ago, some 60 million years before the first appearance of humans.

equation: an expression of a proposition, often algebraic, asserting the equality of two quantities, often used in determining a value of an unknown included in one or both quantities.

fog: a cloudlike mass of minute water droplets near the surface of the earth, which appreciably reduces visibility.

fossil: any remains, impression, or trace of an animal or plant of a former geological age.

geyser: a hot spring that intermittently sends up fountainlike jets of water and steam into the air.

gravity: the force of attraction by which terrestrial bodies tend to fall toward the center of the earth.

greenhouse effect: warming of a planet caused by an accumulation of gases that trap heat in the atmosphere.

Homo sapiens: the species to which modern humans belong; arose about 200,000 years ago.

hormone: a substance secreted by endocrine glands that affects an organ or tissue elsewhere in the body.

ion: any electrically charged atom or molecule.

neuron: a nerve cell, of which the human nervous system has approximately 10 billion.

ozone layer: a layer of ozone gas (composed of three oxygen atoms) 6-12 miles above the Earth that screens out most harmful ultraviolet radiation.

plasma: a fourth state of matter (distinct from solids, liquids, and gases), consisting of a gas of ions; believed to constitute 99% of the universe; also the clear, liquid, noncellular component of blood.

Pythagorean theorem: the theorem that the square of the hypotenuse of a right triangle is equal to the sum of the squares of the other two sides.

rain: water that is condensed from the aqueous vapor in the atmosphere and falls in drops from the sky to the earth.

rainbow: an arc of prismatic colors that may appear in the sky opposite the sun and is caused by the refraction and reflection of the sun's rays in drops of rain.

Richter scale: an open-ended scale indicating the severity of earthquakes. A level of 2.0 is barely felt, 6.0 causes considerable structural damage, and anything above 8.0 causes massive destruction.

software: a set of instructions (a program) that tells a computer what to do.

star: a gaseous celestial body, such as the Sun, located in a *galaxy* (a collection of stars under mutual gravitational attraction) like our Milky Way.

Contributor

Nicole Décuré is an associate professor of English at Toulouse University, in France. She teaches EFL to science and medical students and is head of the university's research team on foreign language teaching and learning.

Whodunit à la E-Mail

Levels
Intermediate +

Aims
Become familiar with
e-mail addresses

Class Time
1¹/₂ hours

Preparation Time
15 minutes

Resources
Copies of e-mail
messages (ideally from
different countries)
Handouts

This multitask activity is designed to introduce students to e-mail before they actually send and receive messages. The procedure demystifies the English used in e-mail messages and allows the students to identify the origin and sender of their messages.

Procedure

1. Before class, print out half the number of e-mail messages as there are students in the class. Cut the messages so the headers are separated from the message sections, which include the signature of the sender.
2. Distribute the handout called "Structure of an E-Mail Message" (see Appendix A).
3. Give a lecture-demonstration, including examples, on the various items in the heading of an e-mail message. Explain that
    ● e-mail messages can originate from various countries
    ● an e-mail address has two parts: the user ID (identification) and the domain name (the part that follows the @ symbol)
    ● the domain name can give the reader a good idea of where the message came from—both the country and the type of organization that sent the message
4. Hand out a list of country codes and organizational identification names used in e-mail addresses (see Appendix B). Have the students work in pairs to guess what the codes and names stand for.
5. Go over the answers to the worksheet as a whole class.
6. Give each student one piece of the cut-up e-mail messages prepared in Step 1. Ask the students to find the person who has the other part of their e-mail message.

7. When all the students have found the corresponding half of their message, have each pair of students answer questions about who sent the message and where it came from (see Appendix C).
8. Lay the reassembled e-mail messages out on a table, and have all the students check to see if they agree with the combinations.
9. Hold a class discussion with the students concerning what they have learned about e-mail addresses and the format of e-mail messages.

References and Further Reading

Pitter, K., Amato, S., Callahan, J., Kerr, N., & Tilton, E. (1995). *Every student's guide to the Internet.* New York: McGraw-Hill.

Warschauer, M. (1995). *E-mail for English teaching: Bringing the Internet and computer learning networks into the language classroom.* Alexandria, VA: TESOL.

Appendix A: Structure of an E-Mail Message

The e-mail message below is from a discussion list. An e-mail message sent directly to an individual will look somewhat different.

An e-mail message has two parts: the header and the body.

1. Below is an example of a *header*.

> **Subj:** NETEACH-L Homepage
> [This tells you what the subject of the message is.]
>
> **Date:** Wed, 19 Jun 1996 9:38 AM PST
> [This tells you what day the message was sent. (This message is from a discussion list. In a message posted to a discussion list, the date and time will reflect when the message was processed by the listserv software, not necessarily when the message was actually sent.)]
>
> **From:** neteach-l@thecity.sfsu.edu
> [This tells you who the message is from (in this case, the mailing list's e-mail address).]

TX-From: frizzy@sfsu.edu (Karla Frizler)
[This tells you the actual person who wrote and sent the message to the mailing list.]

Sender: neteach-l@thecity.sfsu.edu
[This tells you who sent the message to you.]

Reply-to: neteach-l@thecity.sfsu.edu
[This tells you who to send your answer to.]

To: neteach-l@thecity.sfsu.edu (Multiple recipients of list)
[This tells you who else besides you is receiving the message. Sometimes this will be indicated by *cc*, which means *carbon copy*].

2. Below is an example of a *body*.

Hello subscribers!

This is a reminder that there is a wealth of information on the NETEACH-L homepage, including a link to the "Cool Sites" page Kristina puts together for us. You can also find information there about NETEACH MOO sessions and Archives, how to manage your subscription (including unsubscribing), plus details about the illustrious NETEACH team (Frizzy, Ron, Thomas, Kristina, & Greg) and how NETEACH-L got started. You can reach the NETEACH-L homepage directly:

http://thecity.sfsu.edu/~funweb/neteach.htm

or from the Frizzy University Network (FUN) homepage (under "Resources for Teachers"):

http://thecity.sfsu.edu/~funweb

Frizzy

3. Below is an example of a *signature*.

> NETEACH-L: EXPLORING THE ESL-INTERNET CONNECTION
> List Owners: Karla Frizler <frizzy@sfsu.edu> & Ron Corio
> <rcorio@vcu.edu>
> Archivist: Thomas Goldstein <thomas@wolfenet.com>
> Web Mistress: Kristina Pfaff-Harris <kristina@math.unr.edu>
> MOO Master: Greg Younger <youngerg@spot.colorado.edu>
> http://thecity.sfsu.edu/~funweb/neteach.htm

Appendix B: Country Codes and Organizational Identifiers

Directions: Work with a partner to figure out what these common country and organizational codes (abbreviations) stand for. Write your guesses in the blanks.

Countries	
AQ	FR
AR	GR
AT	HK
AU	HU
BE	IE
BR	IL
CA	IN
CH	IT
CL	JM
DE	JP
DO	KR
DK	KZ
EG	MX
ES	NL
FI	NO
PH	PE

NZ	PR
PT	SE
SG	TN
TW	UK
US	VE
QA	ZA

Organizational Identifiers	
COM	NET
EDU	ORG
GOV	INT
MIL	

Answer Key

Countries			
AQ	Antarctica	FR	France
AR	Argentina	GR	Greece
AT	Austria	HK	Hong Kong
AU	Australia	HU	Hungary
BE	Belgium	IE	Ireland
BR	Brazil	IL	Israel
CA	Canada	IN	India
CH	Switzerland	IT	Italy
CL	Chile	JM	Jamaica
DE	Germany	JP	Japan
DO	Dominican Republic	KR	Korea
DK	Denmark	KZ	Kazahkstan
EG	Egypt	MX	Mexico
ES	Spain	NL	The Netherlands
FI	Finland	NO	Norway

PH	Philippines	PE	Peru
NZ	New Zealand	PR	Puerto Rico
PT	Portugal	SE	Sweden
SG	Singapore	TN	Tunisia
TW	Taiwan	UK	United Kingdom
US	United States	VE	Venezuela
QA	Qatar	ZA	South Africa

Organizational Identifiers			
COM	commercial organization	NET	major network support center
EDU	educational/ research organization	ORG	other organization
GOV	government organization	INT	international organization
MIL	military agency		

Appendix C

Directions: After you find the person who has the other part of your e-mail message, look at the complete e-mail message and answer the following questions.

In the Header

1. What is the subject of your message?
2. On what date was it written?
3. Who is the message from?
4. Who wrote the message (if different from the sender)?
5. Who sent the message?
6. Where (to what e-mail address) should you send your reply to this message?
7. Who received this message besides you?

In the Body
8. Summarize the important information in this message:
9. Who signed this message?
10. Is there a signature? If so, write it below. If not, write "no signature."

Contributor

Randi Freeman began teaching Internet skills to ESL students at the American Language Program, California State University, Hayward. She now works at Central Washington University, in the United States.

Detectives in Cyberspace

Level
Advanced

Aims
Use the World Wide
Web for integrated
language practice

Class Time
8–10 hours

Preparation Time
5 minutes/step

Resources
Computer per one to
two students
E-mail and Internet
access
Browser software
Index cards with search
engine addresses
Web search handout
Search engines for
mailing lists

This multifaceted activity teaches the skills necessary to obtain information from the Internet using various resources (search engines, World Wide Web pages, and e-mail lists); it also gives the students a framework with which to evaluate their journey and the information they have gained. The tasks thus encourage the development of both computer and critical thinking skills.

Procedure

1. Ask the students to choose a topic for their search and e-mail it to you.
2. Give the students an index card file of search engine addresses (see Appendix A) and a handout on doing Web searches (see Appendix B).
3. Ask the students to use various search engines to find information on the topic they have specified.
4. Have the students, in groups of four, discuss their findings and analyze their search. For example, they may note differences in the information given by various search engines.
5. Have each group send an e-mail to you describing their findings.
6. Give the students information on e-mail lists to join (see Appendix C).
7. Have individual students join an e-mail list on a topic of their choice.
8. Have the students summarize the discussion on the e-mail list in writing and send the summary by e-mail.
9. Ask the students to form groups and analyze the value of the information gained from the e-mail list.
10. After the students have summarized the information they have found and the experience they have gained, have them send an e-mail with this information to a classmate and a copy to you.

Caveats and Options

1. Have the students choose diverse topics, or help them narrow their searches, depending on the focus of the class. For more oral-aural practice, have the students work in pairs to choose an appropriate topic.
2. To avoid overloading any particular Internet address, give the students each an index card with the address of a different search engine, and have them use only that address until they exchange cards with another person.
3. If the students have taken a library tour, have them perform a search for their topic in a database in the library. Afterward, have them compare the information they found in the library search with that found while searching the Web and reading an e-mail list discussion.
4. The suggested time will vary depending on the speed of the computer and the overall setup of the computer lab. Take possible delays into consideration. Depending on the time available, have the students write more succinctly, with shorter notes or paragraphs, or more elaborately, in essay format.

References and Further Reading

Frizler, K., & Corio, R. (1998). *NETEACH-L: Exploring the ESL-Internet connection* [On-line]. Available: http://thecity.sfsu.edu/~funweb/neteach.htm [February 6, 1998].

Pitter, K., Amato, S., Callahan, J., Kerr, N., & Tilton, E. (1995). *Every student's guide to the Internet.* New York: McGraw-Hill.

Seiter, C. (1994). *The Internet for Macs for dummies.* Foster City, CA: IDG Books.

Warschauer, M. (1995). *E-mail for English teaching: Bringing computer learning networks into the language classroom.* Alexandria, VA: TESOL.

Warschauer, M. (n.d.). *Searching the Internet* [On-line]. Available: http://www.lll.hawaii.edu/markw [February 6, 1998].

Appendix A: Search Engine Addresses

Search Engine	World Wide Web Address
AltaVista	http://altavista.digital.com/
AOL NetFind	http://www.aol.com.netfind/
Electric Library	http://www.elibrary.com/
Excite	http://www.excite.com/
HotBot	http://www.hotbot.com/
Infoseek	hhtp://www.infoseek.com/
Kamus	http://www.he.net/~kamus/mainen.htm
LookSmart	http://www.looksmart.com/
Lycos	http://www.lycos.com/
Metacrawler	http://metacrawler.cs.washington.edu: 8080/index.html
The Mining Co.	http://home.miningco.com/
Search.com	http://www.search.com/
WebCrawler	http://webcrawler.com/
Webtaxi	http://www.webtaxi.com/
Wired Cybrarian	http://www.wired.com/cybrarian
Yahoo!	http://www.yahoo.com

Appendix B: Instructions for Web Searches

1. Identify your research topic.
2. Write down the first search engine's name and address. Use the browser software to go to the search engine's Web address and conduct the search.
3. How many entries did the search engine find?
4. If you have more than 25 entries, try limiting your search:
   - The most basic method is to use quotation marks. For example, entering "Williams University" will make the search engine look for that exact string, whereas removing the quotation marks will result in a search for all the Web pages that contain either the word *Williams* or the word *university*.
   - Another extremely useful method is the use of plus signs to indicate that a word must be included. Note that to achieve the

equivalent of a Boolean AND, the plus sign must also occur before the first word. Here are some examples:

▶ ESL writing (searches for all pages that include either of these two words)

▶ ESL +writing (searches for all pages that include the word *writing*; the pages will be listed with and without the word *ESL*)

▶ +ESL +writing (searches for all pages that include the word *ESL* and the word *writing*)

▶ "ESL writing" (searches for all pages that include the exact phrase *ESL writing*)

▶ +university +"ESL writing" (searches for all pages that include the word *university* and the exact phrase *ESL writing*)

▶ +university +"ESL writing" -Japan (searches for all pages that include the word *university* and the phrase *ESL writing* and do not include the word *Japan*

5. How many entries did the search engine find when you limited your search?

6. Write down a few entries (addresses) that you found especially helpful. Save those pages onto your computer disk.

7. Repeat Steps 2–6 with two more search engines.

Search Engine 2

Name and address:

Number of entries found without limiting search:

Number of entries after limiting search:

Helpful information and addresses (take notes):

Search Engine 3

Name and address:

Number of entries found without limiting search:

Number of entries after limiting search:

Helpful information and addresses (take notes):

8. Summarize the information from the three searches.

9. Write a few sentences about the experience of doing the search. Did it take a long time? Was it useful? Was it enjoyable? Did you learn anything about your research topic or about using search engines? Were there differences in the kind and quality of information you found using the various search engines?

10. Send an e-mail message to your instructor, who will give you his or her e-mail address, and a copy to your e-mail partner about your search, the summary, and your experience of doing the search.

Appendix C: Search Engines for E-mail Lists

Search Engine	World Wide Web Address
Liszt, The Mailing List Directory	http://www.liszt.com/
Tile.Net Lists	http://tile.net/lists/

Contributors

Randi Freeman taught the Internet to ESL students at the American Language Program (ALP), California State University, Hayward, in the United States. She now works at Central Washington University. Ivana Curcic Gordy teaches ESL at the ALP, California State University, Hayward, and at Chabot College in Oakland, California, in the United States.

Actions Speak Louder Than Words!

Levels
Intermediate +

Aims
Become aware of cross-cultural differences in communication
Practice one-to-one oral communication
Learn nonverbal cues for better interviewing

Class Time
About 45 minutes

Preparation Time
5 minutes

Resources
Whiteboard, or overhead projector, transparencies, and pen
Role-play cards
Handout

Nonverbal (along with verbal) communication skills are now being incorporated into many professional skills programs and are considered essential in disciplines that use one-to-one interviewing as their main source of contact (e.g., health sciences, law, business, computer consulting). In a conversation, more than two thirds of the meaning is conveyed via nonverbal communication (Mean, 1990). In fact, people often reveal their true intentions, sometimes contradicting their verbal message, by such nonverbal aspects as facial expression, gaze, gestures, posture and stance, proximity, and touch (Argyle, 1988) and by paralinguistic features such as voice quality (Poyatos, 1988). In a cross-cultural environment, the same action may have different meanings, or different actions may have the same meaning (Schneller, 1992). Consequently, communicators, especially those from a cultural background different from the dominant one in a society, must be aware of the nonverbal cues they are giving to avoid the possibility of ambiguity or contradiction in their communications. Through the use of role plays, this activity helps students recognize the importance of these nonverbal differences.

Procedure

1. Ask the students to recall a one-to-one interview they have experienced (e.g., during a doctor's consultation, at the bank, with a tutor).
2. Divide the blackboard (or an overhead transparency) into two columns labeled *good points* and *bad points*. Ask if the interviewer did anything that made them feel uncomfortable or unimportant (e.g., writing instead of maintaining eye contact while talking). Elicit any good aspects of this interview (e.g., allowing enough time for them to explain the problem). Write the students' answers under the appropriate heading on the blackboard.

3. Ask the students to find a partner for a role-play activity. Explain that there is no right or wrong way to carry out the role play; the students are allowed to be creative (but realistic) with their role.

4. Distribute to each pair of students the matching roles for the role-play scenarios (see Appendix A). Ask the students not to show their role card to their partner.

5. Allow the students a minute or two to think about how they might act as the person they are playing. Tell the students that Partner A begins the role play and that Partner B responds. Also tell the partners to introduce themselves in their role.

6. Have each pair of students enact their role play in front of the rest of the class. Ask those watching the role play to pay attention to the nonverbal cues (body language) of each student. In particular, have them consider the correspondence between the speakers' words and their body language.

7. After each role play, elicit feedback from the students by asking leading questions such as "Did Jenny look like she wanted to talk to Joe?" "Where was Lucy looking?" "Which way was Evan facing?"

8. Conclude by summarizing the points that the students have raised during feedback, and give them a handout that tabulates the perceived meaning of various nonverbal cues (see Appendix B).

Caveats and Options

1. Make up role-play scenarios to suit a specific discipline. For example, have medical students practice their initial consultation with patients, and use differences in age, gender, ailments, or personality to provide a variety of scenarios.

2. Although research suggests that some facial expressions (e.g., smiling) and gestures (e.g., shrugging, beckoning) are universal, there always seem to be exceptions (Argyle, 1988). In addition, defining what a culture is (in particular its overlap with national groups) and how it may differ within subcultures (Mead, 1990) is complicated. Be open to new suggestions about interpretations of body language, and possibly omit any that may not be "mainstream."

3. The length of this activity depends on the number of role plays the class will witness and on the complexity and length of each. As a rule, the feedback on inappropriate nonverbal behavior (e.g., stance, gaze)

diminishes as the class progresses because the students tend to modify their body language by observing the performances of their peers.

4. Appendix B is based purely on subjective observation of behavior and reactions to it in Australia. Revise and amend these to suit local custom, as even people from countries with the same language interpret the same gestures differently.

References and Further Reading

Argyle, M. (1988). *Bodily communication* (2nd ed.). London: Methuen.

Lamp, J., Keen, C., & Urquhart, C. (1996, July). *Integrating professional skills into the curriculum*. Paper presented at the Australian Computer Science Education Conference, Sydney, Australia.

Mead, R. (1990). *Cross-cultural management communication*. Brisbane, Australia: Wiley.

Poyatos, F. (1988). New research perspectives in crosscultural psychology through nonverbal communication studies. In F. Poyatos (Ed.), *Cross-cultural perspectives in nonverbal communication* (pp. 35–69). Toronto, Canada: C. J. Hogrefe.

Schneller, R. (1992). Many gestures, many meanings: Nonverbal diversity in Israel. In F. Poyatos (Ed.), *Advances in nonverbal communication: Sociocultural, clinical, esthetic and literary perspectives* (pp. 213–233). Amsterdam: John Benjamins.

Acknowledgment

This contribution is based on a lesson devised by Clare Rhoden and the author.

Appendix A: Role-Play Scenarios

1a. You are a student and you need an extension on your assignment. You must ask the lecturer to give you the extension.	1b. You are a lecturer in a hurry.

2a. You are a reporter for an educational magazine, and you want to know what studying commerce at Melbourne University is like.	2b. You are a commerce student.
3a. You have an overdue parking fine, and your friend is a lawyer.	3b. You are a lawyer.
4a. You are an athlete with a shoulder injury.	4b. You are a physiotherapy student.
5a. You are a student reporter interviewing a novelist.	5b. You are a novelist.

Appendix B: Sample Handouts

When speaking, it is easy to give a false impression as a result of your body language. Here are possible interpretations of nonverbal communication in Australia.

Action	Possible Interpretation
Posture and Stance	
Leaning forward (e.g., elbow on chin when seated)	Interested, paying attention
Leaning backward	Casual, relaxed, not very interested
Standing with crossed legs	Insecure, not balanced
Standing with legs spread apart	Confronting, challenging
Fiddling with hands	Nervous (speaker) or bored (listener)

| Keeping arms and legs crossed | Serious, closed, not open to suggestions, disagreeing |
| Holding hands behind head | Powerful, dominating |

Facial Expressions

Lowered eyes	Humility, lack of confidence
Insufficient eye contact	Shiftiness, untrustworthiness
Frown	Confusion, lack of understanding, request for clarification
Frown, with nod or shake of head	Sympathy
Smile (when not listening to something funny)	Possible sinister attitude ("I know something that you don't"), a private joke
Smile and nod	Agreement, support
Touch or brush across brow with hand	Vagueness, uncertainty
Tug ear, stroke chin	Thought, reflection, lack of certainty about answer to give

Other aspects of nonverbal communication are personal space and turn taking.

Personal space is the physical distance between the people who are communicating. Are their noses almost touching (a small amount of personal space), or are they 3-4 feet apart (a large amount of personal space)? If you stand or sit closer to speakers than their normal amount of personal space allows, you will make them feel uncomfortable and intimidated. If you are too far away, they will feel as if they are being excluded and will continually move closer to you.

Compromising is the answer here—find a space that is comfortable for you both. If your partner keeps moving closer than you are happy with, rather than move away (and start a chasing game around the room), try turning your body slightly to one side so that you feel there is more space while still looking straight at the person. Likewise, if you feel your partner is too far away (and keeps moving every time you move closer), try just extending your legs (if sitting) or one leg (if standing) to bridge that gap.

Turn taking is the ability to know when your partner has stopped speaking and when you are expected to speak. The speaker often indicates this by prolonging the final stressed syllable of the utterance or by dropping the pitch level of that syllable. It can also be done with body posture. Relaxing the posture, making a gesture with the hand, and directing one's gaze at the listener are all cues for a change in turns.

Speakers often look for confirmation from the listener as they are talking and thus will insert such phrases as *you know*, expecting feedback from the listener in such forms as nods, *mhm,* and *yes* as a sign that the speaker still has the floor and that the listener is still interested.

Contributor

Aveline Pérez teaches academic and professional skills across a range of disciplines to native and nonnative English speakers at the University of Melbourne, in Australia.

Making a Case

Levels
High intermediate +

Aims
Recognize cause and
effect in a case study
Discuss a case study
through role play
Develop fluency

Class Time
1½–2 hours

Preparation Time
3 hours +

Resources
Field-specific case study

Most people are fascinated by disasters. In this activity, which exploits the case study approach in ESP, students take an in-depth look into what went wrong and why.

Procedure

1. Choose a case study from the students' field that involves a failure with a limited number of explicit causes and effects (e.g., the *Titanic* disaster of 1912 for maritime engineers and safety officers).
2. Present the case study as a 20- to 30-minute minilecture while the students listen and take notes.
3. Identify four to six key personnel in the case study (e.g., for the *Titanic* disaster, the designer of the ship, the ship's captain, the president of the shipping company, the watch keeper, wireless operators), and present brief information about their roles in written form to each student. Allow time for questions and clarification after the presentation.
4. Form groups of four to six students, and randomly assign the students the roles of the personnel in the case study.
5. Have the students each prepare an argument defending their role in the case study and explaining why they were not responsible for the failure or disaster.
6. Have students take on their assigned roles and, in their groups, debate the causes of the failure.
7. Have the groups report on their discussions. Ask the students whether it is possible to identify one main cause or a chain of events or to hold one person or a number of people responsible.

Caveats and Options

1. Have the students follow up with investigations of other case studies in their fields.
2. Have the students give oral presentations of case studies following the cause-effect format.

References and Further Reading

Eaton, J. P., & Haas, C. A. (1986). *Titanic—triumph and tragedy: A chronicle in words and pictures.* Sparkford, England: Patrick Stephens/ Haynes.

Contributor

Teresa Thiel is a lecturer for the BEd TESL program in the Faculty of Education, University of Malaya, Kuala Lumpur, in Malaysia.

Good, Bad, Mediocre: The Show Must Go On

Levels
High intermediate +; EFL

Aims
Learn to read theater reviews

Class Time
1 hour

Preparation Time
About 2 hours

Resources
Recent, short theater reviews
List of key words

This activity on understanding English theater reviews is designed for students of the dramatic arts but may be used with others. Its primary aim is top-down reading comprehension. Later on, the same materials can also be used for bottom-up analysis, which the students may be more familiar with.

Procedure

1. Locate several current theater reviews from relevant English newspapers, preferably from at least two different ones, and reproduce these for the students.

2. Prepare a list of key words in the texts you have chosen, and give it to the students at the end of the class before the one in which you do Step 3. Have the students study the key words for the next class.

3. In the next class, give the students a short quiz on the 10 most important words, if necessary. Then have the students quickly scan all the reviews for people's names.

4. After they have located all the names, divide the students into pairs, and have them place the names under the headings *author, producer, director and staging staff, actors and actresses,* and *dramatis personae.*

5. Discuss with your students the textual clues that indicate which names belong under which headings, especially if the play is new and the actors and actresses unknown.

6. Have the students (still in pairs) identify the parts of the text that relate to the author and the script and the parts of the text that relate to the performance.

7. Analyze the text with the students. Let them tell you which plays are worth seeing and why, according to the reviewers. If you have time, ask the students which plays they think are worth seeing and why, and why they would not like to see the other plays.

8. Discuss style differences in the reviews.

9. Analyze long compounds, as in *hall-of-mirrors Borgesian conundrum,* and compare them with groups of words that look like long compounds but are not, as in "to give the *story theatrical life.*" Also show the students how words are formed and used in different ways (e.g., *staging* and *staged* vs. *a stage*).

10. Ask the students to compare one of the reviews with a theater review in their own newspapers, and discuss any cultural differences.

11. For homework, have the students write a short review of a play they have seen or of one of their own performances in English.

Caveats and Options

1. For students in non-English-speaking countries, try to have available suitable theater reviews from both British and U.S. newspapers, though they may be difficult to find.

2. With a heterogeneous group, divide the students into pairs, and let them quietly discuss the reviews while they are working on them.

3. Motivate the students to read in English by bringing them current material on the theater, theater school prospectuses, and theater textbooks. Have them compare these resources to local theater material, if available.

4. Many theater school students believe that concentrating on grammatical structures is of little importance to them even though their vocabulary and grammar are often in great need of brushing up. Using authentic texts to teach structures and vocabulary will help show the students their importance in theater work.

References and Further Reading

Koskinen, L., Mauranen, A., & Virkkunen, A. (1987). Teaching English abbreviated clauses for Finnish readers. *Reading in a Foreign Language, 4*(1), 9-19.

Virkkunen, A. (1987). *Reading comprehension material for theater academy: Reading skills and grammar* (Language Centre Materials No. 60). Jyväskylä, Finland: Language Centre for Finnish Universities.

Virkkunen, A. (1987). *Reading comprehension material for theater academy: Texts and exercises* (Language Centre Materials No. 60). Jyväskylä, Finland: Language Centre for Finnish Universities.

Contributor

Anu Virkkunen-Fullenwider is a lecturer at the University of Helsinki Language Centre, in Finland.

Part II: English for Academic Purposes

Editors' Note

The activities in Part II center on English for academic purposes (EAP). EAP focuses on English taught within an academic setting, most commonly in higher education. Its primary concerns are academic reading and writing, study skills, test-taking strategies, listening and note-taking techniques, and cognitive mapping for content and lecture comprehension. Because one of its major aims is to aid nonnative-English-speaking students in gaining entrance to and succeeding in the university, EAP courses and activities include TOEFL preparation, pre–freshman composition, undergraduate writing, and graduate thesis and dissertation writing.

Talking Business

Levels
Intermediate +; EFL,
tertiary ESL

Aims
Improve oral
presentation skills
Develop a checklist for
peer evaluation

Class Time
45 minutes–1 hour

Preparation Time
15–30 minutes

Resources
Notes for presentation
Videotaped presentation
(optional)

Making a successful presentation depends partly upon the presenter's being aware of the skills by which a speaker conveys a message to a group of listeners. This activity helps develop that awareness by encouraging the students to construct a set of criteria for evaluating a presentation. This checklist of criteria will become a vital tool in later lessons, when the students prepare and give their own and evaluate each other's presentations.

Procedure

1. Give a short presentation to the class on a topic such as "Speaking and Listening" (see Appendix A). Ask the students to take notes as they listen to you.
2. Check that the students have noted the main points.
3. Elicit from the students some of the things you did in your presentation that made it possible for them to follow what you said (the purpose of your presentation) and the things that caused them difficulty. From the suggestions, establish broad headings (e.g., voice, body language, sequence, content, structure and use of examples, explanations, linguistic devices; see Appendix B).
4. Ask the students in groups to brainstorm and make a list of skills that a speaker should have under some or all of these headings.
5. Elicit ideas from the groups, and make a list on the blackboard. Suggest others as necessary.
6. If possible, show a videotape of a presentation, and give the students a chance to practice applying their criteria.
7. Follow up in a later lesson by using the criteria as the basis for the students' delivery and evaluation of presentations.

Caveats and Options

1. In your opening presentation, cover one of the target areas, particularly the linguistic devices involved in making a presentation. To make your presentation even more effective, stress certain aspects while speaking (e.g., by dramatically overemphasizing, using gestures, including long pauses).

2. Information on verbal and nonverbal signals is widely available in many commercial texts, usually in the context of cohesive devices and comprehension of lectures. The simplified information below could be embellished to form a relevant opening minipresentation, or presented at the end or in a later session to give the students some tools for structuring their presentation.

Signals

- Verbal
  - ▶ Cues [Mention various types.]
  - ▶ Emphasis
  - ▶ Repetition
  - ▶ Paraphrase
  - ▶ Connectives
  - ▶ References
- Nonverbal
  - ▶ Voice: stress, pitch, emphasis
  - ▶ Body language

3. Relate the presentation to the type of skills taught to trainee teachers or aspiring lecturers (see Appendix A).

References and Further Reading

Ellis, M., & O'Driscoll, N. (1992). *Giving presentations.* Harlow, England: Longman.

Rea-Dickins, P., & Germaine, G. (1992). *Evaluation.* Oxford: Oxford University Press.

Wallace, M. J. (1980). *Study skills in English*. Cambridge: Cambridge University Press.

Appendix A: Notes for Presentation

Expand or revise these basic notes according to your own perceptions and your students' requirements.

Speaking and Listening

1. Four language skills: listening, speaking, reading, writing (order of learning?)
2. Oral communication requires transmission of message from speaker to listener.
3. Onus on speaker to transmit message in such a way that listener can interpret it, but needs only to operate at level of a specific listener (the "average" listener for the target group)
4. Onus on the listener to interpret the message that is being transmitted
5. Necessity for speaker and listener to have common code (shared medium or language through which message is transmitted and received)
6. Necessity to avoid "noise" in the "channel"

[etc.]

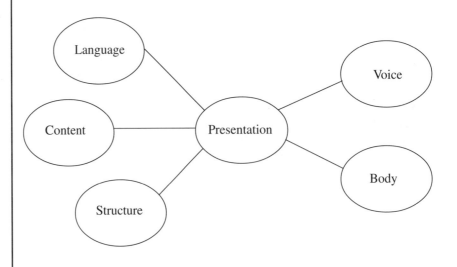

Appendix B: Criteria and Indicators

Criteria		Indicators	
		Positive	Negative
Voice	Volume	Comfortably audible	Too loud/too quiet
	Stress, emphasis	Varied	Inappropriate
	Pitch, tone	Varied	Monotone
Body	Face	Expressive	Nervous or lifeless
	Hands	Expressive, moving	Fidgety or in pockets
	Trunk	Upright, positive	Slouched, leaning
Language	Accuracy	Mostly accurate	Impedes understanding
	Fluency	Acceptable	Impedes understanding
	Vocabulary	Appropriate, accurate	Is too difficult or simple
Content	Interest	Stimulating	Boring, dull
	Level	Appropriate	Facile or complex
	Examples	Relevant, illustrative	Irrelevant, pointless
Structure	Sequence	Is logical	Is confusing
	Signals	Indicate structure	Are inappropriate or not used
	Integration of visuals	Shows timing and balance	Lacks timing and balance

Contributors

Rex Berridge, a teacher educator and formerly an English language adviser with the British Council, is now the director of the Language and Learning Centre, University of Wales, Aberystwyth, in the United Kingdom. Jenny Muzambindo, a teacher educator and specialist in English teaching and the methodology of teaching across the curriculum, is a senior lecturer in English at Belvedere Technical Teachers' College, in Zimbabwe.

Identifying Cultural Eyeglasses

Levels
High intermediate +

Aims
Differentiate between
observations and
interpretations
Learn how personal/
cultural perspectives
influence them

Class Time
2 hours

Preparation Time
20 minutes

Resources
*The Gods Must Be
Crazy II* video
Transcript of the video's
first 3 minutes
Glossary
Handout
Poster board or large
paper
Markers

This activity, intended to be used at the beginning of an anthropology unit, allows students to explore two key terms in the field of anthropology on both a theoretical and an applied basis. The activity provides opportunities for the students to work individually and cooperatively as well as to make cross-cultural comparisons.

Procedure

1. Present a brief description, with examples, of observations and interpretations in the field of anthropology.
2. Show the first 3 minutes of the movie *The Gods Must Be Crazy II* without the sound.
3. Ask the students in groups of three or four to suggest what the movie might be about. Record all the ideas on poster board or a large piece of paper.
4. Pass out the observation-interpretation handout (see the Appendix).
5. Show the movie clip a second time, again without sound. Have the students individually write down what they "see" in the observation column of the handout while they are watching the movie.
6. After they finish watching the movie, ask the students to write their interpretations of these observed movie events in the interpretation column.
7. Ask the students as a group to create a large chart of observations and interpretations based on the movie.
8. Discuss as a whole class the differences in the students' interpretations of observed events and the possible reasons for these differences (e.g., personal and cultural backgrounds, values, perspectives).
9. Pass out a transcript and glossary for the 3-minute section of the movie. Play the movie again, this time with the sound.

10. Divide the students into groups, and have the students find and label examples of observations and interpretations in the movie transcript.
11. If the students do not agree on their answers, encourage them to discuss with each other why they believe something is an observation or an interpretation. Ask each group to give one example from the text of either an observation or an interpretation.
12. Make a second chart of these observations and interpretations.
13. Discuss as a whole class the implications of interpretations being presented as observations or facts in the study of anthropology.

References and Further Reading

Bataille, G. M., & Sands, K. M. (1984). *American Indian women telling their lives.* Lincoln: University of Nebraska Press.

Fisher, M. P. (1986). *Recent revolutions in anthropology.* New York: Franklin Watts.

Kerewsky-Halpern, B. (1983). *Anthropology, the story of people.* New York: Cambridge, the Adult Education Company.

Rosaldo, M. Z., & Lamphere, L. (Eds.). (1974). *Woman, culture and society.* Stanford, CA: Stanford University Press.

Weitzman, D. (1994). *Human culture.* New York: Charles Scribner's Sons.

Appendix: Observation-Interpretation Handout

Directions: You will watch a 3-minute section of the movie *The Gods Must Be Crazy II,* again without the sound. This time, write down things that you observe (see) in the film in the Observations column, and when the movie is finished, write your interpretation of what you saw in the Interpretations column. Do not worry about spelling or finding absolutely perfect word(s) to describe what you see.

Observations	Interpretations

Appendix B: Glossary

Kalahari: desert region in southwest Africa, primarily in Botswana
contentedly: happily
environment: surroundings, setting, climate, habitat
surface water: water that runs on top of the ground
ivory poachers: people who illegally hunt elephants for their tusks
high-tech vehicles: modern, up-to-date trucks and cars
intrude: thrust or bring in without welcome
vast: of very great size, enormous, huge
thirstland: part of a country or area where one is always thirsty; desert
reservoir: natural or manmade place where water is collected or stored
hightail it out of: leave very quickly
isolation: state of being away from other people
hectic: very busy, frantic
domain: area in which the Bushmen live
fringes: borders
survive: live, endure
contrivances: machines, tools
migrate: travel or journey; animals often migrate at special times of the year
gossip: reveal or divulge information, talk about others
patent: government grant to an inventor or an inventor's heirs for a stated period of time, conferring the exclusive right to make, use, license, or vend an invention or process

Contributor

Randi Freeman teaches in the University ESL Program at Central Washington University, in the United States.

Convince the Opposition

Levels
Intermediate +

Aims
Analyze arguments from a film
Develop effective arguments in writing

Class Time
4-6 hours

Resources
Inherit the Wind
Video cassette player

T he film *Inherit the Wind* (Papazian, 1988) provides an interesting way to teach EAP students how to construct a convincing argument. By summarizing and evaluating the opposing arguments on human evolution presented by the attorneys for the prosecution and defense in the film, students develop critical thinking skills and become aware of the elements of a good argument. Students also learn that in developing a convincing argument, they must not only present their own point of view but must also address the opposing point of view. They then choose an issue about which they have a strong opinion and apply their knowledge of effective argumentation to write an essay that argues for their position and convincingly rebuts the opposition's point of view. This assignment encourages students to explore their own beliefs about important issues ranging from abortion to ethnic, racial, and gender bias. The subsequent sharing of students' essays provides a forum for class discussion and possible debates.

Procedure

1. Discuss the events leading to the Scopes monkey trial.
2. Introduce the major characters in the film *Inherit the Wind,* focusing on the two attorneys, Henry Drummond and Matthew Brady.
3. Have the students divide a sheet of paper into two columns labeled *pro* and *con*. Tell them that they will use this sheet to list the key arguments for or against Darwin's theory of evolution made by each attorney (i.e., Drummond's pro arguments and Brady's con arguments).
4. Show the film, having the students take notes as they watch.
5. Have the students in pairs or small groups compare the arguments presented by the two attorneys.

6. Have the students share their findings as a class and write their responses on the chalkboard.
7. Engage the students in a discussion of the effectiveness of each position. Ask them to identify the arguments they found most persuasive and explain why they found those arguments effective.
8. In class, have students write a one-paragraph summary of the arguments they found especially convincing and explain why the arguments were effective. Then have the students share their responses.
9. For homework, ask the students to choose an issue about which they have a strong opinion and write an essay in which they argue their position.

Caveats and Options

1. Use the activity with another film that contains effective scenes of debate or argumentation.

References and Further Reading

Currie, P., & Cray, E. (1987). *Strictly academic* (chap. 8). New York: Newbury House.

Dobbs, C. (1989). *Reading for a reason* (chap. 6). Englewood Cliffs, NJ: Prentice-Hall.

Papazian, R. J. (Producer). (1988). *Inherit the wind* [Film]. MGM Television Productions.

Contributor

Loretta F. Kasper is an assistant professor of English at Kingsborough Community College of the City University of New York, in the United States, where she teaches content-based courses to intermediate and advanced ESL students.

Talking Textbooks

Levels
Intermediate +

Aims
Reinforce formal
schemata of textbooks
Practice reading and
assimilating data from
textbooks
Practice informal
note-taking

Class Time
30–40 minutes

Preparation Time
10–15 minutes

Resources
Self-contained textbook
extracts with clearly
defined sections
Task sheets

This information-gap activity combines reading, speaking, and informal note-taking while allowing students to become familiar with the formal schemata of textbooks. Because the students have to subsequently transmit information to fellow students, the activity encourages purposeful reading and motivates the students to assimilate the main points of the text. As the students must also collect information, they practice listening and informal note-taking skills.

Procedure

1. Before class, cut up the textbook extracts so that you have one section per student. Prepare task sheets (one per student) that consist of an open grid with the names of the various sections in the left-hand column and a blank right-hand column in which the students will take relevant notes.
2. In class, give each of the students one section of the prepared text. Give the students time to read their section and ask any questions they have.
3. Distribute the task sheets to the students. Have them fill in the relevant part of their task sheet with the information from their section and then circulate, asking the other students to give them the information they need to complete the other parts of their task sheet.
4. After sufficient time has passed, check the notes taken by the students against the original information in the texts to ensure that no errors have inadvertently been introduced.
5. Give each of the students a copy of the complete extract (i.e., containing all the sections used) to allow them to check over the other sections at their leisure and see how all the sections fit together.

Caveats and Options

1. Stress to the students the need to assimilate the information in their section of the text. They should pass on only the most relevant information in their section, including whatever details or examples they consider pertinent. Thus, firmly discourage the students from simply reading their texts aloud to the students who need the information.

2. Although this activity is suitable for use with textbook extracts that have a relatively fixed format (e.g., *clinical features, symptoms and signs, management,* and *prognosis* are sections common to most clinical medicine textbooks), it can in fact be done with textbook extracts containing lists of any kind. Another example from the field of medicine is the commonly found lists of factors affecting the epidemiology of diseases. Thus in the case of, say, the epidemiology of coronary atherosclerosis, give the students sections on such topics as smoking, hypertension, diet, stress, race, sex, and age.

Contributor

Paul W. Miller teaches EFL and ESP in the Instituto de Idiomas at the Universidad de Navarra, in Pamplona, Spain.

Competing Explanations

Levels
Advanced

Aims
Explore the explanation
function in sociology
Analyze a text with a
range of competing
explanations
Write a competing
explanations text

Class Time
2 hours

Preparation Time
15 minutes

Resources
Graphs of divorce and
enrollment statistics
Divorce explanations
text

Explaining the causes of phenomena is an important mode of analysis in academic study. The activity described here explores one specific rhetoric of explanation—the summary and evaluation of alternative (or competing) explanations. The text samples are from sociology; the framework for the activity, however, can be applied to other disciplinary contexts.

Procedure

1. Show the students the graph of divorce statistics in the United States (See Appendix A). Ask them what they think are the most probable explanations for the upward trend shown. Make a list of these explanations on the blackboard. Encourage individual students to indicate which explanation they find the most plausible.
2. Distribute the divorce explanations text (Appendix B), and have the students read it. Check the students' comprehension of the text.
3. Ask the students which explanations the writers reject and whether they agree with the explanation offered (e.g., that marital instability has probably always existed and that more liberal divorce laws have merely provided couples with a solution to preexisting marital problems).
4. Discuss the structure and language of the divorce explanations text (see Appendix C for a sample analysis) as follows:
   ● The text presents three different explanations for the phenomenon of rising divorce. The first two are summarized and then rebutted. The final explanation is presented as "the most plausible" one.
      ▶ Ask the students (or show them) how the sequence of *summary + negative evaluation* is realized linguistically.

59

▶ Ask the students why they think the writers have presented their explanation in this way (i.e., ask what rhetorical effect is achieved by presenting and then dismissing alternative explanations).

▶ Summaries of the first two explanations are realized by the following clauses:

"Many people have suggested that . . . ." (Sentence 4)

"Some commentators have gone further and argued that . . . ." (Sentence 5)

▶ Ask the students what other terms could be used for the subjects of these clauses (e.g., *thinkers, theorists, sociologists*). Similarly, elicit from the students other reporting verbs that could be used (e.g., *claim, believe, hold, maintain*). If you wish, teach citation conventions. For example, show the students how to adapt the pattern above if they are summarizing the explanation of an individual scholar (e.g., *Smith (1982) has suggested that . . . .*).

● *Evaluation* of the first two explanations is signaled in two structures:

Structure 1: ". . . the problem with this argument is that . . . ." (Sentence 4)

Structure 2: "But we can certainly be sceptical of such a view, suggesting as it does that . . . ." (Sentence 6)

Unlike the summary clauses, which use verb forms for reporting (e.g., *suggest, argue*), the evaluation clauses use nominals (e.g., *argument, view*).

▶ Ask the students what other nominalized verbal processes might be used here. Have them refer to some of the other verbal processes discussed in the summary section (e.g., *claim, belief*).

▶ Ask the students which words signal that the evaluation being made is a negative one, for example,

"The problem with this argument is that . . . ."

"We can be certainly be sceptical of this view . . . ."

● Contrast these words with the positive *epithet* (Halliday, 1994) used to indicate the final explanation:

> "A more plausible explanation for rises in the divorce rate after the passage of a law is that . . . ." (Sentence 7)

5. Show the students the graph called "Male and Female Enrollments in British Universities" (Appendix D). Ask the students what explanations they can give for the trends shown in this figure (e.g., that males are more attracted to technical subjects than females are). Again encourage debate and disagreement on this issue. Insist, however, that the students adopt an "explanatory" approach.

6. Ask the students to write a short text that outlines the most plausible explanation for the gender imbalance shown in the Male and Female Enrollments graph, using the divorce explanations text as a rough guide. Tell the students to present at least one counterexplanation in their text.

Caveats and Options

1. The activity requires the students to write a paragraph-length text only. In addition, the text they produce will be based only on their own presuppositions of the phenomenon. If you wish, adapt the writing task to be an extended research essay. To do this, give the students (or have them locate) reading materials by different authors that present a variety of explanations for a given phenomenon. If you wish, use the following rubric for the essay: *Critically discuss various explanations offered for* [*Phenomenon X*]. In this version of the task, teach the students about citation conventions.

2. The activity looks at only one rhetoric of explanation, termed *competing explanations*. Use other sample texts to explore other explanation rhetorics, such as *hierarchical explanations*, that are organized around the notion of principal and secondary causes.

References and Further Reading

Halliday, M. A. K. (1994). *Introduction to functional grammar* (2nd ed.). London: Edward Arnold.

Appendix A

Ratio of Divorced Persons per 1,000 Married Persons
With Spouse Present, 1960–1990[1]

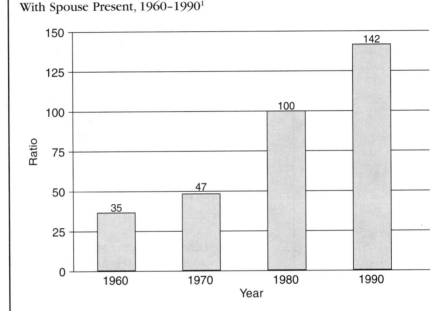

Appendix B:
Divorce
Explanations
Text[2]

[1]As laws and procedures regulating divorce have altered, the divorce rate has tended to increase by leaps and bounds; with each new piece of legislation making divorce more readily available, the rate has risen rapidly for a time before levelling off. [2]Today there is one divorce in Britain for every three marriages. [3](In the USA the rate is one in two.) [4]Many people have suggested that the higher

[1]From *Marital Status and Living Arrangements, March 1990* (Current Population Reports, p. 2), December 1991, Washington, DC: U.S. Department of Commerce, Bureau of the Census.
[2]From *Introductory Sociology* (3rd ed., p. 301), by T. Bilton, K. Bonnett, and P. Jones, 1996, London: Macmillan. Copyright © 1996 by Macmillan Co. Reprinted with permission.

divorce rates reflect an underlying increase in marital instability; the problem with this argument is that we have no way of knowing how many unstable or unhappy marriages existed before legislation made it possible to dissolve them in a public (and recordable) form. [5]Some commentators have gone further and argued that more permissive divorce laws in themselves cause marital breakdown. [6]But we can certainly be sceptical of such a view, suggesting as it does that happily married couples can suddenly be persuaded to abandon their relationship, propelled by the attraction of a new divorce law. [7]A more plausible explanation for rises in the divorce rate after the passage of a law is that unhappily married couples were for the first time given access to a legal solution to preexistent marital problems; in other words, changes in divorce laws are less likely to cause marital breakdown than to provide new types of solution where breakdown has already occurred.

Appendix C: Analysis of Divorce Explanations Text

Introduction to sociological phenomenon and evidence	[1]As laws and procedures regulating divorce have altered, the divorce rate has tended to increase by leaps and bounds; with each new piece of legislation making divorce more readily available, the rate has risen rapidly for a time before levelling off. [2]Today there is one divorce in Britain for every three marriages. [3] (In the USA the rate is one in two.)
Explanation 1 (summary and evaluation)	[4]Many people have suggested that the higher divorce rates reflect an underlying increase in marital instability; the problem with this argument is that we have no way of knowing how many unstable or unhappy marriages existed before legislation made it possible to dissolve them in a public (and recordable) form.

Explanation 2 (summary and evaluation)	[5]Some commentators have gone further and argued that more permissive divorce laws in themselves cause marital breakdown. [6]But we can certainly be sceptical of such a view, suggesting as it does that happily married couples can suddenly be persuaded to abandon their relationship, propelled by the attraction of a new divorce law.
Explanation 3	[7]A more plausible explanation for rises in the divorce rate after the passage of a law is that unhappily married couples were for the first time given access to a legal solution to preexistent marital problems; in other words, changes in divorce laws are less likely to cause marital breakdown than to provide new types of solution where breakdown has already occurred.

Appendix D

Male and Female Enrollments in British Universities[3]

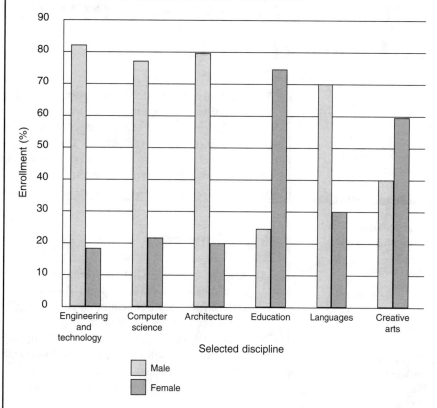

Contributor

Tim Moore works in the Language and Learning Unit at Monash University, in Victoria, Australia.

---

[3]From *Students in Higher Education Institutions 1994/95* (Data Report), 1995, Cheltenham, England: Higher Education Statistics Agency. Copyright © 1995 by the Higher Education Statistics Agency. Reprinted with permission.

Theses and Dissertations: A Guided Tour

Levels
Advanced; postgraduate

Aims
Use techniques of
discourse analysis to
analyze thesis/
dissertation structure
and style
Practice oral
presentations

Class Time
3 hours +

Preparation Time
1 hour +

Resources
Guide to Analyzing
Sample Theses
Extracts from sample
thesis

This activity is designed as an entrée into the thesis genre for students who are writing, or are about to write, a thesis. The Guide to Analyzing Sample Theses (see the Appendix) draws on generalized findings from research into this genre (Hopkins & Dudley-Evans, 1988; Swales, 1990). We have sought, however, to avoid being too reductionist in our approach. Students consider how writing in their own discipline might depart from any generalized model of the thesis and how their own work will differ from any exemplars in their field.

Procedure

1. Ask the students what they believe to be the distinguishing features of a thesis and in what ways they think a thesis is similar to and different from other academic genres (e.g., essays) and nonacademic genres (e.g., popular science magazines).
2. Distribute copies of the Guide to Analyzing Sample Theses (see the Appendix). Discuss any points that need clarifying.
3. Distribute copies of the thesis extracts (see Caveats and Options, No. 1). If necessary, give a very brief overview of the content of the thesis.
4. Ask the students in pairs to use the guide as a basis for analyzing the thesis extracts. Allow at least 30 minutes for this step.
5. When they have finished, ask the pairs to discuss with the class any aspects of the extracts they found interesting, illuminating, or puzzling.
6. For the next class, ask individual students to find a sample thesis in their field and to use the Guide to Analyzing Sample Theses as a basis for conducting their own analysis. Ask them to prepare a short, spoken presentation for the class on any aspect of the sample thesis

they found interesting. If you wish, use the following questions as an outline for the content of the presentation:

- How is X (e.g., organization of the literature review) done in the sample thesis?
- Is it done well?
- How is X likely to be different in my own thesis?

Tell the students to include a short extract from the thesis in the presentation (either as a handout or on an overhead transparency).

Caveats and Options

1. Select the sample thesis carefully. For discipline-specific classes, choose one from the students' discipline. For mixed-discipline classes, choose a thesis on a topic that is both comprehensible and interesting for the students. (For such a group, we used a thesis from the Faculty of Education on right- and left-handed writers.)
2. Select the thesis extracts to exemplify the linguistic and rhetorical features covered in the Guide to Analyzing Sample Theses. Make sure the extracts include samples or whole treatments of all sections, especially the introduction, literature review, and conclusion.
3. A key concept used in the Guide to Analyzing Sample Theses is the *rhetorical move* (Swales, 1981). To introduce this concept to the students, discuss the move structure of a genre with which they would all be familiar, such as the television news broadcast:

Move Structure	
Television News Program	Individual News Story
1. Opening (with music) 2. Summary (headline stories) 3. Headline stories • National • International	1. Introduction by presenter 2. Detailed description by reporter (usually visuals with voice-over) 3. Interview with news actor (optional)

4. Other stories 　● National 　● International 5. Sports 6. Weather 7. Finance 8. Summary 9. Closing	4. Conclusion by reporter

In terms of constituents, suggest to the students that a thesis is akin to the whole news bulletin and that the individual sections of a thesis can be thought of as the individual news stories. Also make the point that although genres have a readily identifiable structure, they usually allow for a degree of variation within it. For example, a news bulletin without a summary would be generically aberrant, but one that included a sports item as a headline story would not. As with all analogies, do not push this one too far!

4. As an alternative procedure, distribute a selection of whole theses to the class. This procedure may be preferable for single-discipline groupings, especially when the subject area's thesis genre is still in the process of development. If you use a selection of whole theses, conflate Steps 3-6 in the procedure. A more-than-adequate pair of biceps will be necessary.

References and Further Reading

Hopkins, A., & Dudley-Evans, T. (1988). A genre-based investigation of discussion sections in articles and dissertations. *English for Specific Purposes, 7,* 113-122.

Swales, J. (1981). *Aspects of article introductions* (Aston Research Reports No. 1). Birmingham, England: University of Aston.

Swales, J. (1990). *Genre analysis: English in academic and research settings*. Cambridge: Cambridge University Press.

Appendix: Guide to Analyzing Sample Theses

Table of Contents

1. How many sections is the thesis divided into? Is a numbering system used for sections and subsections? How many levels are there (e.g., 1.5.2 = three levels)?
2. Which sections are included before the introduction (e.g., summary, acknowledgments)? How are these set apart from the main sections of the thesis (e.g., with Roman numerals)?
3. How long is the introduction? Is a separate review of the literature included? How many sections make up the body of the thesis? On what basis does the body appear to be organized (e.g., methods-results-discussion format, topic areas)?

Summary (Abstract-Synopsis)

> The summary should include at least the following moves:
> - introduction to the area covered in the study
> - statement of the aim of the study and its rationale
> - brief description of method and approach
> - brief description of main findings
> - conclusions

1. Can you readily identify these moves in the summary of your sample thesis? Is the summary clear? Are any other moves included? Do they strengthen the summary? Note that, along with the title, the summary is the most frequently read part of a thesis. Readers will often decide whether to continue reading or not on the strength of the summary.
2. Do you get a clear sense of what the research is about from the summary? Does the summary motivate you to read (some of) the rest of the thesis?

Introduction

1. Look at the opening paragraph. How well does it set the scene?

> Some of the moves in introductions are elaborated versions of the first moves in the summary. In your introduction you should also seek to situate your research within previous research conducted in the field. The following is a sequence of moves typically used in many thesis introductions:
> - introduction to the general area of the study
> - (brief) review of the current state of knowledge in the area
> - indication of gaps, shortcomings, and problems in the research to date
> - statement of the aim of your research, especially how it will fill the gap, solve the problem, and so on

2. Can you identify these moves in the sample introduction? Are the aims of the study transparently clear?

> Another common move attached to the introduction is the *thesis plan* (sometimes referred to as *advance labeling*), as in the following:
> The first chapter outlines the background to the study including its theoretical framework. Chapter 2 reviews . . . . [etc.]

3. Is advance labeling used in the introduction of your sample thesis? Where is it located?

Literature Review

1. Does the thesis contain a separate review of the literature? How long is it? Which citation system is used (e.g., Harvard, Oxford)?
2. How does the literature review (or sections that refer extensively to the literature) appear to be structured? Are different themes covered in different subsections (e.g., theoretical issues, methodological is-

sues, results of previous studies)? Is advance labeling used to indicate how the literature review will unfold?

3. How does the literature review conclude? Does it seek to show how the present study fits in with work discussed in the review?

Body

> In the middle sections (or body) of a thesis, the focus is very much on the study itself. In very general terms, these sections will give an account of
>
> - what was done in the study (e.g., methods, procedures, approaches)
> - what was found (e.g., results, findings)
>
> In some theses, especially those based on experimental models of research, these two elements may be incorporated in separate Methods and Results sections. In theses with a more thematic organization of chapters, these elements might be signaled less explicitly.

1. How do the two elements above appear to be organized in the sample?
2. What level of detail is given for what was done in the study (e.g., subjects, equipment, procedures for data collection, methods of analysis)?
3. How are the findings organized? In a series of separate sections? In what form(s) are the findings presented (e.g., as tables, calculations, examples, extended description)?

Conclusion-Discussion

> Conclusion sections tend to include at least some of the following moves:
> - a summary of the main findings
> - comparison with findings from other research
> - explanations for findings
> - implications of the findings
> - limitations of the research
> - suggestions for future research
>
> Note that these moves do not necessarily appear in the order shown above. Some moves may also be repeated, especially those that deal with the discussion of findings (the first four listed above).

1. Which of the moves listed above can you identify in your sample thesis? In which order do they appear? Are any moves repeated?

> The move called *summary of the main findings* is concerned with making claims about your subject. These often need to be expressed in a qualified way, using expressions like the following:
> On the basis of this study, it would appear that X is . . .
> The findings of this study suggest that X is . . .

2. Can you identify the claims made in your sample thesis? How are these expressed?

References and Appendixes

1. How many pages of references are there? How are individual references cited? (Pay particular attention to "difficult" sources, e.g., nonwritten or unpublished sources.)
2. Are appendixes used? What sort of material is contained in them?

Other Language Matters

1. How does the writer refer to himself or herself in the thesis? Explicitly, using first-person pronouns (e.g., *I, my*)? In the third person (e.g., *the researcher, this writer*)? Implicitly, using passive forms (e.g., *it is thought that*)? Do these patterns vary in different parts of the thesis?
2. How is the thesis referred to (e.g., as *the present study*)? Is a distinction made between the thesis (the written product) and the study (the research process)? How does the writer distinguish between his or her study and other works referred to in the thesis?
3. How does the writer deal with the problem of sexist language (e.g., by using masculine and feminine forms—*his or her*), as in the previous question?

Contributors

Tim Moore and Harriet Searcy work in the Language and Learning Unit at Monash University, in Victoria, Australia.

Appealing to Your Peers

Levels
Intermediate +; EFL;
tertiary ESL

Aims
Develop a sense of
audience in writing
subject-specific texts

Class Time
45 minutes–1 hour

Preparation Time
Variable

Resources
Examples of former
students' written work
in relevant subject
area(s)
Role-play cards
Samples of current
students' written work

Having a sense of audience in writing academic texts is partly a matter of anticipating the expectations of the reader—in this case the person who will be supervising or assessing the text—and partly a matter of appealing to one's academic peers. This activity aims to develop students' appeal to both of these audiences.

Procedure

1. To raise awareness, tell the students to brainstorm in pairs and draw up a short list of what they think are departmental expectations for successful writing in their course of study. Ask the students, "What makes a good piece of academic writing?" Responses might include, for example, *content, evidence of reading, argument, good grammar,* and *spelling*.

2. Give each pair a sample of a former student's writing. Ask them to analyze and discuss it and to decide what they think are its strengths and weaknesses. Phrase the question as "How would you have written this better?" or "How would you respond if someone gave you this piece of writing?"

3. Elicit the strengths and weaknesses, list them on the blackboard, and ask the students what criteria they used to judge the acceptability of the piece of written work (or aspects of it).

4. Ask the students in groups to draw up a set of criteria for appraising students' work and, for each criterion, to include indicators of good or bad practice (see the example in Appendix A).

5. Give the students the role-play cards (see Appendix B). Allowing time for preparation, ask two members of each group to carry out the role play while the others in the group watch and make relevant notes.

Then allow the students a few minutes to reflect on and discuss their performance.

6. If time allows, ask one pair to perform the role play for the whole class. Then allow time for reflection on the role play and on lessons to be learned from it about tutors' and students' expectations of written work.

7. In groups again, ask the students to refine their appraisal criteria and indicators in light of the role play.

8. Ask the students to exchange pieces of their own written work and comment on each other's achievement, using the instruments that they have developed. Stress that the comments should be constructive and designed to help and support their colleagues.

Caveats and Options

1. If the students are not from the same or similar subject disciplines, find student-written texts on neutral topics, or have the students write texts to use in Step 8.

2. To make this activity relevant to the students' needs, have the students look at specific aspects of student writing (e.g., grammar, paragraphing, organization of text, textual cohesion). These aspects could be the focus of the appraisal criteria. What is important here is that, by working out for themselves what their tutors are looking for, the students become more aware of strategies for improving their writing.

3. Omit the role play if time is too short, or expand it if time allows.

References and Further Reading

Livingstone, C. (1983). *Role play in language learning.* Harlow, England: Longman.

Stephenson, B., Salkie, R., Love, A., & Gwete, W. (Eds.). (1992). *English for specific purposes: Theory and practice at the University of Zimbabwe.* Harare: University of Zimbabwe, Department of Linguistics.

White, R., & Arndt, V. (1991). *Process writing.* Harlow, England: Longman.

Appendix A: Checklist for Academic Writing

Criterion	Indicators	Comments
Content	Relevance to title and topic Level: cognitive, affective Interest Evidence of reading: depth and breadth	
Argument	Type: logical, sequential, chronological Clarity and lucidity Originality Exemplification	
Structure	Introduction, body, conclusion Paragraphing	
Referencing	Footnotes or endnotes References: in text or at end Bibliography	
Layout	Writing or typing: size, font, ease of reading Spacing, indention, paragraphing Headings and subheadings Graphics: placement, size, clarity	
Language	Register: lexis, structures Level: cognitive, affective Signposts: connectives, references Grammar: structures, agreement, and so on Spelling	

Appendix B: Role-Play Cards

Role A	Role B
You are a student. You have presented a piece of work to your tutor. Your tutor has called you to his or her office to discuss your essay. You think it is because of your English skills, and you want to ask for special consideration because you are a nonnative speaker of English. You know a lot about English but have problems in actually using it.	You are a tutor. A student has handed you an essay that has serious language faults. [Specify faults or areas of weakness here.] You want to speak to the student about his or her work. You are not an expert in language, but you do know when something does not look right. You have asked the student to see you, and you are going to warn him or her to either work harder or face a failing grade.

Contributors

Jenny Muzambindo, a teacher educator and specialist in English teaching and the methodology of teaching across the curriculum, is a senior lecturer in English at Belvedere Technical Teachers' College, in Zimbabwe. Rex Berridge, a teacher educator and formerly an English language adviser with the British Council, is the director of the Language and Learning Centre, University of Wales, Aberystwyth, in the United Kingdom.

How's Your Genre Awareness?

Levels
Intermediate +

Aims
Become aware of
generic features of
written texts
Recognize academic
argumentation essays
Draft and edit effective
academic texts

Class Time
1-2 hours (initial
activity)
5-6 hours (full cycle)

Preparation Time
1 hour +

Resources
Sample of target genre
List of the genre's key
rhetorical elements
Sample(s) of mass media
genres
Overhead projector,
transparencies, and pen
(optional)
Flawed model of target
genre (optional)

Genre analysis goes on to some extent in all our encounters with texts, and being conscious of this process and the texts encountered in a second or foreign language is a tool for learning. To encourage ESL learners to become more aware of the characteristics of texts they come across in and outside school, teachers can integrate genre analysis into a wide variety of reading and writing activities in the EAP classroom. By understanding how certain mass media genres differ from common academic genres, such as essay exams, research papers, and laboratory reports, learners can become more efficient readers and more strategic writers of a variety of texts. Equally important is to cultivate an awareness of text types and their purposes, structures, specialized lexical items, and other characteristics, which learners can bring to their various encounters with English. Peer editing naturally follows the analysis of the flawed model and brings the perspective of genre analysis to the students' own writing and editing skills.

Procedure

Analysis of Sample of Target Genre (Argumentation Essay)

1. Review the rhetorical structure of an argumentation essay. As a warmup, ask the students to generate a list of the rhetorical elements of an argumentation essay (see Appendix A). Either write or have the students write a complete list on the blackboard and correct it, or distribute copies to the class.
2. Hand out a sample argumentation essay. Have the students work together to read it and identify the rhetorical elements listed, marking them on the essay. (This step will go faster if the students have read the essay before class.)

3. Have the students work together on a more complete genre analysis by describing the following aspects of the essay:
   ● communicative purpose: What is the text trying to accomplish?
   ● audience: Who are the intended readers?
   ● register: How formal or informal is the language?
   ● structure and stages: How is the text organized?
4. Based on cues on the blackboard or an overhead transparency, have the students create a genre analysis form by drawing a grid on a piece of paper. Note to the students that they have already identified the structure and stages. Also ask the students to select words or phrases that provide evidence of the register.
5. When they have finished, have the groups report their answers, or write them on the blackboard.

Analysis of Mass Media Text

1. Before class, find samples of one or more mass media genres for comparison with the target genre (see Appendix B for an example). Use texts of a type that the students can easily find in locally available newspapers or magazines and with which they are likely to be familiar.
2. In class, tell the students that the genre analysis technique applies to all kinds of texts that accomplish all kinds of purposes, including those found in school, business, and the mass media.
3. Distribute the text. Ask the students to identify the kind of text or tell you what it is. Also ask if they think this text is the same as or different from an argumentation essay. Ask only for first impressions, and note responses on the blackboard.
4. To add variety, have the students work in pairs or in new groupings. Either ask them to make new genre analysis forms on their own paper, or supply the forms. Have the students analyze the mass media text, following the same process they used for the sample argumentation essay. When they finish, display or have the students display the analysis on the blackboard.

Comparison of Genres

1. To close this sequence of activities, ask the students to comment on the differences between the two genres, and draw their attention to the ways the text structure and register fit the audience and purpose. They should be able to see that argumentation essays are constructed not to fit an arbitrary set of rules but rather to fit the purpose and academic audience.
2. Give the students further work on writing and evaluating academic argumentation essays, and discuss writers' choices that are not appropriate to the argumentation genre in terms of what kinds of texts they *would* fit.

Analysis of a Flawed Model of Target Genre (Optional)

1. For a follow-up activity, find a flawed model of the target genre that is missing important rhetorical or organizational elements or that is inconsistent in the register and its consideration of intended readers (see Appendix C for a sample).
2. Have the students work in groups to identify the problems in the sample; ask them to prepare to explain how these problems will affect the audience and the accomplishment of the argumentative purpose of the text.
3. To further extend this activity, ask individuals, pairs, or groups to revise portions of the sample essay and share their revisions with the rest of the class.

Peer Editing of Student Work (Optional)

1. If necessary, review the genre of the academic argumentation essay (e.g., if some time has passed since the last genre awareness activity).
2. Have the students work alone to read each others' drafts and identify elements that could be changed or improved to better fit the genre and better convince the intended audience. For this editing activity, keep issues of grammar and punctuation separate from the rhetorical structure and register.

3. Because the students' analytical skills will vary, repeat the activity so that two different students analyze each draft.

Assignment Analysis (Optional)

1. Either bring in or ask the students to bring in assignments from other classes. Select one or two assignments that call for written products of some sort, including such possibilities as a summary, an article review, or a lab report.
2. Ask the students to try to imagine, based on the assignment and their own knowledge, what kind of text product is expected. Have the students use the genre analysis grid in pairs or groups to develop an analysis or description of the text.

Field Work (Optional)

1. Have the students collect samples of good writing from their fields of academic interest and write journal entries analyzing the purpose, audience, register, and structure, including samples of the language used.
2. Tell the students to ask a teacher or teaching assistant what qualities make the chosen text type successful and to write notes on this, either for homework or in class.
3. Ask the students to hand in a completed project consisting of the sample, the genre analysis, and notes on the information offered by teachers. Either assign this as a homework project or structure it in stages, with data collected in the field and analyzed and written up in class.
4. Either ask the students to present their projects to the class, or assemble them into a field work notebook.

Caveats and Options

1. Make sure the students are already somewhat familiar with the rhetorical form of an argumentation essay. The activity does not assume, however, that they have mastered or "acquired" the genre at this point.

2. Appropriate resources are relatively easy to locate:
   - Models of argumentative essays: These can be found in many college composition books, such as *The St. Martin's Guide to Writing* (Axelrod & Cooper, 1997). Or select good models from the work of students in previous semesters. For the key elements, most composition texts also offer some schematic formula with the elements for producing an argumentation essay. This list should be fairly simple, so you may need to adapt what is found in the textbook (see Appendix A for a sample list).
   - Mass media text: The text selected for this activity is a letter to the editor of a newspaper (see Appendix B) because it is a common genre that argues for an opinion but is different from a school argumentation essay in several ways. For example, the audience is a general one of newspaper readers and, possibly, people in positions of power related to the issue addressed; in addition, whereas academic argumentation seeks to demonstrate fairness, letters to the editor may express sarcasm or anger. Another text type that works is magazine columns, which focus more on telling a personal story than on making a formal argument.
   - Flawed model of the target genre: Adapt a student essay from a previous semester. If you wish, include grammatical or word choice errors as part of this text, but they are not needed for the genre focus. Another option is to create your own sample that deviates from the target genre of argumentation essay in register and in rhetorical structure. A good sample will be missing some rhetorical elements and will include some rhetorical elements that do not belong (see Appendix C).

References and Further Reading

Axelrod, R. B., & Cooper, C. R. (1997). *The St. Martin's guide to writing* (5th ed.). New York: St. Martin's Press.

Callagan, M., & Rothery, J. (1988). *Teaching factual writing: A genre based approach.* Sydney, Australia: Metropolitan East Region, DSP Literacy Project.

Conrow, S. (1992). *A case study of two second language writers in a genre-based composition class: Examining process and product.* Unpublished master's thesis, University of California, Los Angeles.

Fahnestock, J. (1993). Genre and rhetorical craft. *Research in the Teaching of English, 27,* 265–271.

Freedman, A. (1993). Show and tell? The role of explicit teaching in the learning of new genres. *Research in the Teaching of English, 27,* 222–263.

Kroll, B. (1993). Teaching writing is teaching reading: Training the new teacher of ESL composition. In J. Carson & I. Leki (Eds.), *Reading in the composition classroom: Second language perspectives* (pp. 61–82). Boston: Heinle & Heinle.

Martin, J. R. (1993). Genre and literacy—modeling context in educational linguistics. *Annual Review of Applied Linguistics, 11,* 141–172.

Swales, J. (1990). *Genre analysis: English in academic and research settings.* New York: Cambridge University Press.

Swales, J., & Feak, C. (1994). *Academic writing for graduate students: A course for nonnative speakers of English.* Ann Arbor: University of Michigan Press.

Appendix A: Rhetorical Elements of the Target Genre

Elements of an Argumentative Essay[1]

1. Introduction
   - gains the reader's attention
   - establishes your qualifications
   - demonstrates fairness
   - states or implies thesis

2. Background
   - presents necessary background information

3. Lines of argument
   - presents reasons to support your thesis
   - demonstrates the ways the argument may be in the reader's interest

[1]From *The St. Martin's Handbook* (3rd ed., pp. 105–106), by A. Lunsford and R. Connors, 1995, New York: St. Martin's Press. Copyright © 1995 by St. Martin's Press. Adapted with permission.

4. Refutation of opposing arguments
   - considers the opposing point of view
   - notes advantages and disadvantages

5. Conclusion
   - may summarize the argument
   - elaborates on the implications of the thesis
   - makes clear what you want the reader to think or do
   - makes a strong ethical or emotional appeal

Appendix B: Sample of a Mass Media Genre

Letter to the Editor

County Budget Deficit[2]

In their attempts to limit budget deficit increases, the Los Angeles County supervisors have decided to curb extensive borrowing that used valuable county real estate as collateral (July 18). I suggest supervisors curb extensive salary and pension increases and consider reductions in these same areas as one way of convincing the electorate that they are really serious about curbing the runaway deficit.

Appendix C: Flawed Model of the Target Genre

Guns Kill

Public figures like John Kennedy, Martin Luther King, and John Lennon have been lost. Postal workers, shopkeepers, and policemen have been lost as well. Gang members have been lost. Sadly, countless children, mothers, and other innocent people have been lost simply because they were in the wrong place at the wrong time. Opinions vary about what should be done, but the fact is that

[2]From "County Budget Deficit," by R. Seidler, July 25, 1995, "Letters to the Editor," *The Los Angeles Times,* p. M4. Copyright © 1995 by Roy Seidler. Reprinted with permission.

guns are killing more and more people every year in American cities. Gun control may not be the whole answer, yet it is hard to believe that controlling the sale of guns is not at least part of the solution.

The controversy over gun control in the United States has continued since the 1960s as the number of guns continues to rise every year. Recent studies show that there are over 200 million guns in the United States today, ranging from small handguns to rifles, shotguns, and a variety of automatic weapons. Some people argue that guns should be outlawed altogether, while others call for strict regulation of gun sales. In recent years, the debate has become heated again during the Clinton Administration, marked by the enactment of legislation banning the sale of semiautomatic and automatic assault weapons. These guns are the weapon of choice for drug syndicates and youth gangs, yet the National Rifle Association fought hard against the law and spent millions of dollars to defeat congressmen who voted for it.

One reason that guns should be restricted is that simply too many people are dying each year. Guns are involved in tens of thousands of deaths and injuries every year in this country. The number keeps growing, and violence has become a significant and frightening part of our national life. The safety of our children and the future of our nation demand that we act to stop or at least slow the killing that has turned our cities into war zones.

Some crazy gun-lovers cling to the Constitutional right to own firearms. These rednecks scream that they need guns to keep themselves safe. They say that crime will only increase if guns are outlawed. They claim they will be more vulnerable if gun control is enacted. Such backwoods gun nuts are really fools. Do they really believe that their right to own guns is valid today? Wake up and smell the coffee!

Another argument holds that guns are really inanimate objects and are not responsible. The often repeated slogan, "Guns don't kill, people kill," is catchy and is true to some extent. Guns would not be a problem in a perfect world. The sad reality, however, is that we live in a society with poverty, unemployment, discrimination, drug addiction, and racial tension. The culture of crime is a reality, and guns make it very easy for violence to be lethal and immediate, adding to the cycle of hate and destruction. With 12-year-olds using machine guns in drive-by shootings, it seems clear that guns are part of the problem.

What we need is a coordinated effort to reduce violent crime. Economic and racial problems must be solved. Communities need to work together, to organize, and to build networks to help each other and fight all kinds of violent crime. Victims' rights groups and police departments around the country are demanding limits on the sale and ownership of handguns and assault rifles to help them win the battle against violent crime in America. It seems reasonable to listen to the requests of law enforcement officers as part of a balanced plan to return to a safe society for all citizens.

It is not time to sit back and wait for others to solve the problem. It is urgent for everyone to act. There are many ways to help, such as joining a citizens group or writing letters to congressmen. The time to act is now.

Contributor

David Olsher is a doctoral student in applied linguistics at the University of California, Los Angeles, in the United States. He has taught ESL/EFL for 12 years, including university-level ESL, public adult education ESL, and EFL at a college in Japan.

Creating Lifetime Genre Files

Levels
Intermediate +

Aims
Become familiar with
written English genres

Class Time
20–30 minutes (initial
presentation)
Ongoing

Preparation Time
1 hour

Resources
Large, ringed notebooks
Blank genre profile
sheets
Completed genre profile
sheet

This lesson is designed to serve as one of the primary activities in an ESP writing course or to serve as a supplement to ESP reading, vocabulary, or grammar instruction. The activity, which entails both independent and instructor-guided learning, provides learners with a useful resource that they can continually use and expand throughout their careers.

Procedure

1. Explain the concept of genres, and show a few diverse examples (e.g., journal article, wedding invitation, grant proposal, poem, insurance policy, letter of resignation, invoice, résumé, obituary).
2. Discuss and list some of the English genres that your students are likely to use during their lives. Mark those requiring immediate instructional attention with an asterisk.
3. Ask the students to begin collecting samples of these written English genres and putting them in a large, ringed notebook for ease of reference. If you wish, point the students to various World Wide Web sites, publications, or other sources to ease the search process. If the students have similar learning needs, have them work together.
4. Distribute copies of the genre profile sheet (see the Appendix), and ask the students to fill out one sheet to accompany each genre sample they obtain. Hand out a completed genre profile sheet for one of the genres shown in Step 1.
5. As the students assemble their individualized collections of English genre samples, draw on the material from time to time during the language course for studies of genre and the contextual, organizational, grammatical, and lexical features that distinguish each type. Studies might include creative analysis and imitation exercises as well as discussions of observed communication differences between

members of various discourse communities. Be sure to add your input on the construction of accurate genre profiles.

6. Ask the students to continue adding genre samples to their personal collections after they complete their English program to encourage self-learning and to build a useful reference for future writing needs. Also have the students include samples of their own work, such as marked drafts and final products, to aid their learning.

Caveats and Options

1. Although creating individualized genre files that can serve all of their anticipated writing needs is productive for English language learners, you might focus on a narrower range of genres during a particular language course to meet the learners' most pressing needs (e.g., university genres for students preparing to begin a specific field of study, business genres for clients training for a particular business venture). The genres you marked with an asterisk in Step 2 might be a reasonable place to begin.

2. Use the genre file as the focus of a subject-specific ESP writing course or as a supplement in an ESP reading, vocabulary, or grammar course.

References and Further Reading

Berkenkotter, C., & Huckin, T. N. (1995). *Genre knowledge in disciplinary communication: Cognition, culture, power*. Hillsdale, NJ: Erlbaum.

Bhatia, V. K. (1993). *Analysing genre: Language use in professional settings*. London: Longman.

Meyer, H. E. (1983). *Lifetime encyclopedia of letters*. Englewood Cliffs, NJ: Prentice Hall.

Porter, J. E. (1992). *Audience and rhetoric*. Englewood Cliffs, NJ: Prentice Hall.

Swales, J. (1990). *Genre analysis: English in academic and research settings*. Cambridge: Cambridge University Press.

Appendix: Genre Profile Sheet

Genre: *Résumé*

Purpose(s): *To market a person's education, work experience, and accomplishments in a persuasive manner to obtain a job interview.*

Audience(s): *Person(s) responsible for personnel decisions (e.g., director of human resources)*

Notes on content and format:

1. *Name and contact information is centered at the top of the page or placed in the upper left margin. The font size is usually larger than that in the body of the document and frequently appears in boldface.*
2. *Education, work experience, achievements, and other material appropriate for the intended reader are usually listed in descending chronological order under these or similar headings. The headings are usually in boldface and placed at the left margin with extra space above and below the heading.*
3. *The document frequently ends with the heading "References" and the line "Available on request."*

Notes on grammar and vocabulary:

1. *The grammatical subject plus the auxiliary or linking verb is usually dropped in most statements related to work experience or accomplishments as in the following:*
   - *Recipient of the XXX Award for . . .*
   - *Awarded the YYY Prize for . . .*
   - *Designed software that . . .*
   - *Developed a training program for . . .*

2. *Other options for "Available on request:"*
   - *Furnished on request.*
   - *Furnished upon request.*

Additional notes:

1. A résumé is usually printed on white or off-white 20- to 24-bond paper with a cotton rag content of 25%.
2. Bright colors and cute graphics are not appropriate.

Contributor

Thomas Orr is an associate professor at the University of Aizu's Center for Language Research, in Aizu-Wakamatsu City, Japan.

A Bridge to Academic Interests

Levels
Advanced

Aims
Become familiar with
the library
Learn to select articles
in a specific academic
area
Respond to written
material
Learn summary writing
and reference format

Class Time
20–30 minutes
(introduction)
60 minutes (orientation)
15–20 minutes/week
(discussion)

Preparation Time
15–20 minutes

Resources
Reading reaction journal
assignment
Library or other source
of readings

This task allows anxious ESL students to begin to learn vocabulary and content related to their academic areas of interest. A reading reaction journal, in which students respond to authentic reading material they have selected themselves, helps familiarize them with the location of relevant journals and texts in the library, gives them experience in writing short summaries of and reference list entries for the articles, and provides an opportunity to share what they have learned in a follow-up discussion with peers.

Procedure

1. Inquire about the students' academic interests.
2. Pass out copies of the reading reaction journal assignment (see the Appendix), and discuss the four parts.
3. Hold a library orientation in which you familiarize individual students with sections of the library pertinent to their studies and the location of copy machines.
4. Tell the students when the journals will be due (i.e., which day of the week and how often—weekly works well).
5. If you wish, have the students meet in groups on the due date to share and discuss their articles.
6. Collect, read, and evaluate the journals. Give feedback on format, and comment on the students' reactions and responses to the written material.

Caveats and Options

1. Require that the students turn in a copy of their article with their journal so that you can evaluate the summaries for accuracy.

2. To cut down on the reuse of journals from previous terms, interview individual students about their reading during your office hours.
3. Have the students present their articles in class.
4. Have the students write research papers based on the articles, provided they are related to the same topic.
5. Count the journals as a percentage of the final course grade.
6. Use the journals as a written dialogue between you and the students.

Appendix

Reading Reaction Journal Assignment

In addition to the textbook assignments, each week you will read and write about an article from your academic interest area. You will need to purchase a notebook to use for your journal. Choose an article of at least 500 words from a magazine, professional journal, or academic text related to your university studies. Please make a copy of the article you choose and turn it in along with your journal each week.

The reading journal has four parts. After you have read the article, please follow these instructions for your entry. (Note: You may put the four sections in any order you prefer.)

1. Reference: In your journal, cite the article in proper American Psychological Association (APA) format. Examples are given below.

Books
Maker, J., & Lenier, M. (1989). *College reading book 2* (3rd ed.). Belmont, CA: Wadsworth.

Journals
Spack, R. (1985). Literature, reading, writing, and ESL: Bridging the gaps. *TESOL Quarterly, 19,* 703-725.

Magazines
Gardner, H. (1981, December). Do babies sing a universal song? *Psychology Today,* 70-76.

2. Summary: Write a two- to five-sentence summary of the article (topic and main ideas). Please do not use a heading from the article. Write the summary in your own words.

3. Reaction: Write a reaction to the article. Include your comments, your questions, whether you agree or disagree with the author, and whether this article has created an interest in continuing to read in this area. Your reaction can be one paragraph long or five pages long. You don't need to try to organize your ideas or write an essay. Just share your thoughts on, feelings about, questions on, and reactions to the material you have read. Perhaps you did not understand the material; that's OK. Write about the areas that were particularly difficult. What makes the text so difficult? Is it vocabulary, complex sentence structure, or something else?

4. Vocabulary: Make a list of the new words you encountered in the text. Try to determine the meaning of each word from the context and with the help of your dictionary. Write a definition of each word in English.

Contributor

Marilyn Rivers is the writing coordinator at the Center for English as a Second Language, Southern Illinois University at Carbondale, in the United States.

Test Your Index Savvy

Levels
Intermediate +

Aims
Practice using an
English index
Practice scanning for
information
Access computer-related
materials and
vocabulary

Class Time
About 30–45 minutes

Preparation Time
20 minutes

Resources
*Essentials of
Computing* and
accompanying software
package
Quizzes and answer
sheets

Being able to find, verify, and accurately quote specific information in texts is an essential skill in any field, particularly fields that require highly specialized vocabulary or develop as rapidly as computer science and engineering. Students need practice in quickly using indexes and scanning for specific information. In addition, this activity helps give ESP students access to authentic English computer science texts, which may initially seem too difficult.

Procedure

1. The first time you use this activity, demonstrate it with one or two questions: Show the students how to
   - identify key words in the question
   - find them in the index to *Essentials of Computing* (Capron, 1995)
   - scan the appropriate page for the answers

   For example, for *A CD-ROM can store up to _____ megabytes per disk*, show the students where *CD-ROM* is located in the index, and have them tell you the answer and its location (660, page 104, paragraph 1).

2. Hand out answer sheets and copies of a quiz composed of 15 or 20 questions on one of the chapters in *Essentials of Computing*, either a version from the Microtest software package (Mackenzie, Sooriarachchi, Hackleman, & Misner, 1995), a quiz of your own, or a version adapted from the ones in Microtest (see the Appendix for a sample quiz).

3. Give the students 15 minutes (or less) to finish the open-book quiz on their own, using the index to help them find the answers. Collect

the answer sheets if you intend to give grades, but make sure the students have also recorded the answers on their test papers.

4. Have the students check their answers in pairs or small groups, using the following steps:
   - Compare answers. Do not discuss problems for which all the group members' answers are the same.
   - Look for the correct answers to problems the group members disagreed on, and write the correct page numbers on the quizzes.
   - If there is time, look for the page numbers for the answers the group members agreed on.

5. Go over the quiz with the students, using one of the following methods:
   - Give points to students who can give the correct answers and page numbers.
   - Particularly when time is short, give the correct locations and answers yourself. Microtest gives the correct answers and pages for the teacher's reference.

Caveats and Options

1. Using authentic materials is important in preparing students to deal with them routinely when they enter regular classes or do research projects in fields such as computer science. *Essentials of Computing* (Capron, 1995) is used for introductory computer courses at U.S. universities.

2. When using authentic materials, have the students carry out the tasks in a way that makes advanced materials accessible to them. Practicing similar skills with the same materials in several ways is useful for maintaining the students' morale and confidence without sacrificing content.

3. When you use the same difficult materials for several activities, keep the activities fairly short, create opportunities for interaction, and provide opportunities for the students to find, understand, and correct errors before they are labeled right or wrong.

4. Multiple-choice quizzes are recommended for several reasons. Scoring and grading take less time and energy, and the students can compare and check answers quickly. In addition, the questions from

the Microtest test bank are in multiple-choice form. For many questions, the students can look up the potential answers in the index or use related vocabulary for personal lists they are developing for class or on their own.

5. Be sure to use well-organized texts with good visuals, good indexes, and clear headings.

References and Further Reading

Benesch, S. (Ed.). (1988). *Ending remediation: Linking ESL and content in higher education*. Washington, DC: TESOL.

Capron, H. L. (1995). *Essentials of computing* (2nd ed.). Redwood City, CA: Benjamin/Cummings.

Kasper, L. F. (1995). Theory and practice in content-based ESL reading instruction. *English for Specific Purposes, 14,* 223–230.

Mackenzie, C. W., Sooriarachchi, M. P., Hackleman, E. C., & Misner, R. J. (1995). Microtest (Version 2.7) [Computer software]. Omaha, NB: Delta Software. (Software package to accompany the 2nd edition of *Essentials of Computing*)

Appendix: Sample Test

Questions 1–22: Scan the index and table of contents in your book to locate the answers.

1. The programming language FORTRAN is/was _____.
   a. developed by Microsoft   b. introduced in 1958
   c. business-oriented   d. the first high-level language

2. The answer to Question 1 can be found in chapter _____.
   a. 5   b. 6
   c. 7   d. 8

3. _____ is *not* part of the textbook's three-part definition of computer literacy.
   a. Awareness   b. Knowledge
   c. Application   d. Interaction

4. The answer to Question 3 can be found in chapter _____.
   a. 1   b. 2
   c. 3   d. 4

5. Five terms are used to refer to *memory*, but _____ is *not* one of them.
   a. internal memory   b. internal storage
   c. primary memory   d. primary storage

6. The answer to Question 5 can be found in chapter _____.
   a. 1   b. 2
   c. 3   d. 4

7. Laptop computers are also called _____ computers.
   a. portable   b. personal
   c. mini   d. notebook

8. The answer to Question 7 can be found in chapter _____.
   a. 1   b. 2
   c. 3   d. 4

9. A _____ converts a digital signal (transmission) to an analog signal and vice versa.
   a. system switcher   b. graphic user interface
   c. modem   d. coaxial cable

10. The answer to Question 9 can be found in chapter _____.
    a. 5   b. 6
    c. 7   d. 8

11. One CD-ROM can store up to _____ megabytes of data.
    a. 250   b. 660
    c. 910   d. 1,200

12. The answer to Question 11 can be found in chapter _____.
    a. 5   b. 6
    c. 7   d. 8

13. A *light pen* is a kind of _____.
    a. graphic input device   b. word-processing software
    c. computer desk lamp   d. CD-ROM

14. The answer to Question 13 can be found in chapter _____.
    a. 1   b. 2
    c. 3   d. 4

15. Grammar and style programs offer _____ that writers can consider to improve their writing.
    a. lists of rules   b. other words
    c. spelling corrections   d. suggestions

16. The answer to Question 15 can be found in chapter _____.
    a. 11   b. 12
    c. 13   d. 14

17. In database management systems, which of the following is *not* one of the three main database models?
    a. hierarchical   b. network
    c. relational   d. managerial

18. The answer to Question 17 can be found in chapter _____.
    a. 11   b. 12
    c. 13   d. 14

19. Cells are used as storage areas in _____.
    a. spreadsheets   b. word-processing programs
    c. databases   d. worms

20. The answer to Question 19 can be found in chapter _____.
    a. 11   b. 12
    c. 13   d. 14

21. The _____ is one of two parts of the central processing unit.
    a. keyboard   b. control unit
    c. floppy drive   d. disk operating system

22. The answer to Question 21 can be found in chapter _____.
    a. 1   b. 2
    c. 3   d. 4

Contributor

Doug Sawyer is an assistant professor at the University of Aizu's Center for Language Research, in Aizu-Wakamatsu City, Japan.

Jigsaw Schema Skim

Levels
Beginning +

Aims
Activate background
knowledge schema of a
reading topic
Improve skimming for
main ideas and retelling
of key points

Class Time
Variable

Preparation Time
45 minutes

Resources
Newspaper or magazine
articles
Overhead projector,
transparencies, and pen

In this activity, a prereading strategy activates students' background knowledge of a topic. The students then skim articles on the topic. The activity encourages the students to share information, check ideas, and summarize, and it greatly assists reading comprehension.

Procedure

1. Before class, locate and copy two or three newspaper or magazine articles on the same topic. Clip the headlines off the articles, and photocopy them on an overhead transparency (OHT). Select 10 key vocabulary items from the articles.
2. In class, write the topic in one word on the blackboard.
3. Have the students form groups of three, write down five words associated with the topic, and write their words on an OHT or the blackboard.
4. Show the students the 10 key vocabulary items you chose from the articles. Ask the students in groups to classify all the words under subtopics on a transparency or on the blackboard.
5. Show the students the OHT containing the headlines of the three articles. Ask them, in their groups, to add to the list of key vocabulary items other words from the headlines or any others that they can think of.
6. Divide the class into three groups. Hand out copies of the articles so that all the students in each group have the same article
7. Tell the students to individually skim the article headline, subheadings, captions, introduction, and conclusion for 3 minutes.

8. After 3 minutes, tell the students to turn the articles over and discuss the points they remember with the other two students in their group.

9. Repeat Steps 7 and 8 once.

10. Have the students form new groups consisting of three students who have each read a different article. Ask each student to explain the main ideas of his or her article to the other group members.

11. Using the OHT or blackboard display created in Step 4, have the new groups check off the subtopics that appear in the articles.

12. Continue doing scanning and reading comprehension activities.

13. Return to the subtopics on the OHT, and ask the students to continue determining which ones appear in the articles.

Caveats and Options

1. Select articles of approximately the same length and difficulty and with overlapping content.

2. Adjust the skimming time depending on the reading level of the class and the length and difficulty of the articles.

3. As they do with all learning strategies, the students need to practice doing this activity in order to become proficient. They may also require preliminary help with such functions as expressing opinions.

4. Do the initial small-group brainstorming as a class if it is strategically and culturally appropriate.

5. Give the students the following suggestions for developing skimming skills:

- Use your background knowledge to help you predict the meaning of the text from the title.
- Check the headings and subheadings.
- Read the introductory paragraph and the conclusion.
- Read the topic sentence for each paragraph.
- Underline key words.
- Look at the pictures. Read the captions under the pictures.

References and Further Reading

Carrell, P., Devine, J., & Eskey, D. (1988). *Interactive approaches to second language reading*. New York: Cambridge University Press.

Chamot, A. U., & O'Malley, J. M. (1994). *The CALLA handbook: Implementing the cognitive academic language learning approach*. Reading, MA: Addison-Wesley.

Silberstein, S. (1987, October). Let's take another look at reading: Twenty-five years of reading instruction. *English Teaching Forum*, 28–35.

Contributor

Ann F. V. Smith has taught ESL/EFL in Britain, Sweden, Canada, and China. Her experience includes program administration, teacher training, and materials development as well as teaching for a variety of special purposes. Currently she teaches English majors at Tokushima Bunri University, in Japan. She holds an MEd from Dalhousie University, in Halifax, Canada.

Listen Up!

Levels
Intermediate +

Aims
Comprehend lectures
Recognize and identify
nonverbal patterns in
U.S. discourse

Class Time
50 minutes
(presentation)
50 minutes (discussion)

Preparation Time
Variable

Resources
Videotaped lectures or
slides of professors in
various lecture poses
Notes on nonverbal
communication in U.S.
discourse

This activity helps the students comprehend academic lectures by recognizing and looking for nonverbal patterns in U.S. discourse. After the teacher discusses and demonstrates the gestures faculty use when lecturing, the students apply the concepts to slides or videos of faculty (ideally from their current courses) and to nonverbal language in their own culture.

Procedure

1. Have the students arrange their chairs in a large semicircle so they can see each other. Model the gestures used for emphasis in lectures in three categories: (a) arms and hands, (b) legs and posture, and (c) head and face (see the Appendix).
2. Have the students discuss how their current content instructors use nonverbal language to emphasize the main ideas in a lecture.
3. Show slides of professors giving lectures, and have the students comment on the gestures. Alternatively, play a segment from a videotaped lecture, and have the students analyze and comment on the gestures.
4. Have the students discuss nonverbal communication practices in their own cultures, noting differences and similarities.
5. Ask the students to attend a lecture, take notes, analyze the lecture for nonverbal emphasis of main ideas, and write a five-paragraph essay summarizing their findings. In the essay, have them discuss the strengths and limitations of their lecture notes, identify the organizational pattern of the lecturer, and analyze the lecturer's nonverbal communication behaviors, voice clues, and transition-word clues.

6. In the following class, have the students share their findings in groups of four. Rotate the students from one group to another until all the students have had a chance to listen to everyone's observations.

Caveats and Options

1. To encourage more dialogue, in Step 3 have the students discuss their reactions in small groups.
2. To spice up the presentation, ask a cooperative professor to deliver a live 10-minute lecture as part of the class.
3. Nonverbal communication, coupled with recognition of transition words (e.g., *OK, therefore, all right*, and *next*), is a powerful tool for student note-taking. The students see a discussion of transition words as more applicable when presented in tandem with gestures and other nonverbal expressions.

References and Further Reading

Culturegrams. (1984). Provo, UT: David M. Kennedy Center for International Studies.

Fitzpatrick, C. H., & Ruscica, M. B. (1995). *Reading pathways.* Lexington, MA: D. C. Heath.

Morris, D. (1995). *Bodytalk: The meaning of human gestures.* New York: Crown.

Morris, D., Collett, P., Marsh, P., & O'Shaughnessy, M. (1979). *Gestures: Their origins and distribution.* New York: Stein & Day.

Seiler, W. (1996). Nonverbal communication. In *Communication: Foundations, skills, and applications* (pp. 114–143). New York: HarperCollins.

Appendix: Emphasis Gestures for Lectures

Category	Gesture
Arms and hands	Steepling
	Open hands
	Pointing
	Writing on the blackboard
	Gripping the podium
	Using the fingers to count out points or ideas
	Clenching the fist
	Using an extension such as chalk, a coffee cup, a ruler, or glasses
	Rubbing palms together
	Rubbing chalk between palms
	Moving hands and arms forward from body
Legs and posture	Walking closer to the audience
	Pacing back and forth with deliberate strides
Head and face	Nodding
	Smiling

Contributor

Gretchen Starks-Martin is an assistant professor in the Academic Learning Center at St. Cloud State University, Minnesota, in the United States.

What's Your Definition?

Levels
Low intermediate +

Aims
Write formal academic
definitions
Use a monolingual
dictionary

Class Time
45 minutes

Preparation Time
15 minutes

Resources
Monolingual dictionary
Overhead projector,
transparencies, and pens
(optional)

The writing of concise and explicit definitions is relevant to all levels of academic and professional study. This activity integrates dictionary skills and definition writing within specific contexts to meet the needs of individual students.

Procedure

1. Present examples of formal definitions following the pattern *word to be defined* + *verb* to be + *general class* + *relative clause showing particular characteristics* (e.g., *a generator is a machine that produces electricity; a marine surveyor is a person who examines ships to discover whether there are any problems with their structures*).

2. Ask the students to find appropriate specialized terminology in a monolingual dictionary and to identify the relative pronouns or adverbs (e.g., *who, which, that; where*) in definitions. Adapt the definitions, if necessary, to a five-part pattern (e.g., "uranium: a heavy metal that is radioactive and is used in the production of nuclear power and in some types of nuclear weapons"; *Cambridge international dictionary of English*, 1995, s.v. uranium) becomes *Uranium is a heavy radioactive metal that is used to produce nuclear power and some nuclear weapons*).

3. Ask the students in groups to prepare five similar definitions for terms in their fields with the assistance of a dictionary.

4. Ask groups to write their definitions on the blackboard or on an overhead transparency, with the headword missing (e.g., *A _____ is a place where the shares of a company are bought and sold*). Have the other students guess the headword that is defined in the sentence and give feedback on the accuracy and clarity of the definitions.

106

Caveats and Options

1. Common mistakes found in the students' writing of definitions are (a) giving an example, not a definition; (b) omitting the general class; and (c) using another form of the defined word in the definition (e.g., *A lawyer is a person who practices law*).
2. In a variation of this activity,
   - Present definitions of new words, some of which are correct and some of which are bluffs (e.g., *An etymologist is someone who studies eating habits. A teetotaler is a person who tastes and grades the quality of tea. An apiary is a place where people keep bees.*).
   - Ask teams of students to guess the correct definitions.
   - Hold a follow-up discussion on word formation (e.g., *-ist, -holic, -ology*).
   - Ask the students in groups to write their own true and false definitions for their peers to guess.

References and Further Reading

Cambridge international dictionary of English. (1995). Cambridge: Cambridge University Press.

Contributor

Teresa Thiel is a lecturer for the BEd TESL program in the Faculty of Education, University of Malaya, Kuala Lumpur, in Malaysia.

But I *Can't* Use My Own Words!

Levels
High intermediate +

Aims
Avoid overreliance on original wording when summarizing
Identify argument structure, main ideas, and key words
Practice paraphrasing

Class Time
1 hour

Preparation Time
10-15 minutes

Resources
Research report abstracts or textbook passages on articles/ reports
Summary Notes Forms

Much ESP writing involves summarizing information found in business or academic reports. This activity focuses students' attention on the overall structure of and the information contained within such reports. In a step-by-step process, students are weaned away from relying on the original text and learn techniques for summarizing the information in their own words through the use of key words, synonyms, and different word forms. The end product of the activity is a paragraph-length paraphrase. This activity is a companion to "Is It Paraphrasing, or Is It Plagiarism?" (p. 111).

Procedure

1. Distribute copies of the Summary Notes Form (see the Appendix), and let the students read through it.
2. Pass out copies of the research report abstract or textbook section.
3. Have the students read through the entire passage once, not making any marks on the passage, if possible, but reading for the information needed on the Summary Notes Form.
4. Ask the students to fill out the Summary Notes Form.
5. Have the students share their summary notes with the class as a whole, and discuss the vocabulary in the reading until you feel that the students have a sense of the passage.
6. Ask the students to write a one-sentence summary of the passage using the completed form (but not the original text). Have the students share their sentence summaries.
7. Ask the students to reread the passage, underlining the key words.
8. Elicit the key words and terms from the students, and write them on the blackboard. Involve the students in negotiating which choices are truly "key."

9. Ask the students to generate all the word forms and synonyms they can think of for each key word listed on the blackboard.

10. Create an outline of the argument structure or parts of the original text (e.g., introduction, purpose or research questions, method, results, discussion and implications) to serve as a guide for the final writing task.

11. Have the students put the passage away.

12. Tell the students to write a one-paragraph paraphrase of the passage, using their one-sentence summary, the argument structure list, and the key words on the blackboard. Emphasize that they should try to use the synonyms and other word forms when possible. Suggest that they use their one-sentence summary as an introduction to the paragraph.

13. Have the students share their paragraphs with each other, checking for completeness, wording, and grammar (word forms).

Caveats and Options

1. Some students might copy from the text as they attempt to write the one-sentence summary. Use this as an opportunity to discuss what would be considered paraphrasing and what would be considered plagiarism. Then introduce the next set of tasks as a way to paraphrase successfully.

2. Consider practicing with short passages about research reports from any reading or writing textbook before using authentic report abstracts. These passages tend to be more accessible for the students, allowing them to focus less on reading and more on paraphrasing until they are familiar with paraphrasing techniques.

3. If the class is composed of students from heterogeneous fields, be careful to choose articles on topics of general interest or accessibility to students, such as studies related to the social sciences. After modeling the techniques with a general passage, place the students into groups based on their field of study. Give them abstracts related to their field, or have them find their own. Then have them go through the summary and key word or synonym tasks as a group and collaborate on or critique each other's one-paragraph paraphrases.

4. Although this task was created for use with scholarly reports, it can easily be adapted to suit any level. Choose shorter, less advanced reading passages, or work at the sentence level with key words, word forms, and synonyms.

Appendix: Summary Notes Form

Preview this list of questions. As you read the passage, look for the information below. Not all readings will contain answers to all these questions. In the boxes on the right, list words or phrases, not sentences, that help answer the questions on the left.

Who or what?	
Where?	
When?	
Why?	
How?	
Conclusions?	

Contributor

Margi L. Wald is assistant director of ESL for the Department of English at the University of Tennessee, in the United States.

Is It Paraphrasing, or
Is It Plagiarism?

Levels
Intermediate +

Aims
Learn what constitutes
plagiarism
Practice paraphrasing

Class Time
40–50 minutes

Preparation Time
20 minutes

Resources
Handout
Published article
Students' summaries of
the article
Reasons form

Teaching the avoidance of plagiarism can be tricky, especially within ESL contexts in which students may not have a clear understanding of what constitutes plagiarism. This activity raises students' consciousness of the difference between paraphrasing and plagiarism. The students then put into practice what they have learned by reflecting on their own texts. The activity is a companion to "But I *Can't* Use My Own Words" (p. 108).

Procedure

1. Collect student-written summaries of one published article. Choose some excerpts from the summaries that demonstrate paraphrasing and some that would be considered plagiarism. Number the extracts. On a copy of the article, mark the location of the information used in each excerpt with a number corresponding to that excerpt.
2. Put the students in heterogeneous L1 groups (if possible), and ask them to choose a reporter.
3. Pass out the handout on approaches to using outside sources in writing (see Appendix A).
4. Have the students in their groups read each description and decide which approaches would lead to plagiarism and which would produce appropriate original work. Tell the students to negotiate until all group members agree on the appropriateness of each approach in a U.S. academic context.
5. Ask each group to report back to the class as a whole. Talk about each group's answers and rationale, and discuss what an academic audience would deem appropriate.
6. Pass out excerpts of students' written work, one copy to each student, and give each group a Reasons Form (see Appendix B). Also distribute copies of the original article with relevant passages noted.

7. Ask the students, again in their groups, to decide whether each excerpt is acceptable by circling *OK* or *not OK* on the form based on their discussion in Step 4.

8. Have each group report back to the class about one of the excerpts, justifying its choice of *OK* or *not OK*.

9. If time allows, have the students rewrite the excerpts they have deemed inappropriate.

10. Ask the students to revise their first-draft summaries, and follow up with an in-class or take-home peer analysis focusing on the appropriateness of each other's paraphrasing attempts.

Caveats and Options

1. Unfortunately, agreeing on where paraphrasing stops and plagiarism begins is not so easy. In addition to various cultures' differing notions, different academic disciplines might also disagree as to what constitutes plagiarism and what is appropriate paraphrasing. Discuss this phenomenon as part of the initiation into a discourse community, especially when (potential) graduate students are in the class.

2. Discussion of Approach 4 in Appendix A sparks much debate and can create anxiety among students. It is true that some phrases (e.g., terms, names) must be taken directly from the original text, as there is no other way to say them. Also, at times the author of the original text has coined a phrase that someone might want to include in a summary. Making the distinction between what must and what must not be paraphrased is sometimes difficult for students because of their level of English. To provide practice, try to pick student excerpts that include both phrases that need to be quoted and those that do not.

References and Further Reading

Bakka, T. (1993). Locking students out. In S. Barnet & H. Bedau (Eds.), *Current issues and enduring questions: A guide to critical thinking and argument, with readings* (3rd ed., pp. 210–213). Boston: St. Martin's Press.

Spack, R. (1990). *Guidelines: A cross-cultural reading/writing text.* New York: St. Martin's Press.

Appendix A: Approaches to Using Outside Source Information in Writing

Swales, J. M., & Feak, C. B. (1994). *Academic writing for graduate students: A course for nonnative speakers of English.* Ann Arbor: University of Michigan Press.

Directions: Listed below are various approaches to take when you want to use information from an outside source. Read through the list, and then decide which approaches are acceptable and which are not. Then get together with your group members and share your answers. You and your group have 10 minutes. Be ready to report your negotiated answer to the class.

1. Taking a section directly from the original source without changing the wording, giving the source, or using quotation marks
2. Taking a section directly from the original source without changing the wording or using quotation marks, but listing a source
3. Taking a section directly from the original source, adding quotation marks and an appropriate citation
4. Changing a few words from a part of a book, magazine, or newspaper and including it in a paper without citing the source
5. Using a paragraph from the original source, substituting synonyms for some of the words but keeping the original sentence and paragraph structure
6. Copying a section from an article, leaving out some sentences, and making your own paragraph with these sentences without using quotation marks or including a citation
7. Taking phrases directly from various outside sources and making a paragraph by combining these phrases with your own words
8. Taking phrases directly from various outside sources and making a paragraph by combining these phrases with your own words and adding citations
9. Taking the message of a paragraph and then rewording and rewriting it, changing the sentence structure, vocabulary, and organization
10. Rewording the message of a paragraph by changing the sentence structure, vocabulary, and organization, and adding a citation for the source

Appendix B: Reasons Form

Directions: Read these excerpts (edited by the teacher) from your comparative summaries. Each refers to the first page of Bakka (1993). Based on the decisions made in the previous task, decide if the wording in these excerpts is acceptable. If not, why not?

1. OK Not OK Reasons:	Some people support bilingual education because it eases the youngster's transition into U.S. culture and it preserves cultural heritage, but Bakka states that there is no impartial evidence that such education improves a student's academic work.
2. OK Not OK Reasons:	Supporters of bilingual education present two reasons: Bilingual education helps the child's entrance into U.S. culture and saves the child's cultural heritage.
3. OK Not OK Reasons:	Various programs exist, but the proponents of bilingual education feel that the international student should be spared the trauma of content courses in English. They feel the method of total immersion is sink or swim.
4. OK Not OK Reasons:	Bakka discusses the supporters of bilingual education, who assert that bilingual education programs are needed, for they make the child's transition into U.S. culture smooth and still allow that child to keep positive thoughts about his own culture and ethnic identity.

Contributor

Margi L. Wald is assistant director of ESL for the Department of English at the University of Tennessee, in the United States.

Lightening the Load

Levels
High intermediate +

Aims
Understand and practice
oral and written
research reports
Interpret and evaluate
information

Class Time
Variable

Preparation Time
2–4 hours

Resources
Between the Lines or
other source with
"issues" content
Research project
guidelines
Group evaluation form
Sample research
proposal

International students studying at U.S. universities must learn how to write research papers and reports, give presentations on research, and collaborate with classmates on assigned group work. This activity provides guided practice and experience in understanding the basic steps and parts of a research report. It also encourages students to collaborate with other students in groups. By conducting interviews and surveys, students practice their language skills, improve their library research skills, and practice interpreting and evaluating information. Finally, the activity integrates language skills across the curriculum as students present an oral report in the core or reading class as well as a written report in the writing class.

Procedure

1. In the core or reading class,
   - Read and discuss the articles in a textbook chapter (e.g., Zukowski/Faust, Johnston, & Atkinson, 1983, chap. 7, "Solving Global Problems"). These readings will provide the background for the research project.
   - Pass out and discuss the research project guidelines (see Appendix A).
   - Brainstorm a list of possible broad research topics for a survey based on the information gleaned from core readings (e.g., poverty, hunger, overpopulation).
   - Put the students into research teams of three or four members corresponding to their interests.
   - Have each group find and discuss library articles related to its chosen research topic. If time allows, have the students present the articles to the class.

2. Meanwhile, in the writing class,
   - Discuss the basic research report format: introduction, method, results, and discussion.
   - Pass out the group evaluation form (see Appendix B), and discuss the scientific method, focusing on the need for a research question to focus the research (i.e., not just "poverty," but "Why does a rich country like the United States have such a large poor population?" or "Is there a difference between the views of international and U.S. students concerning the value of welfare?").
3. In the core class, when the students have acquired enough background on their topics through the library articles, have the groups formulate a research question and write a research proposal in the writing class (see Appendix C for a sample).
4. In the writing class, have the groups prepare questionnaires or survey forms to gather data on the proposal topic. If you wish, have the students pilot test the questionnaire or survey forms on the other groups in the class. Tell the students that each group member should survey 5-7 subjects so that each group will have data from at least 20 subjects.
5. During the core class,
   - Send the students out to survey their subjects.
   - Have the students analyze and interpret their data. Help the students cluster their information into meaningful charts or graphs.
6. In the writing class, have the students collaborate on a first draft of a written report. Give feedback, or have peers do so.
7. In the core class, have the students present oral reports with visual aids and handouts. Give feedback, and have the class do so, too.
8. In the writing class, have the students revise their drafts based on feedback received on their first drafts and oral presentations.

Caveats and Options

1. Help the students choose a research question that is appropriate for a survey or questionnaire, and help them draft questions toward that end. The data received will be much more manageable if you emphasize the importance of focusing the research and help the students maintain that focus.

2. Use the chapters in any social issues textbook or sources as background; many topics are appropriate. In non-ESL settings, the reports could be bibliographic in nature.
3. There are numerous ways to split tasks across courses (e.g., reading and writing, conversation and reading-writing) as long as one course has a writing focus.
4. Have the students write individual final reports.
5. Various group configurations are possible in an EAP course. Either compose research teams of students from similar academic backgrounds and choose topics accordingly, or form teams of students from differing backgrounds, each student contributing expertise from a field (e.g., statisticians working with environmental engineers on the topic of pollution).

References and Further Reading

Brown, J. D. (1988). *Understanding research in second language learning: A teacher's guide to statistics and research design.* Cambridge: Cambridge University Press.

Leki, I. (1995). *Academic writing: Exploring processes and strategies* (2nd ed.). New York: St. Martin's Press.

Zukowski/Faust, J., Johnston, S. S., & Atkinson, C. S. (1983). *Between the lines.* Orlando, FL: Harcourt Brace.

Appendix A: Project Guidelines

Guidelines for the Research Project

Instructions: For this unit you will work in research teams to find information on a particular global issue or problem, share information about the topic with other members of your group, collaborate to create and carry out a survey concerning this topic, and interpret and analyze the results of your survey. Your group will then write two drafts of a report presenting the results and conclusions of your research to the writing class as well as give an oral report (including visual aids) on your research to the core class.

In researching your issue, your group should search the on-line catalogues in the library to locate articles or books on your topic.

In addition, your group should do an Internet search and include at least one reference from the Internet in your report. You may also want to check almanacs or encyclopedias (including electronic ones such as Grolier's or Encarta).

The questionnaire your group develops should be given to at least 20 different subjects in order to provide enough information for you to analyze. Each person in your group will need to talk to 5–7 people. After your group completes the survey, you will need to graph or chart your results on a poster or large piece of butcher paper. This will help you interpret and analyze your information for the written report and for your oral presentation.

Writing Class Task Components

1. Develop focused research questions.
2. Write a research proposal that includes
   - a statement of the issue or problem (with citations)
   - a statement of the purpose of the survey or interviews, including research question(s)
   - a description of the subjects and the materials and procedures
3. Develop a questionnaire and administer it to at least 20 subjects.
4. Write a first and second draft of a survey report that includes
   - an introduction with references to library articles (with citations) and clear research questions
   - proper American Psychological Association (APA) format with headings and subheadings
   - results charts
   - a clean copy of the questionnaire in the appendix
   - references written in correct APA format

Oral Report Guidelines

1. Each group will give a 10- to 15-minute presentation on the results of the survey, allowing time for questions.
2. Each group member should have a speaking part.
3. The presentation should include the components of the written report: an introduction, methods, analysis and results, and discussion.
4. The group should prepare visual aids (e.g., charts, graphs, transparencies, handouts) to help clarify and support the findings.

Appendix B: Self- or Group Evaluation Form

Report Evaluation Form[1]

Answer all applicable questions.

	Yes	No
Abstract		
1. Is the report summarized, including		
● statement of topic and purpose?		
● mention of materials and procedures?		
● summary of results, conclusions, interpretations?		
Introduction		
1. Is the background or rationale behind the study given, including		
● an outline of the issue or controversy?		
● references made to experts or published articles?		
2. Is the purpose stated?		
● Are "research questions" noted?		

[1]From *Understanding Research in Second Language Learning* (pp. 59–61), by J. D. Brown, 1988, New York: Cambridge University Press. Copyright © 1988 by Cambridge University Press. Reprinted with permission.

Methods		
1. Subjects		
● Is there a description of who the people questioned are and whether they have any specialized knowledge of or interest in the topic of the survey?		
● Is a discussion of demographics included in the survey (e.g., age, gender, education, nationality, or other factors that might have affected responses)?		
● Is there a discussion of the participants' interest in and prior knowledge of the topic of the survey? Were the subjects personally affected by the topic?		
2. Materials and procedures		
● Is there a description of the materials used to gather information?		
● Are these materials reproduced in an appendix?		
● Is there a clear description of how the materials were prepared and administered?		
Analysis and Results		
1. Are the arrangement and grouping of data described?		
2. Are statistical procedures noted and explained?		
3. Are the data represented in chart form?		
Discussion		
1. Are inferences and conclusions drawn?		
2. Are these inferences and conclusions qualified and well reasoned?		
3. Are all the research questions answered in this section?		
4. Are the results related to previous research (e.g., library or textbook readings) or plans for further research?		

References		
1. Are all references mentioned in the paper noted at the end of the paper?		
2. Are the references in proper APA format?		
Appendixes		
1. Is a copy of the questionnaire included?		
2. Are other necessary appendixes added?		

Appendix C: Sample Research Proposal

Susan Student
EAP 1 Writer's Workshop
February 20, 1995

Research Proposal
SIU Student Participation in Recycling

Recycling is a vital issue as we approach the 21st century. Not only are people talking about it, but they are also doing something about it. Many recycling programs have been established around the world in order to help alleviate this situation, for people have come to realize that "Planet Earth will not survive the mounds of garbage piling up throughout the world" (Henderson, 1990, p. 12) if the problem is not addressed.

According to reports by the Environmental Protection Agency, the United States and other affluent, first-world countries produce more garbage per capita than less developed nations do (Hirasawa, 1992). Because this topic of recycling is so important, perhaps more so in the United States, it becomes necessary to look at how well received such programs are in developed countries. Therefore, this study attempts to uncover views of young Americans toward the recycling of paper, glass, plastic, and aluminum and how consistently such individuals participate in recycling programs.

METHODS

Twenty-five U.S. college students will be surveyed on the campus of Southern Illinois University at Carbondale. These subjects will be given 10 minutes to complete a questionnaire that focuses on their general feelings about the need for recycling, their recycling practices, and the frequency of such behaviors. The questions will be open ended, allowing subjects to write short responses to any question. Other demographic factors collected will include age, gender, hometown, and major or intended occupation so that these variables may be factored into any results found.

ANALYSIS

All information from the questionnaires will be read and analyzed by three independent readers. Attempts will be made to uncover trends in attitudes and behaviors across all subjects by listing and grouping responses. Comparisons will also be made between what attitudes each subject holds and his or her behaviors to see if any relationship exists. Finally, the researchers will look for connections between attitudes and behaviors of subjects and their gender, age, hometown, and professional focus.

REFERENCES (on a separate page)

Contributors

Margi L. Wald is assistant director of ESL for the Department of English at the University of Tennessee, in the United States. Marilyn Rivers is EAP coordinator for the Center for English as a Second Language, Southern Illinois University at Carbondale, in the United States.

Meeting the Research Community

Levels
Low advanced; graduate

Aims
Meet researchers in students' fields
Learn departmental requirements
Develop field-specific vocabulary
Give short oral presentations

Class Time
Two class periods

Preparation Time
15–30 minutes

Resources
Description of instructor's academic department
Overhead projector and transparencies

International students at U.S. universities often feel a disjunction between their ESL classes (especially if they are enrolled in an intensive program) and the academic world beyond. This may be particularly true of students at the graduate level who plan to become involved in research projects in their major departments. This activity helps bridge the gap and give face validity to ESP courses for such students. It asks students to step outside the English classroom and introduce themselves to the discourse community of scholars and researchers that they will soon join.

Procedure

1. Distribute or display on an overhead transparency a description of your academic department, and give a short model presentation to the class about your department's research activities and graduate programs based on the information contained in the handout.
2. Invite questions or comments about the material in the presentation.
3. Assign the students to research their own departments by interviewing the department head, the academic adviser, or another faculty member. Tell the students to collect in the interview information similar to what you included in the model presentation (see the Appendix).
4. In a subsequent class period, have the students give short (5-minute) presentations based on the information they have gathered from their departments.
5. Following a question-and-answer session, have the student presenters distribute any descriptive brochures provided by their departments regarding graduate programs and research activities.

Caveats and Options

1. Ideally, the description on which this activity is based should briefly list the research activities currently under way, the name of the department head, the credit-hour requirements for graduate degrees offered, the major written and oral requirements for the department's master's and doctoral students (e.g., qualifying exam, thesis, oral defense), and the name of a leading research journal adopted by the department as its model for publication content and format.
2. Allow pairs of students representing the same academic department to plan and give joint presentations, but make sure they divide up the information-gathering chores and do them independently.
3. Do not allow the students simply to take information from the university's graduate bulletin; they must show evidence of actually having interviewed a faculty member from the department.
4. You need not limit students to presenting the types of information contained in the model speech. Any information students can discover related to research activities or graduate student programs in their departments is fair game.
5. The students may need help with the pronunciation of terms before they make their presentations.

References and Further Reading

Barnes, G. (1994). *English communication skills for professionals.* Lincolnwood, IL: National Textbook Co.

Olsen, L., & Huckin, T. (1991). *Technical writing and professional communication.* New York: McGraw-Hill.

Appendix: Sample Handout

Meeting Your Research Community

Objectives

This assignment involves some out-of-class research and a short speech to the class. In the speech you will tell us about the graduate program you are enrolled in or are about to enter. The purposes of this assignment are, first, for you to get acquainted with your academic department and, second, for our class to become aware of the variety of academic programs and research projects going on around the campus.

Field Visit

To gather data for this speech, you must go to your academic department on campus and collect information. Here are some suggested sources:

- Interview the department head or director of graduate studies.
- Interview one or two professors in the department.
- Ask the departmental secretary for brochures or bulletins describing the department's graduate programs.
- Talk to other graduate students in the department.
- Check bulletin boards in the department for samples of professors' published research.
- Visit labs or research field sites.

Data Collection

By the end of your field visit, you should have collected the following information for your speech:

- the location of the department
- the name of the department head
- the size of the graduate faculty and the number of graduate students
- the kinds of graduate degrees offered by the department
- principal areas of research interest among the faculty
- ongoing grant projects in the department
- the number of credit hours needed for each degree
- thesis or dissertation requirements
- qualifying exams, comprehensive exams, and oral defenses required
- seminar course requirements
- any other information that would be useful or interesting to the class

Contributor

Bob Weissberg teaches in the Department of Communication Studies at New Mexico State University, in the United States.

Part III: English for Art and Design

Editors' Note

The activities in Part III involve English for art and design, which focuses on English taught within an art school, school of design, or department of art or design. One of the narrower categories of ESP, its primary concerns are art history (e.g., techniques, media and materials, artworks, structures, historical terms) and the language of the studio (e.g., techniques, media and materials, questions, conditions, and critiques).

Promote the Artist in You

Levels
Intermediate +

Aims
Create an artist's/
designer's statement
Describe and promote
artistic work

Class Time
Variable

Preparation Time
Variable

Resources
Promotional catalogues
about the work of
designers and artists
Visual arts books with
images

In the following project, geared toward students at least one semester into their art or design specialty (in the United States, after the third semester in a bachelor of fine arts program), students create their own promotional catalogues illustrating their work and ideas. For the catalogue, students write personal and professional statements about their inspirations, organize their work into categories, write statements for each work to explain the image in some way, learn and practice writing captions (the format and information under a picture), and write supportive essays on the work of other students. Design catalogues can be created by individual students or can represent the work of an art or design team.

Procedure

1. Bring a few promotional catalogues to class and outline the project.
2. Ask the students to brainstorm about why these catalogues have been created. For example, ask, "How are they different from other books?" "How is written language important in this catalogue?" "Who has editorial control?" "How could these catalogues be useful in business?"
3. Ask the students to observe the structure of the catalogue (e.g., introductory essay, categories for certain work).
4. Ask the students to determine whether they would like to do the project individually, in pairs, or in small groups. If they choose groups, consider requesting that the artists or designers create an art or design collaborative group with a group name, a logo, and an explanation for the choice of each.
5. Divide the tasks that you select into a series of components, which can include the following: title page; contents page; positive statement by a critic (an introductory statement by another student); introduction to the designer or design team (two to three pages),

130

including philosophy, objectives, inspirations, and influences; captions for each image; and 100- to 200-word descriptions of individual images. For material, the students can draw from their previous designs and sketches, perhaps add new ones, and make color copies of photographs of their work.

6. Bring in a few art or design books, or ask the students to bring in theirs from other classes. Ask them to look at the captions and to observe the format. The captions may include, for example, a number, the artist's or designer's name, the title, the year, the medium, and the size. Others may simply offer a brief comment about the design.

7. Ask the students to decide on a caption format to use throughout their catalogue (but emphasize that more than one format exists for writing captions).

8. Ask the students to suggest three different organizational options (e.g., chronologically, by category—posters, logos, package design) for the catalogue; subsequently, have them determine which is the best for their catalogue and explain why.

9. Ask the students to select the typography and layout for the catalogue and justify their choices.

10. Ask the students to generate a finished catalogue of their own work.

Caveats and Options

1. Change the time reference by telling the students to imagine that it is 10–15 years from now. Have them include their résumés (including awards, commissions, and other honors) and histories in the catalogue.

2. Have other students critique the catalogues as promotional material.

Contributor

Robert Preece has designed classes and taught ESP and the language of art and design (LAD) and introductory visual arts classes at schools in Hong Kong, Japan, and the United States. He has published articles on approaches to LAD and the visual arts and has organized art shows. He now serves as contributing editor for Asian Art News *and* World Sculpture News *and as assistant editor for* English for Specific Purposes: An International Journal.

Red Pepper Club Project

Levels
Intermediate +

Aims
Talk about a
collaborative studio
project

Class Time
1–2 hours +

Preparation Time
Minimal

Resources
Red peppers (optional,
but recommended)
Künstlerheim Luise
brochure (optional)
Handout

In specialized language training on the creation and presentation of studio projects, collaborative design speaking projects offer an alternative to having students talk about their work (Preece, 1997). The Red Pepper Club Project is one such activity; it asks students to think, act, negotiate ideas in a group, and speak "on their feet." Visual arts production is downplayed but acts as the vehicle for accelerated, specialized language practice.

Procedure

1. Bring some red peppers to class. Ask the students, in groups, to examine one pepper and brainstorm about its characteristics (e.g., color, line, shape, texture, taste, smell). Ask them to look at the inside as well and report this information. Create a word web of this information on the blackboard.

2. Introduce the Red Pepper Club Project (see Appendix A). Explain to the students that their task is to concentrate on one design aspect of the Red Pepper Club (e.g., fashion design, product design) and present their design concept to the club's owners.

3. Ask the students to work in groups to prepare a brief presentation in order to display their ideas for the class.

Caveats and Options

1. Have the students do the project within a set, in-class time period so that they will spend time communicating ideas quickly rather than concentrating on art production. Quick conceptual sketches on a chalk- or marker board should help them communicate their ideas effectively.

2. Use the activity to supplement a unit on presentation skills development.

3. Use the framework with other fruits and vegetables.

4. Extend the project over two classes. In the first class, brainstorm about the red pepper. For homework, ask the students to find out about red peppers (where they are grown, what dishes they are used in, how they are grown). In the second class, have the students design and present their ideas.

5. Have the students who are not presenting take notes about each project, using the questions in the Appendix as a guide.

6. Have the students write brief essays about their designs.

7. For an additional collaborative design speaking project, have the students present a floor plan (and perhaps an illustration) of a room in an artists' hotel (see Appendix B, the Künstlerheim Luise Interior Design Project, for an example).

References and Further Reading

[Künstlerheim Luise brochure]. Contact Künstlerheim Luise, Luisenstrasse 19, 10117 Berlin, Germany. Telephone: 49-30-280-69-41. Fax: 49-30-280-69-42.

Preece, R. (1997). Art lodging. *World Sculpture News, 3*(1), 12–13.

Preece, R. (1997). Modelling language instruction on collaborative design projects. *Journal of the Imagination in Language Learning, 4,* 108–110.

Appendix A: The Red Pepper Club Project

The owners of the Red Pepper Club (a dance club with a bar and cafe in a very large city) want to create a wild, visually unusual, and spicy atmosphere for their guests. It will be a new place for people to meet and celebrate the spirit of a red chili pepper. They have asked you to select and design one or more of the following:

- a fashion design (e.g., uniforms for waiters, waitresses, the doorman, the bartender, the Red Pepper dancers, and other employees)
- a product design (e.g., chairs, tables, bar, bar stools, drinking glasses, plates, cutlery, bathroom fixtures)
- a graphic design (e.g., a poster, an advertisement for a magazine or newspaper, a brochure, a logo)

- an interior design (e.g., a stairwell, a design for the windows and the dance floor)
- a piece of fine art (e.g., a painting, a sculpture, an installation)

During your presentation, please answer these questions:

1. What characteristics of the red pepper inspired you?
2. What did you decide to create?
3. Describe your design and choice of materials.
4. How does your design help create a "wild, visually unusual, and spicy atmosphere"?

Appendix B: Künstlerheim Luise Interior Design Project

The Künstlerheim Luise is an unusual, low-cost artists' hotel next to the old Berlin Wall in former East Berlin. Each room at the hotel was designed by a local artist in order to create an interesting environment for guests. Many visiting artists and people interested in art stay there because it is cheap (about U.S.$20–$30 per night) and because they can select the room they like. Also, the artists who design the rooms get a part of the money for each night's stay.

1. Using the Künstlerheim Luise as an inspiration, please do the following:
   - Select an area near you that would be an interesting place for an artists' hotel.
   - Design a 14-ft by 14-ft room with furniture for your guests; the bathroom will be down the hall. The design should be low cost but unusual (and unforgettable).
   - Create a floor plan for the room and a presentation outline.
2. Address the following questions in your presentation:
   - What is your main idea or concept for the room? What feeling do you want the guest to have? Why did you choose this?
   - What things in the room express this idea or concept? Describe their design and materials.
   - What will you do about lighting for the room?

- Do you want the viewer to focus on one or more things in the room?
- Explain why the design is low cost.

Contributor

Robert Preece has designed classes and taught ESP and the language of art and design (LAD) and introductory visual arts classes at schools in Hong Kong, Japan, and the United States. He has published articles on approaches to LAD and the visual arts and has organized art shows. He now serves as contributing editor for Asian Art News *and* World Sculpture News *and as assistant editor for* English for Specific Purposes: An International Journal.

Tripping the Art Fantastic

Levels
Intermediate +

Aims
Experience and learn
from the local arts
environment

Class Time
30 minutes (planning)
1–1½ hours (visiting the
exhibition)

Preparation Time
Minimal

Resources
Newspaper reviews of
art shows
Handout
List of current art and
design exhibitions
Museum education
department outreach
materials (optional)

Incorporating tours into the syllabus for a language of art and design class gives the students and teacher an opportunity to take learning outside the classroom and into the local arts environment. The following activity offers one such opportunity.

Procedure

1. Bring in a few copies of a local paper or magazine that lists exhibitions in your local area. Ask the students to select a few shows of interest and determine which are easily accessible and which are not.
2. After deciding upon a show, schedule a day to go to it, make arrangements to get there, and find out about group admission costs and registration requirements (if any). Find out whether the students can attend exhibitions at a discounted cost or free of charge with a student ID card.
3. Contact the site and inquire about educational outreach and publicity material.
4. Introduce the trip objectives by handing out and discussing a list of questions and topics similar to those in the Appendix.
5. Visit the exhibition with the students. After they get a general feeling for it, ask them to address the questions on the handout in small groups and take notes. Gather any postcards, promotional literature, or catalogues that are available to use for posttour activities.
6. In class after the tour, ask a reporter from each group to respond to the questions on the handout.
7. Have the students select a topic from the handout to write about.

Caveats and Options

1. If you are teaching in-service art and design students, at the beginning of the semester ask their visual arts teachers about any upcoming shows or design exhibitions.
2. To gather information about the site and the art that is on view, visit the exhibition, if possible, before you go with the students.
3. Try to go to the site when it is not too crowded. The students may be hesitant to talk about the work and environment in a crowded space.
4. In class, tell the students that they cannot touch the works of art and that they should remain at least an arm's length away from the works. Also, warn them not to use a pen or pencil to point at the picture; the guards (if any) may ask them not to do this.
5. Allow the students to focus on particular aspects of the exhibition outlined in the Appendix.
6. Ask the students to bring postcards of works in museums and exhibitions to class for posttour activities. Remember, however, that these can be limited in scope.

References and Further Reading

Preece, R. (1996/1997). Visual arts learning opportunities for study abroad students in American ESL programs: Focus on tours. *Hong Kong Polytechnic University: Working Papers in English Language Teaching and Applied Linguistics, 2*(1), 115–129. (Available from Editor, Department of English, Hong Kong Polytechnic University, Hung Hom, Kowloon, Hong Kong)

Preece, R., & Tomlinson, G. (1995). *Philadelphia Museum of Art ESL activity* (Instructor and student eds.). Philadelphia: Temple University, Intensive English Language Program. (ERIC Document Reproduction Service No. ED 394 339)

Appendix: Trip to an Art Exhibition

In small groups, discuss and take notes on the following aspects of the exhibition:

The Work on Display and the Exhibition

1. Talk about a specific work or two. (If possible, try to get a color image of the work(s).)
   ● Why did you choose this work over all of the others?

- What do you think about this work?
  - ▶ Subject matter
  - ▶ Use of visual elements and principles of design
  - ▶ Media and technique
  - ▶ Other comments
2. Talk about the exhibition.
   - Is this a good show? Do you like it?
   - Is it well organized?
   - Would you recommend this show to a friend?

Interior Design: Talk about the space in which the art is displayed.

1. Describe the space.
2. Is this space good for displaying art? What characteristics should an art exhibition area have? Give examples to support your ideas.
3. How could the interior design be improved?

Graphic Design and Advertising: Talk about the graphic design (e.g., postcards, posters) for the exhibition. (If possible, get examples of the designs.)

1. Is this good or bad design? Explain.
2. Is there a slogan for the exhibition?
3. What impression or feeling does the graphic designer or advertiser want to create?

Contributor

Robert Preece has designed classes and taught ESP and the language of art and design (LAD) and introductory visual arts classes at schools in Hong Kong, Japan, and the United States. He has published articles on approaches to LAD and the visual arts and has organized art shows. He now serves as contributing editor for Asian Art News *and* World Sculpture News *and as assistant editor for* English for Specific Purposes: An International Journal.

Where Are All the Artists and Architects?

Levels
Advanced

Aims
Create a reference and
resource list for artists
and architects

Class Time
2–4 hours

Preparation Time
Minimal

Resources
Library facilities
Art Index
*Dow Jones News
Retrieval* system
*General Periodical
Index (On-Disc)*

This referencing workshop specifically addresses the gathering of information about artists and architects. In addition to books and videos that deal specifically with individual artists and architects, other easily accessible sources of information that may discuss a particular artist or architect cannot be accessed by a simple subject search using the person's name. These sources include books that provide lengthy histories or surveys of art from a particular country or time period; articles and reviews listed in *Art Index*, and articles and reviews of shows in the *Dow Jones News Retrieval* system and the *General Periodicals Index (On-Disc)*. This activity raises visual arts students' awareness of these sources; it also provides training in writing a reference list.

Procedure

1. Introduce referencing, and review the information that goes into a reference entry (for American Psychological Association, or APA, style, see the Appendix).
2. Divide the students into large groups (four or five students), and have them select an artist or architect.
3. Ask the groups to locate 10 sources about their chosen artist or architect in the library from the following, dividing the task among themselves:
   - two books dealing exclusively with the artist or architect
   - two selections from large survey books (e.g., a history of Western art or architecture)
   - two selections from smaller survey books (e.g., on Italian Baroque art)
   - two or three articles listed in *Art Index*

- two or three articles from *Dow Jones News Retrieval* or *General Periodicals Index (On-Disc)*
4. Ask the students to write complete references for two sources and to bring samples of their research to class. Set up tutorials in which each student shows you the completed references so that you can point out any errors in the reference format.
5. Ask the students to combine and alphabetize the references found by the group and type up a list.

Caveats and Options

1. Check with the visual arts faculty to determine which referencing system they use.
2. As a general rule, selecting different artists or architects will lead to different kinds of references. Your library will probably have more books about the individual work of famous historical artists than about the work of contemporary ones. For these, the students will need to look at books that include other artists or architects and at newspaper and magazine articles.
3. Make arrangements for a librarian to demonstrate basic search procedures.
4. The students do not necessarily need to bring the sources to class, but doing so is useful when problems arise, particularly when dealing with survey books that only have a paragraph about the artist or architect.
5. To create a more expansive list for student reference, include the format for citing a compact disc, a monograph, a videotape, a dictionary, and a World Wide Web site.
6. Ask the students to create in-text references and quotations from a selected source.
7. Incorporate the references in a report-writing project.

References and Further Reading

American Psychological Association. (1994). *Publications manual of the American Psychological Association* (4th ed.). Washington, DC: Author.

Appendix: Reference Handout

American Psychological Association (APA)
Reference List Guidelines

There are many sources in the library on artists and architects. The following are the APA guidelines for citing certain kinds of references. Look closely at the order of the information in the various entries, and pay attention to the punctuation used.

Book with author:
Rawson, P. (1967). *The art of Southeast Asia*. New York: Thames & Hudson.

Book with editor:
Bernard, B. (Ed.). (1986). *The Impressionist revolution*. London: Macdonald.

Book with more than one edition:
Gilbert, R. (1995). *Living with art* (4th ed.). New York: McGraw-Hill.

Journal article:
Hobba, L. (1994). Five uneasy pieces. *Australian Journal of Media and Culture, 8,* 226–226, 267, 268.

Magazine article:
Selenitsch, A. (1995, May-June). Acropolis now. *Architecture Australia,* 48-53.

Newspaper article:
Knithichan, K. (1995, July 31). A time of change. *Bangkok Nation*,
   p. 8.

Review of an art or design show, film, or book:
Preece, R. (1996). Brenda Fajardo and Noel Soler Cuizon at Hiraya
   Gallery [Review of the art show *Panapanahon* (Seasonal Repeti-
   tion and Change)]. *Asian Art News*, 6(6), 88–89.

Contributor

*Robert Preece has designed classes and taught ESP and the language of
art and design (LAD) and introductory visual arts classes at schools in
Hong Kong, Japan, and the United States. He has published articles on
approaches to LAD and the visual arts and has organized art shows. He
now serves as contributing editor for* Asian Art News *and* World Sculpture
News *and as assistant editor for* English for Specific Purposes: An
International Journal.

Part IV: English for Business and Economics

Editors' Note

The activities in Part IV center on the skills taught in English for business and economics (EBE). EBE focuses on English taught within a company, business school, or other professional or corporate setting. Its primary concerns are effective communication and negotiation, technical and business writing, workplace idioms and vocabulary, and business customs and culture. EBE is most commonly taught in private settings (e.g., at corporate offices), though it may also be taught in institutional settings. EBE is also known as BE (business English) and, in the corporate setting, as EPP (English for professional purposes). It is currently the fastest growing form of ESP.

Business Jeopardy

Levels
High intermediate +

Aims
Learn about cultural
institutions commonly
referred to in business

Class Time
1 hour

Preparation Time
30 minutes–1 hour

Resources
List of cultural
institutions
Details on the
institutions
Whiteboard or overhead
projector (optional)

Using the familiar U.S. television game show, *Jeopardy*, this fast-paced game provides the perfect setting for students to recall specific details about cultural institutions as used in business contexts. After researching the institutions, players reinforce their ability to give a quick response, as is often encouraged in academic settings.

Procedure

Before Game Day

1. Give the students a list of cultural institutions to research (e.g., the Federal Reserve system). Either solicit the list from professors in the business department of your college or university, or quickly compile a list by skimming through the *Wall Street Journal* or any other business newspaper or journal. If you wish, have the students in groups research groups of institutions (e.g., government institutions).
2. Give the students the instructions and objectives for Business Jeopardy. You may want to show a short video clip of the television show *Jeopardy* for reinforcement.

Game Day

1. Prepare the categories on the white- or blackboard or on an overhead transparency (see the Appendix).
2. Divide the class into teams of four to eight students each.
3. Read through the categories and explain the point values for the round.
4. Remind the players that they must give their responses in question form.
5. Flip a coin to determine which team will go first.
6. Play the game.

146

Caveats and Options

1. This activity is best done with two facilitators: one to serve as master of ceremonies and one to mark off or erase points from the category board and keep track of points for each team.
2. The facilitators may adapt the rules as they see fit, such as whether the students should raise their hand or press a buzzer to answer, how many times each team member must respond, or whether there will be a Daily Double or Final Jeopardy round.

References and Further Reading

Nunan, D. (1989). *Designing tasks for the communicative classroom.* Cambridge: Cambridge University Press.

Swales, J. (1988). Communicative language teaching in ESP contexts. In C. J. Brumfit (Ed.), *Annual Review of Applied Linguistics, 8* (pp. 48–57).

Appendix: Sample Jeopardy Category

$$$	Federal Reserve System
200	The number of Federal Reserve banks.
400	The Federal Advisory Council is made up of this number of bankers from each Federal Reserve district.
600	This is an informal organization of the presidents of the Federal Reserve banks.
800	This act of 1980 brought depository institutions under Federal Reserve jurisdiction.

Responses
What is 12?
What is one?
What is the President's Conference?
What is the Monctary Control Act?

Contributor

Susan M. Barone is a language specialist in the English for Internationals Department at Vanderbilt University, in the United States.

Persuasive Proposals

Levels
High intermediate +

Aims
Learn the organization
of a solicited business
proposal
Learn what makes a
proposal persuasive
Practice summary
writing

Class Time
1½ hours

Preparation Time
45 minutes

Resources
Business proposal with
a clear problem-solution-
evaluation pattern

Proposal writing is one of the most common types of written documentation in the business world. Most textbooks on business communication highlight the specific sections of the proposal, such as the implementation of the suggested proposal, budget, and personnel. In contrast, this activity sensitizes students to the overall macrostructure of the proposal, that is, the problem-solution-evaluation organizational pattern (see Hoey, 1983) and the way it is realized in various sections of the report (i.e., letter of transmittal, executive summary, introduction, and conclusion). Students become aware of the various linguistic devices used in the three main stages of a proposal and learn that a persuasive proposal identifies a problem or need, proposes a feasible solution, and specifies the benefits of the proposed solution.

Procedure

1. Make three copies of the business proposal. In the letter of transmittal, executive summary, introduction, and conclusion, blank out (a) all the problem (or need) statements in the first copy, (b) all instances of the proposed solution in the second copy, and (c) all evaluative comments (i.e., benefits and advantages of proposed solution) in the third copy. Leave intact the main body of the proposal detailing the implementation, personnel, budget, and other information.
2. Divide the students into three groups of the same size.
3. Give each group a different blanked-out copy of the proposal.
4. Ask each group to fill in the section (i.e., problem, solution, or evaluation of solution) that is missing from its copy of the proposal.
5. Have one member from each group form a new group of three, so that each group contains a student responsible for writing a different section of the problem-solution-evaluation pattern.

6. Ask the three students in each new group to (a) compare what they have written with the original sections of the proposal that the two other members have and (b) discuss the similarities and differences they find. During this discussion stage, circulate among all the groups and take notes on the students' vocabulary usage, their summarizing techniques, and the quality of their end product.

7. As feedback, discuss the three-part organizational pattern, review summarizing and paraphrasing techniques, and emphasize key or useful vocabulary.

Caveats and Options

1. This introductory writing task sensitizes the students to some of the principles involved in proposal writing before they embark on writing a full-length proposal. The students may have difficulty tailoring the summary of the problem-solution-evaluation to the requirements of a particular subsection in the proposal; for example, the letter of transmittal would refer to the problem or need very briefly, whereas the executive summary would give a more substantial overview.

2. To simplify the exercise, confine it to a reading activity: Prepare sentence or short paragraph strips containing pieces of the problem-solution-evaluation parts of the proposal, and have the students identify which subsection of the proposal a particular piece belongs to.

3. Devise similar activities for other types of business writing that employ the problem-solution-evaluation organizational pattern. Sales letters and recommendation reports fall into this category.

References and Further Reading

Hoey, M. (1983). *On the surface of discourse*. London: Allen & Unwin.

Pfeiffer, W. S. (1989). *Proposal writing: The art of friendly persuasion*. Toronto, Canada: Merrill.

Contributor

Lynne Flowerdew is a senior language instructor at the Hong Kong University of Science and Technology, where she coordinates a technical communication skills course.

Triggering Talk Through Ads

Levels
Intermediate +

Aims
Practice making
hypotheses
Analyze the creation of
meaning through figures
of speech in
advertisements

Class Time
1 hour

Preparation Time
1 hour

Resources
Magazine
advertisements related
to students' fields
Overhead projector and
transparencies

This activity is based on advertisements in which the picture is not merely illustrative but is used for generalization or displacement, or as a symbol. Separating the pictures from the text of the advertisement creates an information gap.

Procedure

1. Make two copies and an overhead transparency of each advertisement. Prepare the following task sheets:

   ● Student A: the picture from an advertisement, accompanied by the following text: *This is a picture from an advertisement. In your opinion, which product, company, or charity is it for? Share your ideas with the two other students in your group, without showing them your picture or describing it.*

   ● Student B: the text from the same advertisement, together with the following instructions: *This is the text of an advertisement. What kind of picture do you think it is accompanied by? Share your ideas with the two other students in your group without showing them your text or referring to it.*

   ● Student C: a paper copy of the whole advertisement, with the following lines: *This is a copy of an advertisement. Does it use a generalization, displacement, or symbolic effect? First act as an observer: Listen to Students A and B without giving your opinion. When they have finished, show them your advertisement and discuss with them what they have guessed. Then tell them what you have found and see if they agree with you. Finally, give your advertisement a rating from 1 (very effective) to 5 (a total failure).*

150

2. In class, explain to the students the three main rhetorical effects that may generally be found in advertisement pictures:

- generalization (*synecdoche*, a part for a whole; e.g., a hand or a head that represents a whole person)

- displacement (*metonymy*, applying a word to something that is closely associated to it; e.g., the 1986 IBM advertisement showing a tomato on veined marble. As the text of the advertisement explains, IBM was at that time helping the compilers of the forthcoming edition of the *Oxford English Dictionary*, which would of course include the word *tomato* with its pronunciation in both British and American English. The picture is therefore an example of transfer from container to content. The IBM computers compiling the new edition of the dictionary are represented in the picture by a minute part of their random access memory.)

- symbolism (*metaphor*, a simile without a term of comparison; e.g., the 1996 Microsoft Internet advertisement featuring a heavy ball and chain about to knock down a seedy concrete wall, as the Internet is destroying barriers not only between companies but also within firms)

3. Check that the students understand the generalization, displacement, and symbolic effects.

4. Choose a picture from an advertisement featuring the three effects, and ask the students to find them. An example is a 1994 World Wildlife Fund (WWF) advertisement against deforestation (see the Appendix). The picture shows two small Black children holding seedlings. It is based on a generalization effect: The children and trees are a particular instance of the people and the forests of the third world in equatorial and tropical zones. But there is also a displacement effect from the children to the third-world nations they represent. Finally, the choice of youth, both in the human and in the vegetable realms, induces a symbolic effect of hope.

5. Ask the students to form groups of three. Tell them that two students in the group will receive complementary parts of the same advertisement and that the third student will act as an observer. Tell them not to look at the other students' task sheets.

6. Hand out the prepared task sheets to Students A, B, and C in each group.

7. After about 20 minutes, run a feedback session, using the prepared overhead transparencies of the advertisements. Get the students to report on what their findings were and how they rated the advertisements.

8. Organize a general vote on the best advertisement, and lead an open discussion on the values it promotes.

Caveats and Options

1. Select ads with enigmatic pictures that are clearly separated from the text (outdated issues of magazines discarded by the library can be useful for this purpose). Do not make black-and-white copies of color advertisements if color is a significant factor in the effectiveness of the advertisement.

2. Be sure that the text of the advertisement is not too long. Alternatively, give Part A to weaker students and Parts B and C to stronger students; otherwise, Students B and C might need more preparation time than Student A.

3. It is essential for the success of this activity that the students not look at the other parts of the advertisements before they are told to do so.

4. If you prefer pair work, have pairs of students do Student C's (the observer's) part as a second stage. Prepare the following task sheets:

   ● Student A: the picture of an advertisement, accompanied by the following text: *This is the picture from an advertisement. In your opinion, which product, company, or charity does it advertise? Share your ideas with Student B, without showing that student your picture. Then listen to Student B. When you have both finished, show your picture. Did Student B guess right? Did you guess right? Why? Does this advertisement use a generalization, a displacement, or a symbolic effect? Discuss this with Student B. When you both agree, give your advertisement a rating from 1 (very effective) to 5 (a total failure).*

● Student B: the text of the same advertisement, together with the following instructions: *This is the text of an advertisement. In your opinion, what kind of picture illustrates it? First listen to Student A. Then share your ideas with that student without showing your text or referring to it. When you have both finished, show your text. Did Student B guess right? Did you guess right? Why? Does this advertisement use a generalization, a displacement, or a symbolic effect? Discuss this with Student A. When you both agree, give your advertisement a rating from 1 (very effective) to 5 (a total failure).*

References and Further Reading

Barthes, R. (1964). Rhétorique de l'image [The rhetoric of the image]. *Communications, 4*, 40–52.

Durand, J. (1970). Rhétorique et image publicitaire [Rhetorical figures in the advertising image]. *Communications, 15*, 71–93.

Nolasco, R., & Arthur, L. (1987). *Conversation*. Oxford: Oxford University Press.

Appendix: Sample Advertisement[1]

If the rainforests are being destroyed at the rate of thousands of trees a minute, how can planting just a handful of seedlings make a difference?

A WWF – World Wide Fund For Nature tree nursery addresses some of the problems facing people that can force them to chop down trees.

Where hunger or poverty is the underlying cause of deforestation, we can provide fruit trees.

The villagers of Mugunga, Zaire, for example, eat papaya and mangoes from WWF trees. And rather than having to sell timber to buy other food, they can now sell the surplus fruit their nursery produces.

Where trees are chopped down for firewood, WWF and the local people can protect them by planting fast-growing varieties to form a renewable fuel source.

This is particularly valuable in the Impenetrable Forest, Uganda, where indigenous hardwoods take two hundred years to mature. The *Markhamia lotea* trees planted by WWF and local villages can be harvested within five or six years of planting.

Where trees are chopped down to be used for construction, as in Panama and Pakistan, we supply other species that are fast-growing and easily replaced.

These tree nurseries are just part of the work we do with the people of the tropical forests.

WWF sponsors students from developing countries on an agroforestry course at UPAZ University in Costa Rica, where WWF provides technical advice on growing vegetable and grain crops.

Unless help is given, soil is exhausted very quickly by "slash and burn" farming methods.

New tracts of tropical forest would then have to be cleared every two or three years.

This unnecessary destruction can be prevented by combining modern techniques with traditional practices so that the same plot of land can be used to produce crops over and over again.

In La Planada, Colombia, our experimental farm demonstrates how these techniques can be used to grow a family's food on a small four hectare plot. (Instead of clearing the usual ten hectares of forest.)

WWF fieldworkers are now involved in over 100 tropical forest projects in 45 countries around the world.

The idea behind all of this work is that the use of natural resources should be sustainable.

WWF is calling for the rate of deforestation in the tropics to be halved by 1995, and for there to be no net deforestation by the end of the century.

Write to the Membership Officer at the address below to find out how you can help us ensure that this generation does not continue to steal nature's capital from the next. It could be with a donation, or, appropriately enough, a legacy.

WWF World Wide Fund For Nature
(formerly World Wildlife Fund)

International Secretariat, 1196 Gland, Switzerland.

FOR THE SAKE OF THE CHILDREN
WE GAVE THEM A NURSERY.

Contributor

Marie-Hélène Fries currently teaches in the science faculty of the University of Grenoble, in France.

[1]Copyright © 1994 by the World Wildlife Fund. Reprinted with permission.

Companies at Risk

Levels
Intermediate–high
intermediate

Aims
Acquire professional
communicative
competence
Simulate problems in
professional life
Interpret company
information
Work cooperatively

Class Time
Two or three 50-minute
classes

Preparation Time
2–3 hours

Resources
Case study
Worksheet
Interview script
Colored pencils
Pie charts, graphs, and
pictures (optional)

This activity provides business English instructors with a possible model for preparing and exploiting case studies. It presents some guidelines for developing original cases following the classical four-step case study format, and it suggests ways to use case studies to help business English students acquire professional communicative competence.

Procedure

1. Prepare a worksheet detailing the four stages in a case study (see Appendix A):
   - Stage 1: reading or listening about a company's problem (see the Information File and the Listening File, Appendixes B and C)
   - Stage 2: identifying the problem
   - Stage 3: analyzing the problem (see Problem-Solution Analysis, Appendix A)
   - Stage 4: presenting strategies to solve the problem (see Presentation, Appendix A)
2. Select appropriate case studies (see Appendix B for a sample). Each case study should contain background information on the company that will help the students understand the company's present situation. Also prepare tape scripts for short interviews with the Company at Risk's chief executive officer that contains additional details about its problem (see Appendix C for a sample). Have a colleague help you tape the interviews.
3. In class, group the students in threes. Have the groups work on different cases or, to add some competition to the activity, on the same case. The group that offers the most appropriate solution is the winner.
4. Distribute a copy of the worksheet to each student.

5. Ask the students to read and fill out the worksheet. As they read, check to see that they understand what they are supposed to do: (a) plot a strategy to help the Company at Risk solve its problem and (b) prepare an oral presentation of their strategy. To complete the worksheet, the students select the most relevant information about the Company at Risk (i.e., from the Information File or the Listening File) and the problem it is facing.

6. Assign roles to the students (e.g., marketing consultant, public relations specialist) according to their majors.

7. Tell the students that they can use charts, graphs, and pictures for their oral presentation. Either have the students devise their own visual aids, or give them samples.

8. Before the oral presentations, ask the students to write a short memo to summon their "coworkers" to the meeting. If you wish, ask high-intermediate students to write a short report based on their oral presentation.

9. After each group's presentation, ask the other students to give feedback on the group's performance. Complete the feedback session with your own notes.

Caveats and Options

1. Case studies presuppose that (a) all ideas are useful, (b) everybody can learn from everybody else, and (c) there is no single solution to a problem. Therefore, encourage the students to present alternative ideas, discourage them from criticizing others' language during the feedback session unless their mistakes have caused serious misunderstanding, and, finally, encourage the students to work cooperatively.

2. Increase the length and complexity of the information in accordance with the level of the students. For high-intermediate students, for example, include in the Information File newspaper and magazine articles on topics that are related to the case. Ask the students to interview subject-matter specialists or do library research to get more ideas on how to solve the problem.

3. Ellis and Johnson (1994) is a good source for black-and-white pie charts, graphs, and pictures that the students can use as samples for their strategy presentations.

4. Videotaping the session enriches the experience for the students, as they can immediately review their performance and receive useful feedback. If a video camera is not available, a tape recorder, though less effective, can also be used.

5. Remember that, as with any other activity in a business English course, feedback on performance is more important than feedback on language mistakes.

References and Further Reading

Ellis, M., & Johnson, C. (1994). *Teaching business English.* Oxford: Oxford University Press.

Huckin, T. N. (1988). Achieving professional communicative relevance in a generalised ESP classroom. In D. Chamberlain & R. J. Baumgardner (Eds.), *ESP in the classroom: Practice and evaluation* (ELT Document 128, pp. 61–70). London: Modern English Publications.

Robinson, P. C. (1991). *ESP today: A practitioner's guide.* Hertfordshire, England: Prentice Hall International.

Appendix A: Worksheet

1. The Information File: Read the information about the company at risk. As you read, pay close attention to details and write down those you consider most important. Then check with your coworkers.

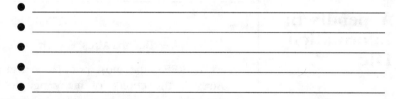

   • _____
   • _____
   • _____
   • _____
   • _____

2. The Listening File: Listen to the manager of the company at risk. As you listen, pay close attention to details and write down those you consider most important. Then check with your coworkers.

   • _____
   • _____
   • _____
   • _____
   • _____

3. Problem-Solution Analysis: Analyze the problems the company at risk is facing. Write them down in order of importance. Then discuss your choices with your coworkers. Together, discuss some possible solutions.

Problems	Possible Solutions
1.	1.
2.	2.
3.	3.

4. Presentation: Plan how you and your coworkers will present the solutions to the problems the company at risk is facing. Here is a list of ideas to help you.
   ● charts and graphs
   ● memos
   ● reports
   ● interviews

Appendix B: Information File

EVERGREEN

Buenos Aires' Favorite Green Restaurant

EVERGREEN, the most popular vegetarian restaurant in Buenos Aires, is the choice of many people whose diet is based on vegetables, fruit, and natural fruit juices.

EVERGREEN is also famous for the quality of its food, which, as its name suggests, is always fresh and green. Prices are another "ingredient" that makes this vegetarian restaurant so popular.

EVERGREEN is now planning to sell its products in other parts of Argentina: Cordoba, Rosario, and Mendoza. More than 30 new employees, including waiters and cooks, will be hired for the company's new "cuisine" adventure.

The owners of EVERGREEN hope to expand the company's annual turnover of $150,000 with this new strategy. So, if you are lucky enough to live in Cordoba, Rosario, or Mendoza and you like "green food," you'll soon have the right place to eat out: EVERGREEN.

Appendix C: Listening File (Tape Script)

EVERGREEN CEO:	Well, the company is now trying to place its products, that is vegetarian food, in other parts of the country; Argentina, I mean. And . . . the structure of EVERGREEN is very small. There's the sales manager, a personnel manager, well . . . the cooks, of course, and waiters and cashiers working in the different restaurants. That's about 35 people in all.
Interviewer:	Are the plans for expansion causing any problems for EVERGREEN?
CEO:	Well . . . yes. As a matter of fact they are. You see, the most serious problem is one of quality. I mean, we are worried about keeping the same quality in the food that will be served in different parts of the country. Quality control is very difficult at a distance. The EVERGREEN head office is in Buenos Aires, and it would be 700 kilometers away from Cordoba, one important selling point we want to approach.
Interviewer:	Is there anything else that worries EVERGREEN?
CEO:	Another problem is product positioning. Cordoba, you see, is a very conservative city, and vegetarian food is not . . . how can I put

this . . . everybody's cup of tea. Besides, I think expansion may also create a problem with the training of the employees. And this is crucial because I believe quality depends on this, too.

Contributor

Julio Cesar Giménez is an ESP instructor at Instituto de Estudios Superiores and at Universidad Empresarial Siglo 21 in Cordoba, Argentina.

Investigate to Collocate

Levels
Intermediate +

Aim
Develop subject-specific
vocabulary

Class Time
Variable

Preparation Time
4 hours

Resources
Computer-stored
versions of specialist
publications
Computer
Concordancing software

This activity involves the students as learners and investigators of language, as they have to analyze real language for themselves. This encourages learners to observe language as it is actually used in their field and develops their specialized vocabulary knowledge in a given subject area.

Procedure

1. Using the concordancing software and the electronic version of a publication, do a search for a key word or concept (e.g., *shares* or *dollar*) in order to locate all articles containing that word.
2. Use the downloading facility to copy to disk the files returned by the search.
3. Use the word-list facility to produce a list of the words in your collection of texts, in descending order of the frequency with which the words are used.
4. Select a frequently used content word from the word list (e.g., *share*), and use the concordancer to produce a concordance (see the Appendix for an example).
5. Use the concordances as the basis of a variety of classroom vocabulary tasks that enable the students to contrast the use of vocabulary in specialized texts with its use in general English (see Tribble & Jones, 1990).

Caveats and Options

1. Electronic publications can provide a ready-made corpus of material (e.g., use the CD-ROM collection of past copies of the *Financial Times* for financial vocabulary). Check that the data can be obtained in what is known as ASCII or text format.
2. This approach can serve as the basis of a closely tailored course (see Roe, 1993).

References and Further Reading

Hales, T. (1995). *Planting seeds: Corpus analysis in reading course production proceedings.* Paper presented at the New Ways in Reading Skills Conference, American University, Cairo, Egypt.

Johns, T., & King, P. (1991). *Classroom concordancing.* Birmingham, England: University of Birmingham, Centre for English Language Studies.

Roe, P. (1993). *Target language: The* Financial Times *Proceedings.* Paper presented at the Second National ESP Seminar, English for Special Purposes: Applications and Implications for Human Resource Development, Universiti Teknologi, Malaysia.

Sinclair, J. (1991). *Corpus, concordance, collocation.* Oxford: Oxford University Press.

Tribble, C., & Jones, G. (1990). *Concordances in the classroom: A resource book for teachers.* London: Longman.

Appendix: Market Movements

Directions: How many ways of expressing market movements do you know? What verbs are often used? Look at the lines taken from market reports in the *Financial Times*. Divide the verbs into groups describing movements up or down.

```
  previous losses of 4.5p. The  shares closed 3p higher at 17p. The F
 staged a strong recovery, the  shares bouncing 9 to 114p in heavy tur
 pesos and Manila Electric A    shares eased 4 pesos to 157 pesos. KUA
 rted in RollsRoyce where the   shares firmed 2 to 104p, in trade of 4
   sellers of Guinness and the  shares gave up 9 to 525p, in trade of 2
ning operation in the US. The   shares jumped 15 to 459p. United News
     volumes this year. Gerber  shares plunged Dollars 4 to 78 to Dollar
 for redundancy payments. The   shares shed 6p to 83p. The decline was
  et expectations, although the shares slipped 2p to 717p on light pro
 BTR, but also to Tarmac. The   shares sped up 6 to 96p, after 97p on t
 93 and remaining a buyer. The  shares retreated 12 to 428p. Bass rec
95m to Pounds 210m range. The   shares tumbled 11 to 169p in heavy tur
 m Monday's SKr922m. Volvo B    shares weakened SKr17 to SKr340 on news
```

Movement up	Movement down

Contributor

Tom Hales is a senior tutor in the Centre for Applied Language Studies at the University of Wales, Swansea, in the United Kingdom.

Speculate, Accumulate, Simulate

Levels
Intermediate +

Aims
Read business and
financial English
Develop speaking
fluency and register
Understand and use
financial trading
vocabulary

Class Time
1 hour +

Preparation Time
45 minutes

Resources
Financial newspaper

This reading-based simulation combines reading and speaking skills. It gives realistic practice in performing real-world tasks with real language. The students use a week of business market reports (gradually introduced by the teacher) to make judgments about future market movements. This requires accurate reading of specialized texts. The aim for the students is to maximize their profits, thereby introducing either a cooperative or a competitive element as appropriate to the students involved. The simulation is adaptable to different markets.

Procedure

1. Collect one week's market reports from a financial newspaper, for example, the "Money Markets" reports from the *Financial Times* or the equivalent in the *Wall Street Journal*. Also collect the same week's market movements (including the values for the starting points and the closing figures of the previous week). Either select a set of shares, currencies, or commodities that figured in much of the trading in the week you collected the articles, or allow the students to select their own using a given budget.
2. In class, give the starting values from the week's market movements, and ensure that the students copy them down.
3. Hand out the first market reports article (e.g., the one for Monday). Have the students choose to buy or sell as a result of what they read.
4. Give the following day's market prices, and have the students calculate their profits or losses.
5. Give the students the market reports article for the second day, and repeat the process until the end of the week or a convenient point at which to stop.

Caveats and Options

1. Rather than doing the entire activity in one lesson, stretch the process out over a week, one article per day. Between lessons, work on any problems identified (e.g., in appropriateness or vocabulary). The students' performance of the task should improve over the period.
2. As with many simulations, you can record the students doing the simulation to help you identify linguistic problems to cover in delayed error correction work.

References and Further Reading

This activity is a "low-tech" version of the author's own computer simulation, FTSim.

Contributor

Tom Hales is a senior tutor in the Centre for Applied Language Studies at the University of Wales, Swansea, in the United Kingdom.

Meet the Press

Levels
Intermediate +

Aims
Practice participating in
and chairing a formal
business meeting

Class Time
25 minutes/meeting

Preparation Time
30 minutes or less

Resources
Business problem
handout
Role descriptors
Language handout
Props (optional)
Name cards (optional)
Peer and self-evaluation
forms

This activity helps ESP students in international business develop the skills and confidence necessary to participate fully in formal meetings.

Procedure

1. Locate or develop a scenario involving a business problem that is appropriate to the interests and level of the students (see Appendix A for a sample). Develop a handout showing the language structures that are used frequently in business meetings.
2. If your class is large, divide the students into two groups.
3. Distribute the scenario and role descriptors (see Appendix B). Assign roles, and ask the students to prepare for their roles for the next class meeting (see Appendix C).
4. Distribute the handout. Review the structures with the students.
5. In the next class, have the students role play the news conference following the format outlined in Appendix A. All people present at the news conference must have a clear understanding of the objectives of the meeting and of the role that they will be expected to play. Each meeting should last about 25 minutes.
6. Have observers complete peer review forms, and have all participants complete self-evaluation forms (see Appendixes D and E).

Caveats and Options

1. Newspapers are an excellent source of current business problems.
2. Business problems may vary in length and complexity. At a minimum, they should be one paragraph long.
3. Require the students to do research to support their positions. For example, have them explore the Internet, interview experts on a

particular subject, or find business articles through the *ABI/INFORM Global Edition*.

4. Include the role plays as part of a unit or module, and have the students acquire background knowledge about a business problem or case through readings, discussions, writing assignments, or other means before they participate in the business meeting. The role descriptors can be commercially prepared or written by the ESP instructor.

5. Use the format to practice participation in other types of business meetings, such as a staff meeting, a meeting of stockholders, a meeting with disgruntled employees, or a union meeting.

References and Further Reading

ABI/INFORM global edition [CD-ROM]. Norwood, MA: SilverPlatter Information. (database of abstracts from articles in management, business, and marketing journals)

Boyd, F. (1994). *Making business decisions: Real cases from real companies*. New York: Addison-Wesley.

Ellis, M., & Johnson, C. (1994). *Teaching business English*. Oxford: Oxford University Press.

Minkoff, P. (1994). *Executive skills* [Audiotape and text]. Englewood Cliffs, NJ: Prentice-Hall Regents.

Scarpino, T. (1991). *Be prepared for meetings: How to lead productive business meetings* [Videotape and text]. San Francisco: Kantola Productions.

Appendix A: Scenario

1. Preparing for the Vitasoy News Conference
   Read the following business situation and answer the questions that follow.

   In 1995 people started to become ill after consuming sour Vitasoy soy milk. On January 9, 1996, Hong Kong's Vitasoy International recalled all paper-packed drinks and shut down its factories so its consultants could determine the source of the contamination. Vitasoy executives have called a new conference to reassure the public through the media.

- What can Vitasoy International do to regain the public's confidence in its soy milk products?
- What can Vitasoy do to protect consumers?
- What can Vitasoy do to reassure its investors?

To run a successful news conference, both the Vitasoy public relations executives and the news reporters must prepare carefully.

2. Conducting the Vitasoy News Conference (about 25 minutes)

Introduction

- The Vitasoy public relations (PR) executives open the news conference by welcoming the reporters and thanking them for attending. They speak clearly and confidently.
- The Vitasoy PR executives state the purpose of the news conference: to inform the public that their company is doing everything it can to determine the source of the contamination and offer consumers only safe, high-quality soy products.

Agenda

- The Vitasoy PR executives invite the news reporters to ask questions.
- When the news reporters ask difficult questions, the executives use appropriate techniques and expressions to answer them.
- The Vitasoy PR executives control the meeting and respond to questions in a calm, concerned manner.

Closing

- The Vitasoy PR executives conclude the news conference by restating their position: Vitasoy International is so concerned about safety that it has recalled all paper-packed drinks and shut down its factories until the source of contamination has been identified. The company will resume production when it is confident that its product is safe.

3. Evaluating the News Conference

Two observers will complete peer review forms for each news conference. In addition, the Vitasoy PR executives and the news reporters will complete self-evaluation forms.

Appendix B: Role Descriptors

Vitasoy Public Relations Executives

Your goal is to chair the news conference and let the public know that Vitasoy International is doing everything possible to protect the safety of its customers by distributing high-quality products. You want the public to be aware that

- Vitasoy has responded quickly and responsibly to the crisis by recalling all paper-packed soy drinks.
- Vitasoy is working closely with local investigators to determine the source of the contamination.
- Vitasoy will resume distribution when it is certain that the soy products are safe.
- [etc.]

International Newspaper Reporters

For a story in the *International Herald Tribune*, you want to find out

- how many people became ill from drinking contaminated Vitasoy soy milk
- how the soy milk became contaminated
- whether a disgruntled employee at Vitasoy might have deliberately contaminated the soy milk
- what steps are being taken to ensure the safety of consumers
- [etc.]

Local Newspaper Reporters

For a story in the *Hong Kong Standard*, you want to find out

- where the contaminated soy milk was purchased
- how Vitasoy International plans to compensate the consumers who became ill after drinking contaminated soy milk
- what consumers should do with Vitasoy soy milk that they have at home
- [etc.]

Financial Newspaper Reporters

For an article in the *Far Eastern Economic Review*, you want to find out

- if Vitasoy International will be able to recover (The price of its shares has plunged, and financial analysts in Hong Kong indicate that the company stands to lose HK$120 million–$155 million from the recall.)
- if and when Vitasoy expects to resume distribution of soy milk
- whether Vitasoy will redesign the packaging of the soy milk cartons and, if so, how much this would cost the company
- what plans the company has to reassure its stockholders that it can recover financially from this crisis
- [etc.]

Appendix C: Role Assignments

For each news conference, decide who will play the following roles:

Vitasoy public relations executives   _____
(to chair the news conference)   _____
                                      _____

International news reporters   _____
(for the *International Herald Tribune*) _____
                                      _____

Local news reporters   _____
(for the *Hong Kong Standard*)   _____
                                      _____

Financial news reporters
(for the *Far Eastern Economic Review*)

Observers (complete peer evaluation
form; evaluate the performance
of the Vitasoy PR executives)

Appendix D: Peer Evaluation of Chairpersons

Vitasoy public relations
executives (chairpersons):

Rate the chairpersons according to the following scale:
  I = ineffective
  S = satisfactory
  G = good

1. Introduction
   _____ used appropriate introductions
   _____ used an effective opening
2. Controlling the Meeting
   _____ dealt with news reporters' questions in a respectful manner
   _____ controlled excessive speaking by individual reporters
   _____ asked for clarification in an appropriate manner
   _____ stated the position of Vitasoy convincingly
   _____ repeated the news reporters' questions when appropriate
   _____ answered questions knowledgeably
   _____ established an appropriate rapport with the news reporters
   _____ worked well together
3. Language Skills
   _____ grammar
   _____ pronunciation
   _____ vocabulary (appropriate for a formal news conference)
   _____ fluency (spoke naturally)
   _____ voice (tone, pitch, stress)

4. Nonverbal Skills
_____ appeared calm and confident
_____ showed concern when appropriate
_____ showed interest
_____ used eye contact to good effect
_____ used active listening skills
_____ used gestures and body language well
5. Overall Performance (Please write your comments in the space provided.)
- What did you like most about the performance of the Vitasoy Public Relations Executives?

- Suggest improvements that the Vitasoy Public Relations executives could make in chairing future meetings.

- How would you rate the overall performance of the Vitasoy public relations executives? (Put an *X* in the appropriate box.)

Poor   Excellent

1	2	3	4	5	6	7	8	9	10

Appendix E: Self-Evaluation of Performance

Name: _____Role: _____

1. What did you like most about your performance?

2. What would you like to improve about your performance?

3. Please rate your overall performance in this news conference. (Put an X in the appropriate box.)

Poor   Excellent

1	2	3	4	5	6	7	8	9	10

Contributor

Jane Jackson is an associate professor and team leader of ESP Research and Curriculum Development at the Chinese University of Hong Kong. She is coauthor of Campus Bound: Passport to Academic Success *(Nelson Canada).*

Slipping Into Problem Solvers' Shoes

Levels
Intermediate +

Aims
Prepare, analyze, and present a case in groups
Understand business ethics
Develop problem-solving and decision-making skills

Class Time
45 minutes–1 hour

Preparation Time
30 minutes or less (if prepared cases are available)

Resources
Handout with cases
Chart paper
Markers

This activity helps students develop the confidence and skills necessary to participate fully in their content courses. In the problem-solving approach used in this activity, the students are encouraged to discuss ideas freely, and differences of opinion are expected. This activity works well if an atmosphere of trust and cooperation is actively promoted in the class.

Procedure

1. Locate a case study that is appropriate to the interests and level of the students (see the Appendix). It can be commercially prepared, or written by the EBE instructor or content specialist.
2. Ask the students to read the case for homework before coming to class.
3. In class, divide the class into groups of four to five students each, preferably at tables. Distribute chart paper and markers.
4. Have the students select one person as recorder and another as reporter, or have one person perform both tasks.
5. Give the groups 10-15 minutes to identify and record on the chart paper the central and secondary problems in the case.
6. Have each group report its findings to the rest of the class by referring to the lists written on the chart paper.
7. Have the groups identify alternative solutions by brainstorming, as the recorder for each group lists the ideas on chart paper. (Try to intervene as little as possible so that the students are encouraged to speak freely.)
8. Ask the groups to evaluate the alternatives proposed and prioritize them, selecting the one(s) most likely to solve the problem or bring about the desired change.

9. Have each group post the chart paper with its proposed solution(s) and present them to the rest of the class.
10. Have the class compare the answers given and discuss the pros and cons of each recommendation.
11. Conclude the session by asking the students to write about which solution they think is the best, giving reasons to support their position.

Caveats and Options

1. Commercially prepared cases are available in most disciplines (e.g., business, social work, psychology, sociology, biology, medicine).
2. Cases may vary in length and complexity. At minimum, they should be one paragraph long.
3. Present the cases in the form of films or videos.
4. Provide a list of questions after the cases to stimulate thought and discussion.
5. Require the students to locate evidence to support their positions. For example, have them conduct library research, explore the Internet, or interview experts on a particular subject.
6. Ask the students to write up their analyses of cases, following specific guidelines.
7. Have the students evaluate their group discussion and make suggestions to improve their next group meeting.

References and Further Reading

Boyd, F. (1991). Business English and the case method: A reassessment. *TESOL Quarterly, 25,* 729-734.

Grosse, C. U. (1988). The case study approach to teaching business English. *English for Specific Purposes, 7,* 131-136.

Kohls, L. R., & Knight, J. M. (1994). *Developing intercultural awareness: A crosscultural training handbook.* Yarmouth, ME: Intercultural Press.

Appendix: Sample Case

1.   Read the following case

Pulling Strings

Michael Torrino graduated from college with a bachelor's degree in international finance. He was a very sharp fellow but did not apply himself well. In fact, the sole reason that he was able to attend one of the best schools in the country was that his family was well off and could afford the high tuition fees. Because he was not on a scholarship and didn't need top marks to stay in school, he spent most of the 4 years partying with his friends, and it showed in his grades.

After he graduated, his parents rewarded him with a summer vacation in Greece. When he got back home, his family started asking him about his career plans. He was very vague about his future and spent almost all of his time relaxing at the beach. His mother decided that she had better pull a few strings and get him a job. Martha Torrino was the president of a prominent insurance agency, so she had many good business contacts. One of the people she contacted was George Gladstone, the director of a small insurance agency in the same city. She and George had gone to college together and were still close. Besides, George's company had just been granted a large contract to do work for her agency.

When Michael's mother approached George, he responded positively and suggested that Martha tell her son to come by for an interview at the end of the week. Michael attended the interview and was granted a job the same day.

Michael was not very excited about the job but thought that it might be an easy way to make some money. After all, he was smart enough to know that, by hiring him, Gladstone hoped to get even more contracts with his mother's firm. How hard could the job be?

Three weeks into the job, Michael had already made enemies. In fact, most of his workmates couldn't stand him! Whenever he was asked to do errands, he would go on long breaks and forget to finish them. When a more challenging task was assigned, he would try to get one of the other employees to do it for him, claiming that Gladstone would be happy that they were helping him out. Michael began arriving later and later each morning, and he was the first one out the door at night.

By the second month, his coworkers had had enough. Several of them went to see the manager of the unit and complained that Michael was lazy and not pulling his weight. The manager, who had intended to talk with Michael about his job performance, decided that she couldn't put it off any longer. She called Michael into her office and began to voice her concerns when Michael became very hostile and warned her that she could get into a lot of trouble if she hassled him. The manager had heard that Michael was well connected and was not at all sure how she should respond.

2. In groups, discuss the following questions.
   ● Who are the key players?
   ● What problems do they face?
   ● How should Michael's manager respond to him? (Try to think of several different suggestions, and note both the strengths and the weaknesses of each.)
   ● What would you do if you were in the manager's shoes?
   ● Are there policies that the agency should adopt to prevent this situation from occurring again?

Contributor

Jane Jackson is an associate professor and coordinator of ESP curriculum research and development at the Chinese University of Hong Kong. She is coauthor of Campus Bound: Passport to Academic Success *(Nelson Canada).*

Start With an Ad

Levels
Intermediate +

Aims
Practice basic language skills in a content lesson on marketing

Class Time
6-8 hours

Preparation Time
45 minutes-1 hour

Resources
Newspaper or magazine
Textbook excerpt
Taped lecture on marketing
Comprehension questions

In this activity, students experience an actual college content class within the secure environment of the ESL class. The lesson offers students a basic introduction to the content area—marketing—and encourages them to think about their own behavior as consumers and about effective marketing techniques. The activity's four-stage approach—prereading, reading, analysis, and expansion—engages students in hands-on activities designed to encourage both active involvement in learning and analytical and creative use of the English language. The taped lecture affords the students the opportunity to listen to an authentic classroom lecture with fast-paced speech and to practice note-taking. Subsequent class discussion of the lecture experience teaches the students how to identify the main points in the lecture. The essay prompt assigned in the expansion stage of the activity produces some very creative thinking as the students invent their own products.

Procedure

Prereading

1. Ask the students to bring in an advertisement from a newspaper or magazine.
2. Cover the name of the product, and ask the students to guess what is being sold.
3. Have the students explain why they chose that particular advertisement.
4. Point out the elements (e.g., color, characters) that make the advertisement effective.

5. Have the students discuss whether they would be likely to buy the product on the basis of the advertisement.
6. Familiarize the students with vocabulary used in the content area of marketing.

Reading

1. Assign the textbook excerpt (e.g., Kolter, 1988) for homework.
2. Discuss the reading in class on the following day; ask the students to identify the key points in the text.

Analysis

1. Play the taped lecture on marketing (e.g., Ruetten, 1986, Lecture 8, "Basic Marketing").
2. Ask the students to take notes on the important points in the lecture.
3. Have the students summarize the main points in the lecture.
4. Ask the students to explain what helped them identify the important information in the lecture.
5. Point out the techniques the lecturer used to emphasize important information (e.g., restatement).

Expansion

1. Give the students the handout of comprehension questions (see the Appendix). Allow them to use their lecture notes to write answers to these questions.
2. Ask the students to write an essay for homework in which they design a new product, identify the target market, and explain how they would market this new product.

Caveats and Options

1. This activity has been successful with both intermediate- and advanced-level ESL students. The students especially enjoy the prereading task, which stimulates lively discussion about the advertisements themselves and about comparisons between advertising in the United States and in the students' native countries.

2. The activity helps alleviate the students' anxiety about their ability to understand mainstream academic English by exposing them to the types of listening, speaking, reading, and writing activities they can expect to encounter in mainstream courses.

3. Use this activity as the marketing segment of a multicontent course or as one topic in a single or paired content course focusing on marketing.

References and Further Reading

Brinton, D. M., Snow, M. A., & Wesche, M. B. (1989). *Content-based second language instruction*. Boston: Heinle & Heinle.

Kasper, L. F. (1994). Developing and teaching a content-based reading course for ESL students. *Teaching English in the Two-Year College, 21*, 23–26.

Kolter, P. (1988). Market targeting. In L. W. Holschuh & J. P. Kelley (Eds.), *Academic reading: A content-based approach* (pp. 67–70). New York: St. Martin's Press.

Ruetten, M. K. (1986). *Comprehending academic lectures*. New York: Macmillan.

Appendix: Sample Comprehension Questions

Directions: Use your lecture notes to help you answer the following questions.

1. List and define, with examples, the three market-coverage alternatives discussed in the textbook excerpt, "Market Targeting."

2. Do you think it is possible to create a need or a desire for a product that has never existed before? Think of and list three or four products sold today that were not available 20 years ago. What types of needs do you think each one satisfies in the consumer?

3. List and define the four types of marketing utilities discussed by the lecturer on the tape you heard in class. Use specific examples in your answer.

Contributor

Loretta F. Kasper is an assistant professor of English at Kingsborough Community College of the City University of New York, in the United States, where she teaches content-based courses to intermediate and advanced ESL students.

Write Better and Be a Company Director!

Levels
Advanced

Aims
Simulate a business setting
Engage in cooperative learning

Class Time
3 hours

Preparation Time
4 hours

Resources
Reports produced by previous year's students
Reading from assigned text (optional)

This task-based activity motivates students be more enthusiastic about writing and produce better end products because they take up managerial roles in the local business context. The students enjoy being in the managerial positions and thus have strong motivation to participate in class during this activity. It also gives them the incentive to read authentic company reports carefully, as they have to set up their own companies. The companies and the students' roles can be used for other business communication activities because students find writing to each other more realistic than writing only to the teacher.

Procedure

1. For homework, ask the students to read some of the reports produced by former students (see the Appendix). Alternatively, ask them to read a relevant chapter from their business communication course book.
2. In the next class, talk about the format, style, content, and tone of annual reports.
3. Ask the students each to select a specific line of business that interests them. Form groups of four or five based on the students' interest in or knowledge of a specific line of business.
4. Inform the students that they will be creating a company devoted to that line of business, and ask them to brainstorm ideas for the company. When they have made a decision, ask them to write down the nature of their company on the blackboard. Have other groups who want to pursue the same line of business think of another type of company, preferably one that can do business with the companies already listed on the blackboard.
5. After all the groups have decided on the nature of their companies, ask them to brainstorm, and have a group secretary write down, an

181

imaginary history of their company, their respective posts in the company, and their responsibilities. If time allows, ask them to talk about the future prospects of the company as well.

6. For homework, ask each group member to complete different parts of the report (see the Appendix for a sample).
7. In the next class, ask the students to exchange their writing and do peer correction.
8. Ask each group to make an oral presentation so that the whole class knows what kind of businesses there are in the group's "business world."
9. Tell the students to keep their posts and their companies for other business writing assignments in later lessons (e.g., meetings and minutes, memos and letters, reports and proposals).

Caveats and Options

1. Because the tasks are based on the local business setting, the students do not need to learn a foreign culture in order to understand the practice exercises.
2. If there is not enough time for the students to write a report that includes a history, last year's performance, future prospects, and other components, have them write a description of the company and the personnel involved. Then have the different groups write to each other.
3. Annual reports from big companies in Hong Kong or any other city are useful reference materials for the language and style used in formal documents.
4. If the students have a course book, have them refer to the chapter on reports (e.g., Bovee & Thill, 1995, chap. 14).

References and Further Reading

Bovee, C. L., & Thill, J. V. (1995). *Business communication today.* New York: McGraw-Hill.

Lai, E. F. K. (1992, April). Teaching business writing through a status-raising simulation. *English Teaching Forum,* 35–38.

Appendix: Sample Student Report

Sahara Hotel Management Corporation

The Sahara Hotel Management Corporation was established on 1 January 1965. It is the oldest hotel management company in Hong Kong with more than 20 years' experience of developing and managing deluxe class hotels around the Asian region.

The first Sahara Hotel was opened in Hong Kong in July 1965 at Tsimshasui. Our strategy is to concentrate on providing our patrons with high standard of service and on increasing operating efficiency. Our hotels cater to a wide range of clientele, including tourist and business travellers, and they are well known for their consistently high standard of service.

In its preliminary stage, our corporation encompassed four countries and more than 5,000 employees. Sahara Hotels were founded in Hong Kong, Manila, Bangkok, and Seoul. The Hong Kong headquarters and the regional liaison offices are responsible for all of Sahara's activities in the territories. The Sahara Hotel in Bangkok is the largest hotel owned by the corporation and has 925 rooms and suites. Besides, there are seven restaurants and bars including a nightclub, 24-hour room service business centre, and two all-weather tennis courts. Moreover, our hotel view information service is available through the TV, providing guests with immediate access to the latest information on the stock exchange, weather, and world news.

During the past 20 years, the corporation has gone through various stages of development and overcome numerous difficulties to become what it is today. The business of the corporation has diversified greatly from its early days, when it concentrated solely on hotel ownership and management, to being involved today with other multifaceted business interests, such as the Sahara Health Club, the Sahara Florist, Camel Travel Ltd., and the Sahara Lounge. Among the subsidiaries, the Sahara Health Club, a very popular health club in the Asian region, is fully equipped with the advanced facilities of a full-sized gymnasium.

The 1970s marked an important milestone in the history of the corporation. The advances in transportation and communication technologies along with increasing economic interdependence among nations have fostered steady growth in international commerce and travel. This trend towards multinational operations has extended to service industries, including the ownership and management of hotels.

President, Daisy C. C. Chong
Miss Chong, who has extensive experience in the hotel industry, was transferred from The Sahara (Bangkok) Hotel in 1970. She oversees the management and operation of the hotels within the group and its related businesses in Hong Kong, Thailand, the Philippines, Korea, and the People's Republic of China.

She has been developing contacts with government agencies concerned with supplying hotel-related services; directing studies of agency services, policies, procedures, and staffing; and measuring long-term and short-term programme objectives.

As president of the Group, Miss Chong developed and instituted a project in Bangkok in 1975 and has successfully generated, on an average basis, an annual revenue of U.S.$20 million.

Vice President—Sales and Marketing, Brenda W. Y. Chui
Miss Chui, after graduating from Oxford University in the United Kingdom, joined the Group in 1980 as a marketing executive. With her enthusiasm and strong desire to succeed, she worked her way up and in 1987 was appointed to the well-deserved position of vice president for sales and marketing of the Group.

Miss Chui's primary responsibilities are to research, analyse, and interpret the market sources in order to plan and implement the marketing strategies and to accomplish prescribed goals by coordinating with the marketing managers of various operations. Aside from this, Miss Chui is actively involved in the planning of marketing strategies, both short-term and long-term, for individual operations. In order to promote and upgrade the Group's image, she has been carrying out promotional campaigns and organizing exhibitions, seminars, and prestigious advertisements.

Miss Chui's self-confidence and her ability to think quickly and to work under extreme pressure have enabled her to interact with customers, hotel developers, and hotel executives.

Last Year's Performance

The operating and financial results of the Group for the year under review exceeded expectations with record revenues. The hotel's average room occupancy reached 80%, with a 15% increase in average room rate over 1987.

The year 1988 marked a breakthrough in the realization of our endeavours in Shanghai, China. The Shanghai Hotel was completed and opened in February 1988 under our management. In addition, the groundbreaking ceremony of the May Flower Hotel in Beijing was held on 5 March 1988. Our equity joint venture project with the Jining Group of Shanghai has been progressing well and has been actively pursuing business opportunities. At present, several other projects in and around Shanghai are under negotiation.

According to the information supplied by the Hong Kong Tourist Association, the total number of visitors to Hong Kong for the year 1988 increased by 9%. Four countries, namely Japan, Australia, the United States, and the United Kingdom, together accounted for 56% of the total incoming visitors.

The hotel industry will certainly experience keen competition although confidence in the tourist business remains strong. We are conscious of the challenge and prepared to meet the competition in order to sustain our growth.

Future Prospects

In 1990, we anticipate current earnings from our company's principal divisions, hotels and properties.

As a matter of fact, the rapid growth in travel in the past few decades has broadened the scope of hotel markets. In some ways, a hotel, no matter where it is located, now competes for guests with hotels all over the world. Competitive pressures and economies of scale will continue to encourage the internationalization of hotel chains over the foreseeable future. Our long-term plans are threefold.

First, set up a wholly owned five-star hotel in Jakarta, Indonesia. With the decline in income from oil and gas exports, tourism as a foreign exchange earner has become increasingly important to the economy and is currently the sixth-largest earner. In recognition of its importance, the government has eased visa procedures ad now allows foreign airlines to operate directly to sightseeing spots like Bali.

Second, inaugurate a resort in Maldives, Sri Lanka, a newly developed sightseeing and holiday place. By 1992, there will be a 200-room continental-style hotel with well-equipped facilities for activities like waterskiing, golf, and tennis.

Third, reestablish the Repulse Bay Hotel in Hong Kong. The hotel will be pulled down and will be replaced by four luxurious residential blocks with a commercial complex. This project is scheduled for completion by the end of 1995 but will not contribute to the Group's earnings until 1997.

Contributor

Eva Fungkuen Lai is program director of the English Section, Independent Learning Center, at the Chinese University of Hong Kong.

Nice Meeting You

Levels
High intermediate +

Aims
Develop language and
presentation skills for
professional meetings

Class Time
2–3 hours over two
class periods

Preparation Time
5 minutes

Resources
Conference/meeting
room
Whiteboard and markers
(or facsimile)
Notepad and pen
Examples of good visual
aids
Video camera, clips of
meetings, viewing
equipment (optional)

This two-session activity is designed to introduce students or working professionals to the language and social behavior expected at English meetings in the learners' target vocation or profession. In addition to the instruction provided by the teacher, the learners practice their skills in a realistic setting where they can receive immediate practical feedback.

Procedure

Session 1

1. Invite your students or clients to share their knowledge of and experience with meetings conducted in English.
   - During the discussion, list characteristic features of the genre on the whiteboard. The list may include such features as purposes (e.g., discuss and resolve a problem), common expectations (e.g., adhere to an agenda), and special vocabulary (e.g., *make, second, discuss, vote on,* or *table a motion*).
   - If they are available, show a few short video clips of illustrative meeting segments.

2. Ask your students or clients to prepare to take part in a mock meeting.
   - As a class, select a theme (e.g., increasing productivity at XYZ Corporation).
   - Determine each participant's role and duties (e.g., chairperson: write up and distribute an agenda, begin the meeting, direct the discussion, close the meeting; participants: share analyses of the problem and offer solutions).

● If visual aids are frequently used in the meetings that your students or clients are training for, offer some instruction in the appropriate selection and use of visual support for such meetings. Show some good examples of the options.

Session 2

1. If possible, have your students or clients meet in a genuine conference or meeting room where all participants can sit around a large conference table and face each other. Place the whiteboard near you at one side of the room to display written input during the meeting. If a different setting is commonly used for meetings, arrange for the students to practice in that setting.
2. If a video camera is available, set it up so that the entire meeting can be filmed from one wide camera angle.
3. Have your students or clients conduct their mock meeting while you take notes on their presentations and language usage. When a participant begins to search for a word or phrase during his or her presentation, without interrupting the flow of the meeting, write appropriate options on the whiteboard next to you so that all the participants can see the information.
4. Depending on need, "freeze" the meeting every 15-30 minutes to share observations. Point out both strengths and weaknesses in the operation of the meeting and in the use of English. Suggest better alternatives.
5. When the mock meeting ends, review the behavior and language of the meeting from the material you have collected in your notes. View the video of the meeting (if available), paying particular attention to the strongest and weakest aspects of the students' or clients' performance.
6. Provide further practice opportunities, if needed.

Caveats and Options

1. Describe as accurately as possible the specific features of meetings that your students or clients are likely to participate in. The description must include likely topics, meeting purposes, appropriate behavior, the physical environment, and the special and high-frequency

language that is commonly employed. Textbooks may not provide enough detail, so you may need to gather this information from knowledgeable informants in the target vocation or profession or from personal observations of actual meetings.

References and Further Reading

Comfort, J. (1995). *Effective presentations.* Oxford: Oxford University Press.

Reel, J. (1994). *Speech acts used in business meetings (and elsewhere).* (ERIC Document Reproduction Service No. ED 369 271)

Contributor

Thomas Orr is an associate professor at the University of Aizu's Center for Language Research, in Aizu-Wakamatsu City, Japan.

Wanted: Editors, Journalists, Reporters

Levels
Intermediate +

Aims
Brainstorm vocabulary and ideas
Develop writing skills in the workplace
Recognize a newsletter's impact on a corporation
Build awareness of EFL training
Create a team atmosphere

Class Time
Minimal

Preparation Time
A few minutes

Resources
Sample newsletters
Headlines from magazines or newspapers

This newsletter project at the workplace not only helps students communicate and develop reading and writing skills but also demonstrates the newsletter's impact on the corporation and builds awareness of EFL training. It creates a team atmosphere at work while giving students the benefit of exercising their independence in selecting their own themes and topics, focusing on content rather than form. As students practice the language in open-ended situations in an authentic context, they become authors and build each other's self-esteem and confidence, thus helping overcome their language handicaps.

Procedure

1. Tell the students that they will be publishing an in-house newsletter. Make sure they know what a newsletter is, and discuss what it takes to be a journalist or reporter.
2. Show the students the sample newsletters (see the Appendix).
3. Discuss and make suggestions for the newsletter's contents. Brainstorm a possible name (e.g., for a brewery, *What's Brewing?*).
4. Nominate editor(s). (For the first issue, select someone who already feels comfortable with the language.)
5. Encourage the editor(s) to assign specific writing tasks and to set a deadline for contributions.

Caveats and Options

1. For the first newsletter, be sure to give the students a lot of encouragement. Ask, remind, and help each participant as necessary. Once the process has begun, let the students work on their own.

2. Participants do not necessarily need to be in the same EFL/ESL class, but they should share a workplace or occupation.

3. Match the assigned tasks to the participants' proficiency and skills in order to avoid frustration; suggest tutoring for weaker students, or team them with stronger students.

4. Have less proficient students contribute by selecting materials, typing, or photocopying if they are not ready to write yet.

5. Make sure every issue has a different editor or editors.

6. Make sure relevant contact people, management, and the training department get copies of the newsletter when it is completed.

7. Some suggestions for content are a sports page, a social page (e.g., to announce birthdays, weddings), surveys, interviews, literature, games and puzzles, and comics. Of course, if the content of the newsletter is occupationally related (e.g., contains process instructions, charts, and graphs), it is more likely to impress company personnel.

8. Do not correct errors unless they interfere with effective communication, but include a brief comment on why you do not; it will discourage criticism and misunderstandings when nonparticipants read the newsletter.

**Appendix:
Sample
Newsletter
Excerpt[1]**

What´s Brewing ?

Brewer´s Newsletter # 2

JUNE Issue 1994

Copyright : Quilmes English Team.
Printed in Quilmes, Argentina. All rights reserved
No part of this publication may be reproduced, stored in a retrieval system or transmitted , in any form or any means , electronic, mechanical photocopying, recording, or otherwise , without the prior written permission of the publishers.

[1]Copyright © 1994 by the Quilmes English Team, Cervecerma y Malterma Quilmes, Quilmes, Argentina. Reprinted with permission.

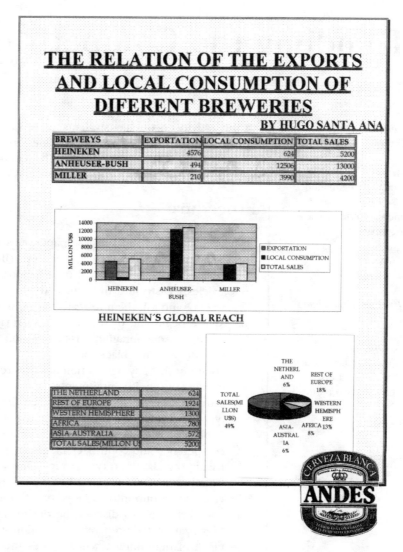

THE RELATION OF THE EXPORTS AND LOCAL CONSUMPTION OF DIFERENT BREWERIES

BY HUGO SANTA ANA

BREWERYS	EXPORTATION	LOCAL CONSUMPTION	TOTAL SALES
HEINEKEN	4576	624	5200
ANHEUSER-BUSH	494	12506	13000
MILLER	210	3990	4200

HEINEKEN'S GLOBAL REACH

THE NETHERLAND	624
REST OF EUROPE	1924
WESTERN HEMISPHERE	1300
AFRICA	780
ASIA-AUSTRALIA	572
TOTAL SALES(MILLON U$)	5200

Contributors

Liliana Orsi and Patricia Orsi have been teaching and administering EFL programs at the workplace in Argentina since 1984. They have been TESOL ESP Interest Section presenters.

Handling the Competition

Levels
Intermediate +

Aims
Practice negotiation
Use *be able to* to
increase effectiveness in
negotiations

Class Time
1 hour

Preparation Time
20 minutes

Resources
Business-related article
that details a dispute
between two parties
Chart of target
structures

This activity encourages students to use various forms of *be able to* as an alternative to *can* and *could*. Business professionals who incorporate this structure into their speech will enhance the authority with which they resist demands and make commitments and concessions in a negotiation.

Procedure

1. Select a magazine or newspaper article that outlines a business dispute between two organizations. (Business magazines and the business section of a local newspaper are reliable sources for such articles.) Distribute the article to the students the day before the activity, and ask them to read it as homework.
2. At the beginning of the next class, review the major issues of the dispute by encouraging class discussion. It may be helpful to outline the issues on the blackboard.
3. Point out that any negotiation involves resisting demands and making concessions and commitments.
4. Introduce the target structures (see the Appendix), and discuss the types and levels of commitment that these expressions represent. Explain that the use of these structures creates an impression of competence and control, elements vital to successful negotiation.
5. Divide the class into two groups. One will represent Organization A from the article, and the other will represent Organization B. Subdivide each group into teams of two to four students.
6. Ask each team to discuss the desires and demands of its assigned organization and prepare a negotiation strategy. Emphasize the importance of determining which issues the team holds to be nonnegotiable and which it may be willing to concede.
7. Match each A team with a B team.

8. Instruct the students to simulate a negotiation between the two organizations. Encourage them to use the target structures as they respond to the requests and demands of the opposing side.

9. Continue until each negotiation reaches a satisfactory compromise or an impasse. Follow up with a class discussion on how use of the target structures enabled the groups to influence the outcome of negotiations by creating an image of competence and authority in the speaker.

Caveats and Options

1. Encourage the students to justify their positions by using clauses beginning with *since*, *because*, *as*, *due to*, and *due to the fact that* with the target structures.

2. Encourage the students to make agreement and disagreement conditional by using *unless*- or *if*-clauses after the target structures.

3. Audio or video record one of the negotiations, and play it back for analysis during the follow-up discussion.

Appendix

Resisting Demands

I'm afraid	we won't be able to	+ *verb* (+ *optional noun*).
	we wouldn't be able to	
I don't think	we will be able to	
	we would be able to	

Making Commitments and Concessions

I think	we will be able to	+ *verb* (+ *optional noun*).
	we might be able to	
	we would be able to	
	we should be able to	

Contributor

Carolyn Reseland is the assistant director of the Executive English Program at Global Language Institute, St. Paul, Minnesota, in the United States.

The Client Always Comes First

Levels
Intermediate; adults

Aims
Analyze data and
express them as graphs
Write a draft for a
presentation
Discuss and support
viewpoints

Class Time
1½ hours

Preparation Time
20 minutes

Resources
Data on product sales in
note form

This activity provides ESP learners with opportunities to practice real-life professional situations and to develop learning and communication strategies. These include analyzing information and expressing it in another symbolic code, working cooperatively, preparing for a presentation, drawing conclusions, and justifying one's viewpoints.

Procedures

1. Set the context and the students' role by saying, "You work in the operational research department of an advertising agency. Your main function is to compile and analyze data related to products that the agency handles. You have recently collected data on the sales performance of a Vitamin C health drink in your country. Your task is to analyze these data."

2. Distribute copies of the collected data (see the Appendix), in the form of notes.

3. Tell the students to work in pairs to analyze the data, paying particular attention to seasonal influences on such sales. Ask them to transform this information into a graph to show to a new client of the agency.

4. Inform the students that they will meet with the new client on the following day. To prepare for the data presentation, recommend that they write a draft of what they will say. Elicit from them the points they should cover in their presentations, writing pertinent information on the blackboard as the students provide it (e.g., mention the source of data, call the client's attention to the graphs, explain the pattern of the curve, introduce the variables, and explain their influence on the product's sales performance). Write the vocabulary they may need on the blackboard. You may also wish to add some language structures that the students have recently practiced.

5. Have the students present their graphs and explain the information they display.
6. Tell the students that, after going through the presentation of the data, the client will probably ask them to suggest a course of action for effective advertising that will improve sales performance. Hold a group discussion for this task.

Caveats and Options

1. Setting the context clearly and providing a communicative purpose for the activity enables the students to carry it out more effectively.
2. The information in the notes also works as a form of language input. If you wish, have the whole group discuss it before the pairs proceed to the drawing of the graphs.
3. Drawing graphs—that is, translating written information into another type of representation—is often difficult for students. The reverse process is also difficult, especially if they have to explain the distinctive patterns of a graph. Working in pairs makes it easier for the students and fosters self-confidence.
4. If the students are unfamiliar with graphs, give them copies of various types of graphs used to show sales curves (available in most business English course books). You may even wish to take the opportunity to teach the students how to build graphs using a computer spreadsheet program such as Excel. This is often possible when teaching in a company or in the research center of an institution.
5. Writing a plan for the presentation on the blackboard helps the students develop their ideas more coherently and appropriately. The vocabulary and structure list (also on the blackboard) works as a source of ideas while allowing the students to put recently learned and practiced language to effective use.
6. During the group discussion (Step 6 above), encourage the students to use linking devices.
7. This activity is relevant to ESP students who work in market research, advertising, marketing, and sales. It may be adapted to other fields, such as production (analysis of output), finance (performance of various types of investments), and accounting (analysis of balance sheets, profit and loss statements).

8. This activity was prepared for adult EFL students; therefore, some of the learning strategies involved in this activity may not apply to younger learners.

References and Further Reading

Ellis, M., & O'Driscoll, N. (1989). *Giving presentations*. London: Longman.

Hughes, G., Pilbeam A., & West, C. (1989). *Business talk*. London: Longman.

Microsoft Excel 97 [Computer program]. (1997). Redmond, WA: Microsoft.

O'Driscoll, N., & Pilbeam, A. (1989). *Meetings and discussions*. London: Longman.

Sandler, P. L., & Stott, C. L. (1988). *Manage with English*. Oxford: Oxford University Press.

Appendix: Sample Sales Data

Sales Performance of a Vitamin C Drink

Source = retail audit sales data

Distinctive pattern = peak in the summer months

Shape of the curve: ⇨ upward trend as of midspring
⇨ downward trend as of early autumn

Two variables: ⇨ variation in amount of advertising (low advertising during autumn/winter)
⇨ price barrier (due to low sales, price increases in autumn/winter)

Contributor

Maria Alice Capocchi Ribeiro has been an EFL teacher for 19 years and is a materials writer at Centro de Linguistica Aplicada, Yázigi International, in São Paulo, Brazil.

Charm Your Way to Success

Levels
High intermediate

Aims
Build confidence in
starting conversations
with native speakers
Practice communication
strategies

Class Time
Several periods over
consecutive days

Preparation Time
20 minutes

Resources
Worksheets
Videos (optional)

Small talk is a component of the language of business that is often overlooked in business English courses. This four-stage activity (based on Dick, 1986) helps students of business English assess instances in which social conversation is appropriate and develop their social and conversational skills. After all four stages have been completed, they are integrated into a conversation.

Procedure

All Stages

1. Provide a brief explanation, modeling with feedback, controlled practice, and free practice.
2. Have the students practice in the following sequence:
   - Student A makes an opening statement or asks an open question on an appropriate topic (nonthreatening, culturally and environmentally appropriate, easy to talk about).
   - Student B gives an appropriate answer plus some free information in words, body language, or tone.
   - Student A listens for the free information and, using the free information, gives a two-part response consisting of an appropriate personal disclosure plus an appropriate open question.
   - Students A and B alternate roles using the formula above.
3. Do not go on to the next stage before the students have mastered the previous one. As the students practice, check their progress and give advice and feedback.
4. For each stage, provide useful phrases that are suitable for the level and needs of the students.
5. Discuss cross-cultural issues in social business conversations.

Stage 1: Opening a Conversation (see Appendix A)

1. Get the class to brainstorm ideas on where they might talk to a stranger (e.g., a business-related party vs. a restaurant or cinema).
2. Get the class to brainstorm some simple topics with which to start a conversation. (Suitable topics are universally easy to talk about, are appropriate to the situation, and do not make the other person feel uncomfortable.) Discuss appropriate lexical phrases if necessary.
3. Discuss *open questions* (questions that invite further information) versus *closed questions* (questions that can be answered with *yes* or *no*). Review the language of questions if necessary.
4. Group the students in pairs. Have them practice asking each other open questions. Encourage the students to gradually increase the pace of the questioning.
5. Form the class into groups, and ask them to think of topics and related topics (e.g., topic: immediate physical surroundings; related topics: crowds, buildings, weather, pollution).
6. Have the students return to their partner in Step 4, and ask each pair to prepare a simple statement and an open question for each topic (e.g., "I've never seen such a large crowd"; "How many people do you think are here?"). Ask them which is better to use with a stranger—the statement or the question.
7. Give the pairs some simple situations, and have them prepare conversation openers. Comment on these as necessary.

Stage 2: Identifying Free Information (see Appendix B)

1. Explain *free information* as information not directly asked for that is expressed in words, tone, or body language. For example (free information is in italics),

   Partner A: I've never seen such a large crowd.

   Partner B: Me neither, not since *I came here from Bangkok*.

2. Have the students form pairs and take turns for the following steps. Emphasize that the students should go as slowly as necessary.
   - The partners decide on a situation.
   - Partner A makes an opening statement (either a statement or a question) as in Stage 1 above.
   - Both partners stop and check: Is the opening appropriate? If a question, is it open?
   - Partner B responds with an appropriate reply plus some free information.
   - The partners stop and discuss: Was the opening statement (open question or appropriate statement) OK? What was the free information?
3. Have the students continue changing roles till they have mastered this process and can do it reasonably quickly.

Stage 3: Using Free Information to Make a Reply (see Appendix C)

1. Explain how to use the free information to make a two-part reply: (a) an appropriate self-disclosure on the topic of the free information and (b) an open-ended question on the topic of the free information (e.g., "I've never been to Bangkok. What's it like there?").
2. Explain that the appropriate level of personal disclosure depends on the relationship of the two people and the cultural and social situation.
3. Have the students practice as in Stage 1, Step 2, but add one reply, as follows:
   - The partners decide on a situation.
   - Partner A makes an opening statement as in Stage 1 above.
   - Partner B responds with an appropriate reply plus free information.
   - (new step) Partner A gives a two-part reply (disclosure plus free information) as above.
   - The partners stop the conversation. They determine (a) if the opening statement, open question, and reply were appropriate and, for the two-part reply, (b) what the free information was and whether the question was open.

4. Check the understanding of each pair. Continue till the students have mastered the conversational technique and can do it reasonably quickly.

Stage 4: Starting and Continuing a Conversation Naturally and Effortlessly (see Appendix D)

1. Review the process introduced and practiced in Stages 1–3.
2. Ask the students to conduct a conversation in this way for a few minutes. After the opening statement and response, each student, in turn,
   - listens for (or observes) free information
   - gives a two-part response on the topic of the free information, consisting of an appropriate self-disclosure and an appropriate open-ended question
3. Have the students continue, slowly at first but faster (more naturally) as they practice.
4. Explain that in real life the principles work well and that the students do not have to follow the guidelines rigidly.

Caveats and Options

1. Vary the activity with demonstration skits and invited observers.
2. Have the students form groups of three instead of pairs. Ask the groups to observe each other and make comments on the language or the procedure, or appoint a formal observer in each group, who analyzes the process, stopping after each step if necessary.
3. Extend the steps in the stages with language activities as necessary.
4. If you wish, have the students record each step, play the tape back, and analyze whether they have been successful. Make sure that the conversation openers and situations are realistic for the target culture.
5. Explain how open questions can be "more open" or "more closed."
6. Find a videotaped interview. Watch for closed and open questions and free information in words and body language, and check examples of language that are actually used. Show sample portions of the video to the class. Discuss and analyze the conversations.

7. Find a video of a social conversation, and analyze the steps, noting which elements are present and which are absent. Alternatively, do a role play with another teacher, or have the students do role plays.
8. Ask the students to start a conversation with a native speaker they do not know outside class and report to the class on what happened. (Make sure the students do this in a safe, appropriate situation. Warn them that not all strangers may be willing to participate in such a conversation.)

References and Further Reading

Dick, B. (1986). *Learning to communicate*. Brisbane, Australia: University of Queensland, Department of Psychology.

Appendix A: Opening a Conversation

1. Form pairs.
2. Consider where you might talk to a stranger in English: A business party is OK. A plane is OK. How about a restaurant or cinema?
3. Discuss how you can start a conversation with a stranger at a business party.
   - Suitable topics are those which are universally easy to talk about, are common to both of you, are appropriate to the situation, and do not make the other person feel uncomfortable. A possible topic would be the crowd at the party or an unusual room.
   - Voicing a strong opinion to a stranger is not the best strategy with which to start a conversation.
4. What is an open question?
   - An open question is one that invites further information and cannot be answered with *yes* or *no*.
5. What words do you use to form open questions?
6. Why is it better to use an open question than a closed one to start a conversation?

7. How can you start a conversation?
   - You can make a statement or ask an open question. A statement may be safer. For example,
       "I've never seen such a large crowd at a party."
       (simple statement)
       "How many people do you think there are at this party?"
       (open question)
8. Practice some simple conversation starters.
   - Choose a location first. Think of some examples. Do not continue the conversation.
   - Then choose another location, and think of some examples.
9. When you have finished this exercise, check with your teacher.

Appendix B: Identifying Free Information

1. Form pairs (Partner A and Partner B).
2. What is free information?
   - It is any information the other person gives you that you didn't ask for. It is *free*.
3. How can you give free information?
   - You can give free information in words, in your tone of voice, or in your body language. For example,

       Partner A: I've never seen such a large crowd. (conversation starter)

       Partner B: Me neither, not since *I was at a similar party last year.* (free information)
4. Practice giving a simple conversation starter and reply. Identify the free information.
   - Decide on a typical situation together. Discuss the details of this situation.
   - Partner A: Make an opening statement or ask an open question to start the conversation.
   - Partner B: Make a suitable reply and give some free information.

- Listen and watch for the free information.
- Discuss the opening statement and the free information. Are they OK?
- Now change roles.

5. When you have done Step 4 two or three times, check with your teacher.

Appendix C: Using Free Information to Make a Reply

1. Stay with your partner. Consider the following:
   - Why would you want to listen for free information? [possible answer: Free information can be used to make a reply.]
   - A good reply has two parts:
     ▶ some information about yourself using the topic of the free information (not too deep)
     ▶ an open-ended question on the topic of the free information
   - Why do you give some personal information? [possible answer: because it is a conversation and not an interview. A conversation needs a balance of information from both people.] For example,

     Opening: "What a large crowd!"
     Reply 1: "It's not as crowded as it was last year." (free information = *was there last year*)
     Reply 2: "I've never been to one of these functions before. How do you like them?" (personal information + open question)

2. Continue working in pairs. Give an opening statement, then use the free information, but add one reply as follows:
   - Decide on a situation together.
   - Make an opening statement or ask an open question to start the conversation
   - Make a suitable reply and add some free information.

- Listen and watch for the free information. Then give a two-part reply (information about yourself using the free information plus an open question on the topic).
- Stop here. Together, discuss the opening statement, open question, or appropriate statement. What was the free information? Did Partner A use the free information to give a two-part reply? Was Partner A's question open ended?
- Now change roles and decide on a different situation.

3. After you have finished, check with your teacher. Then go on to the next exercise.

Appendix D: Extending the Conversation

In pairs, start and continue a conversation for a few minutes.

1. Decide on a situation together.
2. Make an opening statement, or ask an open question on an appropriate topic (nonthreatening, culturally and environmentally appropriate, easy to talk about).
3. Give an appropriate answer plus some free information in words, body language, or tone.
4. Listen and watch for the free information. Then give a two-part reply (information about yourself using the free information plus an open question on the topic).
5. Now continue the conversation in the same way. Both of you should
   - listen and watch for the *free* information
   - give a two-part reply (information about yourself using the free information plus an open question on the topic)
     Tip: If you get stuck, stop and analyze what went wrong. Did you use the free information? Did you use an open question? Check with your teacher.
6. Analyze the reasons some conversations worked better than others.
7. (optional) Try the conversation strategy you have been practicing with a stranger at a party, a taxi driver, or someone sitting next to

you on a plane. Be sure to choose someone who appears to want to talk. Do not choose someone who is busy or in a dangerous place. Realize, however, that if the person does not want to talk, it is not your fault. Try someone else.

Contributor

Tim Roskams has taught general English, English for academic purposes, and ESP for several years in a tertiary context in Australia. He currently teaches business English, English improvement strategies, and academic writing at the Chinese University of Hong Kong.

Putting Workplace Product Catalogues to Work

Levels
Any

Aims
Practice spoken and
written communication
skills
Learn about trade and
professional products

Class Time
10-15 minutes/task

Preparation Time
Minimal

Resources
Workplace product
catalogues

Using workplace product catalogues as a resource allows the teacher to plan a range of possible activities that support aims within the curriculum. Some common features of these catalogues, which can be used to practice English and learn more about safety, are (a) color photos of products, (b) organization of products by type of protection (e.g., clothing, respirators, gloves, hard hats, hearing protection), (c) safety standards statements, (d) technical tables (e.g., measurement conversions, chemical resistance ratings), (e) safety warning signs, (f) short product descriptions, (g) short introductions for each category of product, (h) a table of contents, (i) important user information and warnings, (j) environmental protection statements and facts, (k) an alphabetized list of products, (l) pricing information, and (m) ordering procedures.

Procedure

1. Collect a variety of workplace product catalogues. Keep them on hand in the classroom or resource center to adapt for a variety of teaching purposes.
2. Allow the students (or content instructors) to choose the product catalogues that relate to their fields of interest.
3. Do any of the following activities. Some focus primarily on language; others, on organizing ideas with language as a supporting skill.
   - Have the students perform word searches in stretches of text.
   - Ask the students to collect similar types of products in a single category (a modification of card or board games).
   - Have the students match a text to a photo or drawing.
   - Set up a competition for the students to find technical information in a table.

- Have the students select and argue for choosing a particular product over others, given local conditions.
- Create a classification grid for similar but slightly different products; then have the students identify and fill in specific features.
- Have the students expand telegraphic descriptions in the catalogue to full sentences.
- Create role-play scenarios involving a salesperson and customer discussing a specific product (perhaps at a conference exhibit), and have the students enact these scenarios.
- Assign the students the task of explaining the role of a product in their trade or profession.
- Have the students develop criteria for evaluating particular products.

Caveats and Options

1. Catalogues can be found at local organizations, businesses (e.g., auto or bicycle repair shops, dentists, doctors, hospitals, food services, transportation, laundries, dry cleaners, hairdressers, barbers, photographic processing shops, public security and workplace safety organizations, hotels, gas stations), or industrial sites. If you are a regular customer or client, they are usually happy to give you old catalogues and may even begin saving them for you. In non-English-speaking countries, check with organizations serving international populations and involved in joint ventures, or approach a product company yourself.

2. Catalogues, though valuable sources of scientific or technical content, are sales documents designed with the interests of the company in mind. They are not designed to teach content. However, safety products catalogues often have extensive supporting tables and appendixes and a full range of products that can be used by students in scientific and technical fields as classroom references.

3. Some tasks do not require all the students to have the same edition of a catalogue. The same task can apply to a variety of products or other specialized content.

4. Some catalogues, such as safety product catalogues, can be used in various workplaces.

5. Use the catalogues whole if you have enough for two or three students to share one, or cut up the catalogues for specific tasks. The required preparation will vary depending on the task, the number of catalogues available, and whether you or the students do the preparation. For example, the students can identify products they wish to talk about, then cut out the product descriptions and the pictures separately for use in a matching activity. Be sure you can rematch (or keep a record of) cut-up sections.

References and Further Reading

van Naerssen, M., & Brennan, M. (1995). *SciTech: Communicating in English about science and technology*. Boston: Heinle & Heinle.

Contributor

Margaret van Naerssen, of the University of Pennsylvania in the United States, is a specialist in communication for specific purposes, materials development, and second language acquisition and is currently interested in nonnative English speakers in the workplace.

**Part V: English for
Legal Purposes**

Editors' Note

The activities in Part V involve English for legal purposes (ELP). One of the narrower categories of ESP, ELP focuses on English taught within a law school, law office, or other legal setting. Its primary concerns are written cases and judgments, lawyer-client consultation, legislation, contracts, and agreements.

Trial by Jury

Level
Advanced

Aims
Learn about the legal
system in the U.S. and
other Western countries
Learn debate and
decision-making skills

Class Time
Two class periods

Preparation Time
30 minutes

Resources
Note cards
Vocabulary list

After the appearance of some well-publicized U.S. trials on television around the world (e.g., O. J. Simpson's, Susan Smith's), many students have raised questions about the particular process of a trial. This activity fosters a greater understanding of the U.S. legal system by placing the students in the roles of the parties involved, presenting them with the necessary vocabulary, setting the stage with three possible scenarios, and allowing the students themselves to present and try the case.

Procedure

1. Prepare a list of vocabulary covering all areas of a trial and the members involved (see Appendix A).
2. On each note card, write the name of a character in the trial and his or her purpose. With the exception of the juror cards, all the cards will contain certain facts regarding the case (see Appendix B).
3. In the first class, ask the students if they remember seeing the O. J. Simpson case, other trials on television, or TV shows such as *LA Law*. Elicit some of the terms on the vocabulary list through such questions as "What do we call the place where the trial is held?" and "What do we call the people who saw something and who come to tell what they saw?"
4. Hand out the vocabulary list, and discuss each term. Follow this discussion with a brief explanation of how a trial proceeds (e.g., first the prosecution presents its case, then the defense).
5. Explain that the class is going to take part in a trial in the next class and that each person will have a role to play and a certain amount of information to work with. Mention that each person will receive a card and should prepare a statement or argument at home. Tell the students that the members of the jury will know the crime for

which the person is accused; their task is to keep an open mind and listen to the case carefully.

6. Distribute one card to each person in the class. For greater success, give the judge and attorney cards to more assertive students.

7. Have the students read their cards silently, and ask for any final questions before they leave the class.

8. In the following class, begin by asking if there are any additional questions.

9. Turn around three desks at the front of the class so that they are facing the class. Have the accused, the prosecution's lawyer, and the defense lawyer move to these positions. Ask the witnesses to come to the front row of the class. Ask the jury to move to the back. (The judge should still be sitting down.)

10. Announce that the trial will now begin. Ask everyone to rise, and ask the judge to come forward and sit at the podium or in a chair at the head of the class. Act as the bailiff/moderator, telling the students to rise and sit and keeping the trial moving.

11. Ask the accused to stand, and read out the allegations. Have the judge announce that the trial will begin with the prosecution's argument.

12. Following the argument of the prosecution, allow the defense attorney to make his or her statement.

13. Ask the witnesses to give their statements.

14. Give the members of the jury about 5 minutes to discuss what they have heard and come to a verdict. While this is taking place, call for questions from the students who are not on the jury.

15. When the jury has come to a verdict, have the judge ask the foreman of the jury to state it.

16. Have the judge announce the sentence.

17. Use any remaining time to discuss the findings and to answer any remaining questions about what took place during the activity.

Caveats and Options

1. This activity works best with a class of up to 20 students. A class of 20 would have 12 jurors, 1 judge, 1 accused, 2 lawyers, and 4 witnesses. Break a larger class into halves, give each a scenario, and hold two separate trials. This, of course, would double the

amount of time required but would reinforce the vocabulary and skills being presented.

2. In a very confident, advanced class, pass along the role of moderator to the judge. Intervene only if the trial runs into a snag or if you are running short of time.

3. In some EFL contexts this activity could be seen as too democratic, and some crimes may seem inappropriate for class. Use discretion in selecting topics.

Appendix A: Vocabulary List

the accused	the defense	judge
acquittal	evidence	jury
attorney	foreman	the prosecution
case	guilty	sentence
client	indictment	trial
conviction	innocent	verdict
court	"innocent until	witness
crime	proven guilty"	

Appendix B: Possible Trial Scenarios

Scenario 1: "Les Misérables"

The accused has been arrested for stealing a loaf of bread.

● The prosecution might argue that stealing is a crime and must be punished.

● The defense might argue that the accused only stole to feed his or her family.

Scenario 2: The Litterbug

The accused has been arrested for throwing a soft-drink can on the ground.

● The prosecution might argue that littering is irresponsible and makes the area less beautiful.

● The defense might argue that the accused was simply throwing the can into the trash but missed.

Scenario 3: Is It Art?

The accused has been arrested for drawing graffiti on a wall of the school.

- The prosecution might argue that the accused has caused a lot of damage to the school.
- The defense might argue that graffiti is art and that this act was actually a tribute to the school.

Sample Cards for Scenario 1

Witness 1: The Baker	Member of the Jury
You saw the accused enter your bakery and take a loaf of bread without paying. He then ran out of the bakery. You screamed at him, but he didn't stop, so you called the police.	The accused has been brought to trial for stealing a loaf of bread. Listen to the facts carefully and with an open mind. Take notes on the evidence presented. Then you and your fellow jury members must decide if the accused is innocent or guilty.

Contributor

Shawn M. Clankie is currently in the graduate linguistics program at the University of Cambridge, in the United Kingdom.

Empathetic Communication

Levels
Intermediate +

Aims
Learn client
interviewing skills
Maximize client's
willingness to answer
Understand the use of
empathy in a
communicative situation

Class Time
30–40 minutes

Preparation Time
15 minutes

Resources
Role-play information
cards

This activity uses role playing to demonstrate the need for empathy in the legal profession. Students role-play lawyer and client in cases in which the client has a particularly sensitive issue to discuss. Various degrees of empathy are demonstrated, and the role plays are critiqued with respect to the lawyer's effectiveness in dealing empathetically with the client.

Procedure

1. Prepare role-play information cards for the students who will take the role of the client. Include a problem that the client is faced with, preferably one that is embarrassing or difficult to discuss (e.g., being arrested for drunk driving, finding a spouse with a secret lover, being fired for stealing office supplies). Alternatively, have imaginative students invent the client's problem.

2. In class, describe the importance of empathy in establishing rapport with a client. Discuss how many professionals, including lawyers, doctors, counselors, and ministers, must obtain (often sensitive) information from their clients in order to do their jobs. Emphasize that creating an atmosphere of trust and confidence is thus extremely important.

3. As an example, take the role of the lawyer first. Ask for a volunteer to describe a recent encounter with authority (e.g., receiving a parking ticket, talking to an unhappy landlord). Face the class and interview the volunteer student. Demonstrate (with humor) extreme examples of both poor and excessive empathy and the effect of both.

4. Distribute the role-play information cards to the students who will take the role of the client, and discuss the role play with the class. Ask

the students about facial expressions and body language as well as the language used by the lawyer to establish rapport.

5. Write on the blackboard or distribute a handout with the kinds of expressions used to show empathy (e.g., *I understand, I see, I'm sorry about that*).

6. Repeat the introductory demonstration, this time playing the client while a student plays the lawyer. Ask the class to critique the performance.

7. Repeat the introductory demonstration, this time with two students playing the lawyer and client. Ask the class to critique the performance.

8. Have the students do the role play in pairs, with one student as the lawyer and the other as the client.

9. Conclude with a class discussion about the students' feelings during their interview.

Caveats and Options

1. Learning how to establish rapport with clients is a part of the curriculum at an increasing number of U.S. law schools. The role play described above is often used in law school classes with native speakers and is ideal in an ESP context, too, because it teaches a professional skill while increasing awareness of the communicative process in general.

2. Adapt the lawyer-client exercise to other contexts (e.g., doctors and patients).

References and Further Reading

Redmount, R. S., & Shaffer, T. L. (1980). *Legal interviewing and counseling*. New York: Matthew Bender.

Shaffer, T. L., & Elkins, J. R. (1987). *Legal interviewing and counseling in a nutshell* (3rd ed.). St. Paul, MN: West.

Contributor

Brady Coleman, who has a doctorate in law from Columbia University, is currently completing an MA in applied linguistics at the University of Leicester, in the United Kingdom, and teaches legal English at the College of Law, Seoul National University, in Korea.

Read, Sift, Summarize, and Use

Level
Intermediate +

Aims
Understand and
summarize facts,
decisions, and reasons
Read cases in law texts
Use cases in written
discourse

Class Time
1 hour

Preparation Time
45 minutes–1 hour

Resources
Legal case text
Handouts

This activity teaches strategies that enable students to read cases more effectively, isolate the relevant facts in regard to a legal principle, and use them in written legal discourse. The sequence of exercises develops reading, comprehension, summarizing, note-taking, and writing strategies suitable for legal discourse. It also assists the students in separating important from less important facts. Because the case selected is coordinated with the students' study in mainstream classes, the activity clarifies students' understanding of the legal principle embedded in the case and develops their understanding of legal discourse.

Procedure

Stage 1

1. Locate a case relevant to the students' current study in their mainstream class, and prepare it as follows (see Appendix A for an example):
   - Photocopy or type the case with the paragraph immediately preceding it. Paste it onto another sheet of paper.
   - On the left side of the case, number the lines at intervals of five.
   - Below the case, write an exercise requesting the line numbers for the following information:
     ▶ the legal principle
     ▶ the facts of the case
     ▶ the court's decision
     ▶ the reasons for the decision
2. Explain to the students the types of information contained in a case.
3. Hand out the prepared case, and ask the students to fill in the missing line numbers.

Stage 2

1. Create an exercise that sequences in note form the events in the case, the decision, and the reasons (see Appendix B). Omit some information from the notes.
2. In class, have the students read the facts of the case and fill in the omitted details.
3. Ask the students to write a summary of the facts, the decision, and the reasons.

Stage 3

1. Create an exercise with a variety of discourse markers or sentence beginners for each "move" in the section of legal discourse that states the law—that is, the section in which a case is integrated with the legal principle before it is applied to a particular set of facts (see Appendix C).
2. Instruct the students to select a sentence beginning for each move and integrate it with the summary of the facts, decision, and reasons they completed in the previous exercise.

Caveats and Options

1. Use the three stages of the activity either individually or as a sequence (whether in the same lesson or in consecutive lessons), depending on the competence of the class.
2. This activity is especially suitable for an adjunct class (e.g., Legal Language for Commercial Law, a class that focuses on academic strategies for the study of law and language use in legal discourse while utilizing the law content of the mainstream subject).
3. Use the three stages (either as a sequence or as individual activities) for an ESP program focusing on English for law.
4. Use the activity to help the students compile summaries in preparation for open-book examinations. Include the case summaries with the appropriate legal principle.

References and Further Reading

Crosling, G. M., & Murphy, H. M. (1996). *How to study business law: Reading, writing and exams* (2nd ed.). Sydney, Australia: Butterworth's.

Appendix A: Understanding Information in a Case

Cases summarized in legal texts usually consist of the following information:

- the name of the case
- the facts
- the court's decision
- the reason(s) for the decision

Read the following case and indicate the lines where the above information occurs.

Social or domestic arrangements[1]

[402] As was noted earlier [401], it is presumed that the parties to agreements involving social or domestic matters do not intend any *legal* obligations to arise therefrom. This presumption is clearly based on common sense, for it is hard to imagine that the parties could intend otherwise. This presumption was applied in the following case.

5

Balfour v Balfour [1919] 2 KB 571, Balfour, a civil servant in Sri Lanka (then known as Ceylon), and his wife were holidaying in England. When the holiday was over the husband returned to Sri Lanka without his wife who, for health reasons, remained in England. Prior to his departure, the husband promised to pay his wife £30 per month until such time as she joined him in Sri Lanka. The reunion did not eventuate as the parties agreed to live apart. In the meantime, the husband failed to keep up the payments and the wife sued for breach of his promise. She was unsuccessful. The court held that although the parties had not expressly indicated their intention in regard to the legal enforceability of the agreement, the presumption was clearly against enforceability. Their agreement involved matters of a social or domestic nature and there were no facts to rebut the presumption which applies in such cases.

10

15

20

---

[1]From *Understanding Contract Law* (pp. 77-78), D. Khoury and Y. Yamouni, 1990, Sydney, Australia: Butterworth's. Adapted with permission.

During the course of his judgement, Atkin LJ stated: 'It is necessary to remember that there are agreements between parties which do not result in contracts within the meaning of that term in
25 our law. The ordinary example is where two parties agree to take a walk together, or where there is an offer and an acceptance of hospitality. Nobody would suggest in ordinary circumstances that those agreements result in what we know as a contract, and one of the most unusual forms of agreement which does not constitute a
30 contract appears to me to be the arrangements which are made between husband and wife. It is quite common, and it is the natural and inevitable result of the relationship of husband and wife, that the two spouses should make arrangements between themselves— agreements such as are in dispute in this action—agreements for
35 allowances, by which the husband agrees that he will pay to his wife a certain sum of money, per week, or per month, or per year, to cover either her own expenses or the necessary expenses of the household and of the children of the marriage, and in which the wife promises either expressly or impliedly to apply the allowance
40 for the purpose for which it is given. To my mind those agree- ments, or many of them, do not result in contracts at all . . . . They are not contracts, and they are not contracts because the parties did not intend that they should be attended by legal consequences . . . They are not sued upon, not because the parties are reluctant to
45 enforce their legal rights when the agreement is broken, but because the parties, in the inception of the arrangement, never intended that they should be sued upon. Agreements such as these are outside the realm of contracts altogether' (as 578-9).

the legal principle: line _____ to line _____

the facts: line _____ to line _____

the decision: line _____ to line _____

the reason(s):   line _____ to line _____

Appendix B: Understanding the Facts of a Case, the Decision, and the Reasons

1. Using the case you have already studied, complete the following notes on the facts of the case (Lines X-XX).

   Balfour (husband) v Balfour (wife)
   - Mr. and Mrs. B, holidaying in England.
   - Mr. B returned home, Mrs. B stayed.
   - Before leaving, Mr. B promised_____ until reunited.
   - Mr. B and Mrs. B stayed apart.
   - Mr. B_____
   - Mrs. B sued for breach of promise.

2. Complete the following notes for the court's decision (Lines XX-XX).
   - Mrs. B was_____ because_____

3. Complete the following notes on the reasons for the court's decision (Lines XX-XX).
   - Some agreements do not result in contracts.
     Example: hospitality
                  fl
           no contract
   - A usual form or agreement not constituting contract:

     _____
                fl
     make arrangements between themselves
     e.g., _____
                fl
     not contracts because _____
     _____

4. Summarize.
   - The facts of the case:

   - The decision:

   - Reasons for the decision:

Appendix C: Using a Case in Legal Writing

Usually, a legal argument for a problem question includes an identification of the issue, a summary of the appropriate law, and the application of the law to the facts of the problem question. In Common Law, the law is the legal principle and a case.

Using the summaries you wrote previously, complete the following segment of a legal argument. Because there is no one way of framing sentences, several alternatives are provided below. However, these are examples only, not absolute ways of introducing the information in your writing.

Legal Principle

The presumption with social and domestic matters is that ...

Facts

This can be seen in Balfour v Balfour, where . . .
or The case of B v B demonstrated *or* exemplified that . . .
or In the case of B v B, . . .

Decision and Reasons

The court decided that . . .
or It was held that . . .
or Atkin LJ stated that . . .

Contributor

Glenda Crosling is a lecturer in language and academic strategies in Language and Learning Services at Monash University, in Victoria, Australia.

Part VI: English for Science and Technology

Editors' Note

The activities in Part VI involve English for science and technology (EST). EST focuses on English taught within an academic science or engineering department, a laboratory, a scientific or technological company, or any other scientific or technical setting. Its primary concerns are the reading and writing of technical reports (particularly research reports, proposals, feasibility studies, and lab reports), technical oral communication, and the understanding and use of subtechnical and, to a lesser extent, technical vocabulary. It is the oldest form of and was once synonymous with ESP.

Developing Your Engineering Ears

Levels
High intermediate +

Aims
Segment engineering
lectures into
information phases
Identify information
types within phases

Class Time
1 hour (ongoing)

Preparation Time
30+ minutes

Resources
Videotaped university
engineering class
Video cassette recorder
and player
Overhead projector,
transparencies, and pen
Handout

This activity requires engineering students to listen to a lecture and decide which phase of the lecture contains certain information. They must also determine the type of information contained in each phase. The activity aids students in chunking information into predictable categories.

Procedure

1. Present a brief description of the segments of an engineering lecture (topic, problem, solution).
2. Play a video clip (preferably starting just before the start of a topic) of 8–12 minutes, depending on the students' level and the difficulty of the clip.
3. Distribute a handout (see the Appendix) indicating the typical components of an engineering lecture. Ask the students to mark whether the section type or information in the lecture is present on the handout. If another information type is present, ask the students to note it.
4. Have the students compare their answers. Then elicit the answers from the class and mark them on an overhead transparency of the handout.
5. Play the video clip again, and ask the students to check their markings and take content notes. Ask them to note any difficulties they had in ascertaining whether information was present or not.
6. As a class, discuss the correct answers, the content, the variance of the real lecture from the handout's categories, and any problems the students had.
7. Play the clip a third time, and have the students continue taking content notes.

Caveats and Options

1. Be sure to introduce subject-specific (e.g., *modiolus elasticity, moment of inertia*), local geographical, cultural, or other vocabulary (e.g., *two-by-fours, beam*) either in a class activity or in a reading assignment as a prelistening activity. This is necessary even for graduate students because they may already know the subject-specific concept but not the English word for it.
2. The introduction to this activity may entail only identifying whether or not the phases are present. In subsequent uses, expand the depth of analysis of information types to include the type of emphasis, the language used, and so on.
3. As the students become more proficient, have them take notes instead of marking a handout.
4. Use a transcript of a lecture, if available.

References and Further Reading

Bame, J. (1994, March). *Content listening: Integrating bottom-up with top-down processing.* Paper presented at the 28th Annual TESOL Convention, Baltimore, MD.

Hutchinson, T., & Waters, A. (1980). Communication in the technical classroom. In *ELT documents special: Projects in materials design* (pp. 7–36). London: British Council.

Olsen, L., & Huckin, T. (1990). Point-driven understanding in engineering lecture comprehension. *English for Specific Purposes, 9,* 33–47.

Appendix

This list of information segments, information types, and other occurrences was gleaned from six lecture transcripts and is not meant to be exhaustive.

Directions: In the column on the left, put a check mark (✓) if the information indicated is given in the video clip. If it is not, do not mark it. If another type of information is there, note it.

Topic
Backgrounding
    Previous lecture reference
    Real-world reference

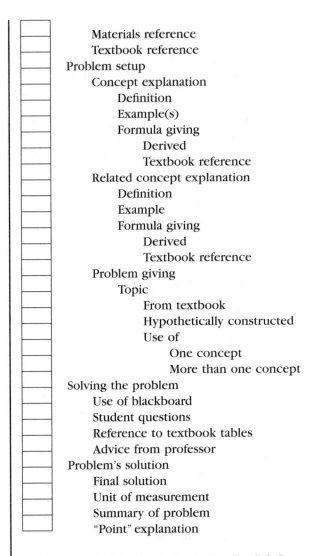

```
Materials reference
Textbook reference
Problem setup
    Concept explanation
        Definition
        Example(s)
        Formula giving
            Derived
            Textbook reference
    Related concept explanation
        Definition
        Example
        Formula giving
            Derived
            Textbook reference
    Problem giving
        Topic
            From textbook
            Hypothetically constructed
            Use of
                One concept
                More than one concept
Solving the problem
    Use of blackboard
    Student questions
    Reference to textbook tables
    Advice from professor
Problem's solution
    Final solution
    Unit of measurement
    Summary of problem
    "Point" explanation
```

Contributor

Jim Bame teaches in the Intensive English Language Institute at Utah State University, Logan, Utah, in the United States.

A Word in Your EIA

Levels
Advanced

Aims
Expand and
contextualize lexis

Class Time
One 90-minute session
or two 45-minute
sessions

Preparation Time
1 hour

Resources
Video sequence
Videotape player
Lexis cards
Simulation scenario

When specialized lexis is tied to local context not necessarily within the learners' experience, visual clues may facilitate recognition. Specialized lexis contrasts and overlaps with everyday language. Environmental impact assessment (EIA) specialists, like other professionals, need to negotiate with laypeople. This task helps students of EIA assimilate new lexis and simulates a EIA public meeting, where they can explore the distinctions between specialized and nonspecialized use of lexis and the role of bias in language.

Procedure

Video Setup

1. Locate a suitable video sequence (an appropriate video for an EIA group might be a sequence of varied landscape scenes).
2. Prepare two types of lexis cards based on the video (see Appendix A), including a balance of new and known vocabulary and noting the order in which the terms appear in the video. One type should reflect specialized terms, and the other type should reflect emotional responses to the video sequences in everyday language. Make enough sets of cards for your class when divided into pairs or groups of three to four students. Scramble the cards within each set.
3. In class, divide the class into pairs or small groups. Give half of the groups a scrambled set of the specialized lexis cards, and the other half, a scrambled set of the "everyday" lexis cards.
4. Ask the students to confer within their groups on the meaning of the terms on the cards in order to pool their knowledge.
5. Show the video sequence once without stopping (without sound, if you wish, especially if that is likely to distract). Have the students

reorder the scrambled cards while watching to reflect the chronological sequence in which the items appear.

6. Ask the students to agree on a sequence of cards within their group. Then have the groups compare their sequences with those of other groups with the same type of lexis cards. Allow brief discussion on discrepancies. (If needed, give a recommended or "model" order.) Discourage discussion of these items between groups with different types of cards.

7. Show the video again to confirm the sequence, stopping where uncertainties have emerged.

8. Encourage the students to identify likely users and contexts for the terms on their cards and any instances of bias.

9. Ask the students to suggest synonyms and alternative items of their own.

Simulation

1. Present the students with the scenario for the simulation (see Appendix B), and give out the role cards, making sure that members of the specialized lexis groups receive Role Cards 4, 5, 6, and so on.

2. Ask the students individually to briefly (a) brainstorm likely environmental impacts based on the scenario, using their local knowledge of the area involved (from the video) and (b) assess their character's personal response to the proposal.

3. Allow a short time for students with the same role card to confer on their approaches.

4. Integrate the "specialists" and "nonspecialists" into groups of a suitable size, and ask them to perform the simulation.

5. Observe and monitor the groups' simulations (videotape them if possible). Note especially the participants' negotiation of meaning in the target lexis and appropriateness of use.

6. In subsequent group discussion, offer observations and show the relevant video footage. Focus on appropriateness of usage and identification of bias.

Caveats and Options

1. To aid in classroom management, use different-colored index cards for the two sets of lexis cards and the simulation role cards.
2. Adapt the activity for various contexts (e.g., the impact of possible urban developments on architecture and communities).

References and Further Reading

Neat, T. (1984). *Hallaig: The poetry and landscape of Sorley MacLean* [Videotape]. Argyll, Scotland: Eagle Eye Productions/Scottish Heritage Video Collection.

Welsh Office Agriculture Department. (1994). *Environmentally sensitive areas: Wales (Cambrian Mountains extension)* [Pamphlet] (ESA/2 CM). Cardiff, Wales: Central Office of Information.

Appendix A: Terms for Lexis Cards

Specialized Lexis	Everyday Lexis (with bias)
marshy grassland habitat	patch of bog/marsh
unmanaged dry stone walls	tumble-down/broken down/ neglected walls
unenclosed natural rough grazings	unspoiled natural grassland
invasions of scrub and bracken	useless, weed-infested land
unimproved meadows	old-fashioned meadow
poorly drained fields	muddy fields
high stocking rate	overgrazed land
dwarf shrub heath	purple heather moors
habitat restoration work	encouraging wildlife replenishment
traditional farm dwellings	old farmhouses

Appendix B: Simulation Scenario and Role Cards

Scenario: The landscape in question is the site of a proposed golf course development. A meeting has been called for affected members of the public to express their concerns and perspectives and for the environmental impact team to offer an informed specialist response to the proposal, pointing out likely impacts and suggesting mitigation.

Role Card 1	Role Card 2
Proprietor of small guesthouse. Winter income dependent on landscape painting courses.	Farmer owning but not living on 50% of the marshland in question. Currently unable to use this land for stocking because it has site of special scientific interest (SSSI) status.

Role Card 3	Role Card 4 [5, 6, etc.]
Family living adjacent to area designated for development. Relatively low property value. Family places high value on privacy and access to unspoiled natural resources of the surrounding countryside.	Representative of local environmental assessment group. Specialist interest in traditional communities, water courses, woodland, and so on.

Contributors

Rex Berridge, a teacher educator and formerly an English language adviser with the British Council, is head of the Language and Learning Centre, University of Wales, Aberystwyth, in the United Kingdom. Pauline Worthington is presessional coordinator at the English Language Unit, University of Wales, Aberystwyth, Penglais Campus, in the United Kingdom.

Getting to Know Our Working Tools

Levels
Low intermediate

Aims
Scan a text for
information
Use nouns and
adjectives with
measurement units

Class Time
35–40 minutes

Preparation Time
5 minutes

Resources
Magazines with
descriptions of ships
Figures of two identical
vessels
Maritime news column
from local newspaper
(optional)

Following a simple routine of questions and answers, this open but guided activity provides opportunities for oral interaction and negotiation of meaning among peers. By scanning texts, selecting targets, and designing pictures, the learners are engaged in making up their own information-gap activity and are challenged to solve their peer's.

Procedure

1. Hand out to each student a copy of *The Nautical Magazine* (or any other magazine with descriptions of ships) together with a sheet containing figures like Figure A in the Appendix.
2. Have the students work on their own to study the information provided and choose from the magazine any vessel that satisfies the requirements of any figure on their sheet.
3. Still on their own, ask the students to complete only one of the figures by (a) identifying the type of vessel they are dealing with, (b) giving it a name, and (c) labeling the corresponding dimensions with appropriate data (see the Appendix, Figure B).
4. Ask the students to work in pairs. Have them take turns gathering data on their partner's vessel and picturing it by asking and negotiating orally.
5. Ask the students to compare their figures and check whether the exchange of dimensions, numerical figures, and measurement units has been accurate.

Caveats and Options

1. Using both nouns and adjectives to describe certain dimensions (e.g., *length-long*) versus using only nouns to describe others (e.g., *draft*) may confuse the students. Clarify by contrasting such sentences as *The tug is 36.8 meters long, The tug has a length of 36.8 meters, The*

tug's length is 36.8 meters, and *The tug is 36.8 meters in length*, or *The tug has a draft of 2 meters* and *The tug's draft is 2 meters*.

2. Offer pairs who have solved the problem quickly the possibility of making up their own vessels and resuming the activity.

3. As a further activity, distribute copies of the week's local newspaper (in particular, the maritime news column) so that the students can work with data on vessels that are in the harbor and observable.

4. Tailor this activity to technical students in general by adapting the figures to their needs. For example, instead of vessels, give the students sketches of tools and other instruments they need to be familiar with.

Appendix

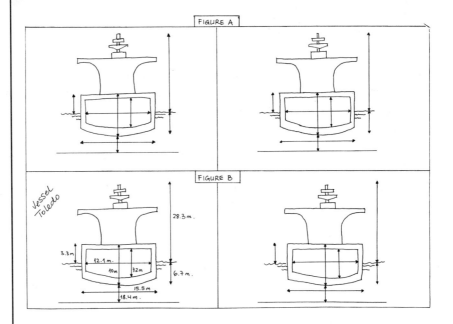

Contributor

Ana Bocanegra has recently completed her PhD and lectures in nautical and marine engineering English at the Faculty of Maritime Studies, University of Cádiz, in Spain.

Minds Meeting

Levels
Advanced

Aims
Work in teams with a
specific agenda
Express a plan as a
flowchart
Write minutes of
meetings

Class Time
1 hour

Preparation Time
30-60 minutes

Resources
Task sheet
Agenda sheet
Meeting agenda handout
Overhead projector,
transparencies, and pens

This activity simulates a workplace project team meeting. It closely integrates several language activities: practicing with professional workplace procedures, using language for planning and decision making, and recording oral interactions in both diagrammatic and written forms. Because the students are expected to produce a flowchart to demonstrate the coordination of a project, the verbal interaction is engaging and purposeful. The homework exercise of writing up the minutes, in which accuracy of form and content are important, is also experience based.

Procedure

1. Devise a task sheet outlining a problem, the solution of which can be addressed by groups and then recorded as flowcharts. Alternatively, use the task in the Appendix.
2. Explain to the students that they will be taking part in a workplace simulation. In a meeting, they will plan a project, a secretary will take minutes, and they will record their plan as a flowchart. The team leader of each group will present these results on an overhead transparency (OHT).
3. Divide the class into teams of four or five students, preferably at tables.
4. Choose team leaders and give them each an OHT and a pen.
5. Give each team member a copy of the task sheet and an agenda sheet.
6. Instruct the teams to select a secretary to take notes and a scribe to draft the flowchart.
7. Direct the teams to spend 20-25 minutes discussing the plan in response to the task sheet and drafting the flowchart, making it as realistic as they can, while the secretary takes minutes.

8. Direct each team to draw its flowchart on an OHT.
9. Ask each team leader to present the team's flowchart, briefly justifying the team's decisions.
10. Direct each team to look at the secretary's notes and clarify anything that is not clear, as each team member will need to write up the minutes of the meeting.
11. Photocopy each team's notes, and give the copies to team members.
12. Assign the writing up of the minutes as homework.

Caveats and Options

1. The activity is most successful with a class that has a professional orientation. It was devised for engineering students but can be used with students of business, computing, and the like.
2. Precede the activity by a session in which you discuss the purpose and practice of taking and writing up minutes, preferably providing a sample or two. If not, do so at the beginning of class.
3. For Step 7, put the task sheet on an OHT to keep all the students focused.
4. Depending on the students' language and interest levels, encourage them to make the flowcharts as detailed as they want, imagining the processes in time and space. If you wish, introduce an element of competitiveness, again depending on the overall class dynamics and your objectives.
5. Note that the team leader's presentation need only be short.
6. Either assess the minutes yourself, or have the students do so.

Appendix: Task and Agenda

Task: You are the manufacturing manager of a company that makes office equipment. Your market research shows that there is a demand for the development of a new product: an automatic envelope sealer. You are meeting with a small, executive project team to plan the project. The group is aiming to coordinate the activities of the following departments: design, sales, production, packaging, warehouse, and delivery. These departments need to

know what they have to do and which other departments they need to cooperate with. Your group must
- appoint a secretary to take minutes (All the students will be given a photocopy of the minutes at the end of the lesson.)
- conduct the meeting in accordance with the agenda
- draw up a flowchart to show the desired progression of events and the coordination of the departments

You will be required to write up the minutes from the photocopy for homework.

Austral Office Equipment
Project Team Meeting
Agenda

1. Business arising

   1.1 New product

2. Manufacturing plan and responsibilities of departments

3. Development of flowchart

4. Other business

Contributors

Rosemary Clerehan, head of Language and Learning Services, Monash University, in Victoria, Australia, teaches both adjunct courses and individual sessions and conducts research in the field of academic English. Glenda Crosling is a language and academic strategies lecturer in Language and Learning Services, Monash University, in Victoria, Australia. She has worked extensively with engineering students and is particularly interested in workplace communication.

A Genre to Remember

Level
Advanced

Aims
Take responsibility for
development as writers
Analyze discipline-
specific written
discourse
Recognize the
connection between
reading and writing
Read critically

Class Time
10–12 hours over a
semester or quarter

Preparation Time
2 hours

Resources
Library and Internet
sources on technical
writing

Upper-division writing courses in EST often serve students from a variety of disciplines, including the sciences, the social sciences, engineering, and even business administration. It is often difficult to tailor instruction to the diversity of writing tasks and rhetorical conventions students encounter in their own discourse communities. Furthermore, students at this level may already be doing a considerable amount of writing outside of their writing course, whether in their content courses, for their dissertations or theses, or even for publication. In this context, they may not see the value of extensive ESL writing assignments. In lieu of such assignments, the instructor can offer this course-long project to involve the students in gathering and analyzing both samples of technical genres from their discipline(s) and other useful resources for technical writing. The students then organize their findings in a handbook, which they can continue to refine and refer to throughout their professional lives.

Procedure

1. Ask the students to bring to class examples of writing genres common in their disciplines, including research articles, abstracts, proposals, lab reports, progress reports, feasibility studies, résumés, memos, and anything else they can find.
2. Lead the students in brainstorming questions to explore and discourse features to analyze in their samples. Draw on technical writing concepts the class is familiar with (e.g., paragraph organization, citation forms, foregrounding and backgrounding of information, treatment of given or new and general or specific information, parallel form, repetition of key terms or topics) as well as specific grammatical features, such as verb tenses and noun and pronoun

usage (see Huckin & Olsen, 1991; Swales, 1990; Weissberg & Buker, 1990).

3. Divide the students into groups of three or four, with each group focusing on a specific sample type or genre. Have the students discuss their samples and identify which discourse features and conventions are common to all their samples and which ones vary among them.

4. At the end of the lesson, have each group report its findings to the entire class. If several groups have analyzed the same or similar genres, see what generalizations the class can draw from the findings of the small groups.

5. Repeat this cycle periodically throughout the semester or quarter. Have the students continue this analysis on their own at home and then collect and label their samples in a three-ring binder. The students may elect (a) to photocopy pages from their samples to mark up or (b) to cut out selections, mount them on the page using tape or glue, and then annotate them. Have the students choose samples that demonstrate particular discourse features or rhetorical conventions.

6. At the same time, ask the students to collect, organize, and label other writing resources as part of their handbooks. Examples include proposal-writing guidelines, helpful articles from engineering magazines, and tips from writing center pages on the World Wide Web. They might also compile lists of discipline-specific count and noncount nouns, useful transition words and phrases, or unfamiliar scientific phrasal verbs and idioms. Encourage the students to collaborate with their peers as well as with their advisers and other mentors, but make sure the students cite all published works.

7. Set aside short show-and-tell times for the students to bring in their handbooks and report on their findings, either in small groups or to the entire class.

8. At the end of the semester or quarter, collect and grade the handbooks as you would a major writing assignment.

Caveats and Options

1. You may want to start with the research article as the first genre to analyze, as the students are usually quite familiar with it and its rhetorical features are fairly conventionalized.

2. To help the students develop their critical analysis skills, encourage them to look for samples of both effective and ineffective writing and to explain why they feel one sample works and another does not.
3. This activity works well as a follow-up to Don't Take My Word for It! (p. 257).

References and Further Reading

Frodesen, J. (1995). Negotiating the syllabus: A learner-centered, interactive approach to the teaching of academic writing. In D. Belcher & G. Braine (Eds.), *Academic writing in a second language: Essays on research and pedagogy* (pp. 331–350). Norwood, NJ: Ablex.

Huckin, T., & Olsen, L. (1991). *Technical writing and professional communication for nonnative speakers of English* (2nd ed.). New York: McGraw-Hill.

Swales, J. M. (1987). Utilizing the literatures in teaching the research paper. *TESOL Quarterly, 21,* 41–67.

Swales, J. M. (1990). *Genre analysis: English in academic and research settings.* Cambridge: Cambridge University Press.

Weissberg, R., & Buker, S. (1990). *Writing up research: Experimental research report writing for students of English.* Englewood Cliffs, NJ: Prentice Hall.

Contributors

Laurie Cox teaches academic ESL at Georgia Southern University, Statesboro, Georgia, in the United States. Ruth Munilla is the director of ESL at Lehigh-Carbon Community College, Schnecksville, Pennsylvania, in the United States.

Techno-Jargon

Level
Intermediate +

Aims
Practice giving clear definitions

Class Time
2 hours

Preparation Time
Minimal

Resources
Strips of paper

Many students quickly learn the jargon of their subject. Some of this jargon even becomes loan words in the L1. However, when challenged as to the exact meaning of the jargon, students are often at a loss to explain it in English. This activity forces students to think about the jargon they use and find ways to define the words in English so that a nonspecialist can understand them.

Procedure

1. Ask your class to identify technical jargon in their subject area. Examples in computer science are *RAM, ROM, mouse, motherboard, CPU, clock speed, DRAM, DMA channels, math coprocessor, I/O card, data path,* and *BIOS.* Write these words on the blackboard, or get your students to compile a list on paper.

2. Write each of the jargon words on a strip of paper.

3. Distribute the strips equally among the members of the class.

4. Tell your students to write clear and simple definitions for the words they receive and to make sure the definitions are comprehensible to nonspecialists. Set a time limit for completing the task. Circulate and help where necessary.

5. When the time is up, ask the students to come to the front of the class one by one and read a definition without saying what the jargon word is.

6. Have the class guess the jargon word from the definition. If the definition is unclear, ask the class to challenge the student giving the definition and have the student try to make it clearer.

Caveats and Options

1. Do the last part of the activity as a game, with points given for clear definitions and for how quickly a team guesses the jargon word.
2. This activity can be useful before having the students write a report.

Contributors

David Gardner is a senior language instructor in the English Centre of the University of Hong Kong. Lindsay Miller is an assistant professor in the English Department at City University of Hong Kong.

New Encounters With Unidentified Functional Objects

Levels
Low intermediate +

Aims
Describe form, function, and purpose of stationary objects

Class Time
10–20 minutes

Preparation Time
5 minutes

Resources
Desk drawer or empty cardboard shoe box

The aim of this activity is for students to practice the physical description of stationary objects and to explicate their function and purpose. A student brings to class a "mystery" object, which is kept hidden, and describes it. The class has to guess what the object is. The object is then disclosed.

Procedure

Preteaching

1. Teach and give the students practice in the description of objects (e.g., *it is ___ wide, the thickness is ___, it weighs ___*) and expressions of function or purpose (e.g., *it is used to ___, its purpose is ___*).
2. Have the students practice describing everyday objects in detail and explaining their function.
3. Have the students practice writing a detailed description of an object as seen by someone who does not know its name or function. (See the Appendix for two sample descriptions.)
4. Ask a volunteer student to bring an object to class to be described in the same way. Ask the student to prepare the description and to keep the object's identity a secret.
5. Before class, check that the student has brought the object, knows the English name for it, and has prepared the description. Place the object out of the sight of the other students, in a drawer or shoe box.
6. When you are ready to start the exercise, ask the student to take your place and describe the object. Write difficult words on the black- or whiteboard if necessary.

7. Ask the class to guess what the object is. Have the student who guesses correctly explain the function of the object, take it out of the box, and pass it around. Tell the class to ask questions, and have the student who brought the object give more information on its use or function. If no one guesses correctly, have the student who brought the object give more clues about the function or use until someone has guessed.

8. Repeat the exercise every week until every student has brought an object or until the class is tired of the exercise.

Caveats and Options

1. Be sure to use an appropriate first object, as it will set the standard for the rest of the exercise. When the exercise goes well, a competitive spirit develops among the students, who produce excellent descriptions. On the other hand, if the students see the first exercise as unchallenging, their interest will wane rapidly (for an excellent description of a shoehorn, see Kempton, 1994, p. 47).

2. Technology students may bring parts of engines, motors, or sports equipment, some of which may be surprising for a noninitiate.

3. If an object lends itself to a drawing exercise, the students bringing the object to class may wish to turn the description into drawing instructions. Be sure that the student prepares these carefully, bearing in mind that the class will actually try to draw the object being described.

4. With advanced students, rename one or two objects or rewrite their description in "techspeak" to practice compound words and "chained" noun groups (Tenner, 1986). For example, glasses are renamed "a stereoscopic image correction system" (p. 51).

5. If your students keep portfolios, have them select the best descriptions and drawings and place them in the portfolios.

References and Further Reading

Kempton, A. (1994). *English for science*. Paris: Belin.

Petitjean, A. (Ed.). (1987). Les textes descriptifs [Descriptive texts]. *Pratiques, 55.*

Tenner, E. (1986). *Techspeak, or how to talk high tech*. London: Kogan Page.

Appendix: Sample Descriptions of a Simple Object

Object 1

Description: The object is made of heavy cloth and either metal or plastic. It is rectangular, long, narrow, and quite thin. It consists of two rows of teeth that are brought together or apart by a small sliding piece. It exists in various lengths and colors.

Function: It is a fastener used for closing openings, especially in clothes or bags.

Name of object: A zip, zip fastener, or zipper

Object 2

Simplified description: The object is a copper cylinder with one end drawn out as a spout. A portion of the cylinder is wider, with some holes on one side. Opposite the spout is a small apparatus made of leather and copper studs, with wooden handles. The leather part is folded and can open and close to allow a controlled airflow into the cylinder.

Function: The object is a device used to tranquilize bees. The part of the cylinder with holes in the copper serves as a firebox. The small apparatus opposite the spout is a bellows attachment used to direct smoke as desired.

Name of object: A (bee) smoker

Contributor

Josiane Hay teaches in the Language Department at Joseph Fourier University, in Grenoble, France.

Briefing From Parts to Whole

Levels
Low intermediate +

Aims
Determine main ideas
and supporting details
Create graphic
organizers for briefings

Class Time
1 hour

Preparation Time
15-30 minutes

Resources
Articles on technical
topics
Overhead projector,
transparencies, and pen
(optional)

By using articles related to their fields of work or study, students can apply the reading techniques learned, develop their critical thinking skills in English, and practice giving oral presentations in a classroom setting. This practice will help prepare them for their professional lives.

Procedure

Prebriefing Activities

1. In magazines or manuals, find an article or several articles on technical topics, such as aircraft flying, maintenance, and electronics. If your students are in the same field, use a longer article with several distinct sections and assign a different one to each group of students. If the students are in various fields, locate several articles, and have each group select the one they feel most comfortable discussing.
2. In class, divide the students into small groups or pairs. Distribute a copy of the article(s) or reading(s) to each group.
3. Tell each group of students to
   ● discuss the topic of the article or reading
   ● decide what the audience needs to know (determining the main idea and supporting details)
   ● decide how they will present the information to the rest of the class in an interesting and meaningful way (e.g., use overhead transparencies or realia, design word maps or webs, make a handout with an outline of the presentation)
   ● create two or three postbriefing questions for the listeners to answer
   ● decide what section each member will present

If the students' reading or speaking skills are at a low-intermediate level, tell the groups to summarize or paraphrase the information and use the result to give the briefing.

Briefing

1. Give the groups 3–5 minutes, depending on the length of the excerpt, to present their portion of text.
2. Encourage the listeners to take notes and ask questions to clarify or challenge what the presenters have said.

Postbriefing Activities

1. Ask the speakers to answer any additional questions that the listeners have.
2. Have the listeners answer the questions that the speakers have prepared, unless they have been covered previously.
3. If time permits, have the speakers ask the listeners to contribute any additional information that they have on the topic. If the speakers have presented a particular problem, ask the listeners to provide possible solutions.

Caveats and Options

1. This activity can be used with any field of specialization (e.g., medicine, engineering) in which the students may be expected to give oral briefings during their academic studies or professional lives.
2. As part of their homework the previous day, ask the students to find an article or reading that they would be interested in discussing.
3. In an advanced class with a lot of experience, create a reading jigsaw:
   - Divide a technical article into the same number of parts as there are groups (ideally three to four members per group).
   - Have the members of each jigsaw "home group" discuss the main ideas and prepare themselves to summarize their segment of the article. (See the Appendix for jigsaw groupings.)
   - Reconfigure the groups such that one member of each home group is now in a different "satellite group." Tell the group members to take turns presenting their portion of the text to others.

● Once all the students in the satellite group have presented, have the students determine the correct order for the various portions of the text.

References and Further Reading

Dörnyei, Z., & Thurrell, S. (1992). *Conversation and dialogues in action*. Englewood Cliffs, NJ: Prentice Hall.

Hutchinson, T., & Waters, A. (1987). *English for specific purposes*. Cambridge: Cambridge University Press.

Kessler, C. (Ed.). (1992). *Cooperative language learning: A teacher's resource book*. Englewood Cliffs, NJ: Prentice Hall Regents.

Klippel, F. (1984). *Keep talking: Communicative fluency activities for language teaching*. Cambridge: Cambridge University Press.

Ur, P. (1981). *Discussions that work: Task-centered fluency practice*. Cambridge: Cambridge University Press.

Appendix: Jigsaw Groupings

Home Groups

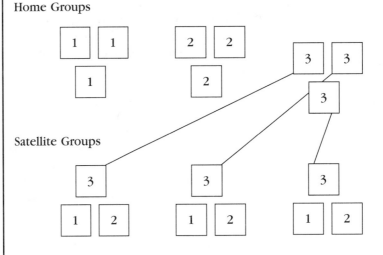

Satellite Groups

Contributor

Lisa A. Hima is an ESP curriculum project officer at the Defense Language Institute English Language Center, San Antonio, Texas, in the United States. She has been an adult education ESL teacher for 20 years in the United States, Mexico, and Japan.

Let Your Subject Do the Work

Levels
Low advanced

Aims
Practice identifying
inanimate subjects with
active verbs
Discuss limits of
anthropomorphization
in scientific English

Class Time
1 hour

Preparation Time
15 minutes

Resources
"Earthwatch" column
(newspaper)
"Science News of the
Year" column (*Science
News*)

This activity helps students recognize how often inanimate subjects with active verbs occur in scientific prose. The students first identify examples of the structure in a text in their own fields or majors and then explain to their classmates why they think the structure was used in that context. In this way, students have a chance to explain why such a structure may not be possible in their native languages, thereby helping overcome their reluctance to use it in their own scientific writing in English.

Procedure

1. Present a brief description, with examples, of inanimate subjects with active verbs (e.g., *A thermometer measures temperature*).
2. Distribute a copy of a recent "Earthwatch" column to each student. This column, which is published in many U.S. newspapers, describes the week's earthquakes, hurricanes, record temperatures, natural disasters, and other natural phenomena.
3. Ask the students, working in pairs, to underline all the occurrences of inanimate subjects with active verbs in the column.
4. When they are ready, ask the students in a general class discussion to tell what they have found. Write the examples on the blackboard, and discuss any difficulties.
5. Distribute a copy of the "Science News of the Year" column to each student. In this column, published every December in *Science News*, a weekly news magazine of science, the news of the year is categorized by field (e.g., astronomy, biology); give the students each a category that reflects or is related to their specific field.
6. Ask pairs of students who are in the same field to work together to underline every instance of an inanimate subject with an active verb in their column.

7. Ask each pair to write an example from their specific column on the blackboard and explain to the class why they think the verb was chosen in that case.
8. Ask the students to find three examples of inanimate subjects with active verbs in their textbooks, journals, or other reading sources.

Caveats and Options

1. Inanimate subjects with active verbs are particularly difficult for students whose L1s (e.g., Japanese) do not allow this structure. They tend to use a passive structure (e.g., *Temperature is measured with a thermometer*) or a wordy circumlocution (e.g., *If we want to measure temperature, we use a thermometer*) in place of a sentence with the more direct active verb. It is generally not a problem for other students.
2. Devote vocabulary lessons to what inanimate and abstract subjects can do, that is, the kinds of objects verbs with inanimate subjects can take. For example, a thermometer can *measure* (temperature), *increase* (reliability), *reduce* (errors), *indicate* (temperature), *record* (changes in temperature), and *provide* (accurate measurements). A thermometer cannot, however, *assess* (temperature), *protect* (reliability), or *prove* (hypotheses).
3. Hand out sentences containing errors with inanimate subjects and active verbs from the students' compositions, and ask classmates to correct them.

References and Further Reading

Banks, D. (n.d.). *Writ in water: Aspects of the scientific journal article.* Bordeaux, France: Université de Bretagne Occidentale, ERLA.

Kojima, S., & Kojima, K. (1978). *S* (inanimate subject) + *V* + *O*: A syntactical problem in EST writing for Japanese. In M. T. Trimble, L. Trimble, & K. Drobnic (Eds.), *English for specific purposes: Science and technology* (pp. 198–226). Corvallis: Oregon State University.

Master, P. (1991). Inanimate subjects with active verbs in scientific prose. *English for Specific Purposes, 10,* 15–33.

Contributor

Peter Master is associate professor in the Department of Linguistics and Language Development at San José State University, California, in the United States.

Becoming a Topic Detective

Level
Intermediate +

Aims
Develop speed-reading
and presentation skills

Class Time
1-2 hours

Preparation Time
Minimal

Resources
Library
Strips of paper

Science and technology students at universities often have difficulty locating source material for their subjects and spend long periods of time reading articles that might not be relevant to the task they have to do. The activity described here helps students refine what they want to know about a topic and gives them practice in doing a library search within a set time limit.

Procedure

1. Begin the class with a discussion of the types of journals or magazines the students have to read in their content area.
2. Ask the students for some common topics within their area of study. Write these on the blackboard (e.g., *building and construction: safety at work, sick building syndrome, geosynthetics; manufacturing engineering: electronic assembly systems, retrofitting, computer-integrated manufacturing*).
3. If the members of the class are studying
   - the same subject, ask them to discuss some of the topics on the blackboard to find out what they know about the topics. Also ask them to try to identify what they do not know about the topics.
   - various subjects, ask them each to think about a topic of their choice and to try to identify what they do not know about the topic.
4. Give the students each a slip of paper. Have them each write on the paper a statement such as *I am going to find out what causes sick building syndrome*. Several students can have the same topic.
5. Check the statements your students have written, and if any appear too broad, get the students to focus them more.

6. Inform the students that they have an hour to go to the library, look through the popular journals or magazines there, and gather information on their topic. Tell the students that they must try to find more than one article on the topic and that they must quickly read the articles they find and write down the main points.
7. Have the students return to class and exchange their information in small groups. Have the students tell the group what they wanted to find out and what they did find out.

Caveats and Options

1. If necessary, do an introduction to the library before trying this activity.
2. Use this exercise to start a larger project on a topic of the students' choice.
3. Spend another lesson on the formal presentation of the topics and on what the students found out in their library search.
4. Many journals and magazines (e.g., *Science News, Newsweek, Time, New Scientist*) contain short articles on scientific and technical subjects that can easily be read within 10-15 minutes. Try to identify these journals or magazines before class.

Contributor

Lindsay Miller is an assistant professor in the English Department at City University of Hong Kong.

Don't Take My Word for It!

Level
Advanced

Aims
Learn the concept of a
discipline as a discourse
community
Interview members of
the discipline
Learn the importance of
writing in professional
life
Write for a real
audience

Class Time
5–8 hours over a
semester or quarter

Preparation Time
1–2 hours

Resources
Interviewees from the
students' disciplines
Interview guidelines

Many graduate students in EST/ESP courses have already encountered difficulty writing in their discipline(s) but are only vaguely aware of what their problems are and how to address them. Years of ESL instruction and ever-more-intricate grammar rules do not seem to transfer to writing tasks done for their professors, for journal editors, and for other professional audiences. By having the students interview these insiders directly, the ESP instructor can encourage the students to see that technical writing involves a struggle to communicate their ideas to peers in their discourse communities. This interview project also solves the dilemma of what to have students write about when they represent a variety of disciplines, because the first writing assignment evolves naturally as the students attempt to present their findings to a real audience (i.e., their classmates). Students searching for ultimate solutions to their writing problems discover that a technical writing course is only the beginning of a lifelong process of honing their skills as writers and professionals in their fields.

Procedure

1. Introduce the concept of *discourse community* in a class discussion. Distribute guidelines for the interviews (see Appendix A), and ask the students to arrange interviews with their advisers, another professor in their department, and someone who is working in the field in a nonuniversity setting.
2. In groups or as a class, have the students brainstorm interview questions concerning the role of writing in their future work.
3. Have the students conduct the interviews over a 2-week period. Ask the students to report informally on the status of their interviews as they take place. Help students who are having difficulty arranging interviews, and make sure everyone is on the right track.

4. Have the students write up the key points of their interviews in an informal report. Encourage the students to
   ● include recommendations for other students who share their discourse communities
   ● be creative and consider their purpose and audience as they select a format that will clearly and effectively convey the information they consider significant, interesting, or surprising
   ● use visual aids, such as lists, charts, and graphs, to emphasize key points and summarize their findings
5. Ask the students to present a short oral summary of their findings in class, allowing time for questions and comments from the rest of the class.
6. Have the students hand in three copies of their report. Keep one copy, and distribute the others to two classmates to read at home, reinforcing the idea that they are indeed a real audience for this valuable information.
7. Respond to the students' interview reports as you would to any major writing assignment, highlighting areas where they have effectively communicated information or applied strategies they have discussed in class.
8. After you and the students have read all of the reports, lead the class in a discussion of the organizational choices students made in their reports and their effectiveness in fulfilling the purpose of the project.
9. Have the class summarize major themes, similarities, and differences in writing across the disciplines and hypothesize reasons for these differences (e.g., between people employed in industry and in the university). Have the students comment on the implications of the findings for them as new writers in their discourse communities.

Caveats and Options

1. The interview project serves as an excellent starting point for a learner-centered course and as a point of reference throughout the course because the students will have had firsthand experience with many of the concepts that will be presented (see Appendix B for a sample course timetable).
2. In our experience, the students' advisers are often eager to talk about their writing experiences, to direct the students to colleagues whose

writing they respect, and to refer them to contacts outside the university.

3. This project is a good starting point for A Genre to Remember (p. 242) because by the end of the project the students will have collected many good samples of important genres in their discipline(s).

References and Further Reading

Belcher, D. (1994). The apprenticeship approach to advanced academic literacy: Graduate students and their mentors. *English for Specific Purposes*, *13*, 23–34.

Hutchinson, T., & Waters, A. (1987). *English for specific purposes: A learning-centred approach*. Cambridge: Cambridge University Press.

Johns, A. (1990). Coherence as a cultural phenomenon: Employing ethnographic principles in the academic milieu. In U. Connor & A. Johns (Eds.), *Coherence in writing: Research and pedagogical perspectives* (pp. 209–226). Alexandria, VA: TESOL.

McKenna, E. (1987). Preparing foreign students to enter discourse communities in the US. *English for Specific Purposes*, *6*, 187–202.

Appendix A: Sample Interview Guidelines

Task

For this project you will interview your adviser, another professor in your department, and someone who is working in your field in a nonuniversity setting. You will ask them general questions about the writing they do as part of their jobs as well as what they like and do not like in the writing of others. Finally, you will ask them for good samples of writing in your field.

Guidelines

1. Conduct a face-to-face oral interview, or a telephone interview if you cannot meet in person.

2. Use the questions below as a guide, and add questions of your own about technical writing in your field. Take notes, write them up in an informal report, and submit the report along with the other materials you collected from your interviewees. You may use a tape recorder if your interviewee gives you permission to do so.

3. Arrange your meetings in advance—don't just stop by. Ask your interviewees if they can meet with you for a short time, no more than

about 30 minutes, to talk about the importance of writing in their field, the kind of writing they do regularly, and any advice they can give you from their experience to help you write more clearly. Also, ask them if they can provide you with any guidelines they use for technical writing and samples of the kind of writing that is done in your field. If you plan to use a tape recorder, ask permission to use it at this time, and explain that it will help you take notes.

4. Arrive on time, and thank your interviewee for giving time to help you in this project. Thank your interviewee again after the interview is done.

5. Don't write your notes on the question sheet, because you probably won't have enough room. Instead, write the question number on a separate sheet of paper, and take notes there. You can show your interviewee these questions if you need to, but it's best if you keep this sheet and ask the questions.

6. IMPORTANT: You don't have to discuss every one of the questions below, and you will probably discuss topics related to technical writing that are not included. These questions serve only to get the dialogue started. Your interviewees will have plenty of their own ideas to share about writing in their fields.

Suggested Interview Questions

1. Your Interviewee's Own Writing
   - How important is writing in your position? How much time do you spend on writing during an average week? What kinds of writing do you do—e-mail messages, technical reports, proposals, feasibility studies, progress reports, memos, letters, instructions, journal articles?
   - What do you do first when you start to work on a longer paper? How do you get started? How do you get feedback from other people? How do you revise your papers?
   - Do you ever collaborate with other people on papers? When and how?
   - For you, what is the most difficult aspect of writing?

2. The Writing of Others
   - When you read a report or journal article, what part do you look at first? Second? Are there any parts you might skip?
   - What makes students' writing (or the writing of others) difficult to read; that is, what are the biggest problems you see in their writing? What would you like to see in students' writing?
   - What suggestions do you have for me as I work to improve my writing in this field?

Samples of Writing

1. Do you have any samples of the kind of writing I might do in the future, such as technical reports, proposals, feasibility studies, progress reports, memos, letters, instructions, or journal articles? Which, if any, do you consider particularly good examples of clear writing?
2. Do you have any printed guidelines for writing, for example, for specific journals, for writing in this department, for writing for a particular course or activity?
3. Do you have any sample bibliographies or reference lists that you could give me?

When You Finish the Interviews

Collect all the writing samples in a folder. Review your notes from all three interviews, and try to organize the information into an informal report. Include any conclusions you came to after the interviews and any recommendations for other students in this class or in your field. Use any format you like—use visual aids like charts or graphs if they help you. We will read each others' reports and talk about the findings in class.

Appendix B: Course Timetable

	Week															
	1	2	3	4	5	6	7	8	9	10	11	12	13	14	15	16
Strand 1	Why technical writing?		Survey of genres I: The research article					Survey of genres II: Short reports, proposals, résumés/cover letters, other genres							Evaluation and synthesis: Where do we go from here?	
Strand 2			Analysis of coherence issues, discourse features of well-organized writing													
Strand 3			Analysis of linguistic forms and grammatical issues in context													
Task 1		Conduct interviews, write up reports	Hand in interview reports, present findings to class, discuss report format choices/rationales					Revise interview reports	Turn in revised interview reports, present to class, discuss revision strategies						Final in-class essay	
Task 2		Collect samples of style guides, genre conventions, coherence issues, grammatical features; analyze, bring to class, discuss						Organize samples into individual writing handbooks		Turn in writing handbooks, present to class						
Conferencing		Hold biweekly instructor-student conferences to discuss projects; work on other content-area writing assignments													Final instructor-student conference	
	1	2	3	4	5	6	7	8	9	10	11	12	13	14	15	16

Contributors

Ruth Munilla is director of ESL at Lehigh-Carbon Community College, Schnecksville, Pennsylvania, in the United States. Laurie Cox teaches academic ESL at Georgia Southern University, Statesboro, Georgia, in the United States.

Get Your Terms in Order

Levels
High intermediate +

Aims
Identify the
relationships among
technical terms

Class Time
1 hour

Preparation Time
15–30 minutes

Resources
Short general-interest,
semitechnical text
Short texts from
students' subject areas
Worksheet

Comprehending special-purpose vocabulary involves more than just understanding particular technical terms. It also often involves understanding the relationships among these terms. This activity shows how students can be encouraged to explore the relationship between technical terms in specific-purpose written texts.

Procedure

1. Before class, choose a short, special-purpose text in a subject area that will be of general interest to the particular group of students you are teaching (e.g., Du Bay, 1989).
   - Identify the key vocabulary items in the text, and use them to prepare a worksheet and answer key (see Appendixes A and B).
   - Prepare prereading comprehension questions that focus on the main point(s) of the text.
2. Ask the students to read the text to find answers to the comprehension questions.
3. Ask the students to discuss their answers to the questions in pairs. Then have a feedback session in which the class discusses the general content of the text.
4. Hand out the worksheet. Ask the students to reread the text and underline each of the vocabulary items that appear on the worksheet.
5. Ask the students, working in pairs, to sort the vocabulary items into ones that have a "kind of" relationship with each other and ones that have a "part of" relationship with each other, as in the example shown in Appendix A. Allow the students to refer to their dictionaries to complete this task if they need to.
6. Give the students the answer key, and have them check their answers.

7. Give pairs of students who are in the same field a short, field-specific text, and ask them to draw up a chart that illustrates the relationship between the technical items in the text, as they have just done.
8. Ask the students to prepare a presentation in which they explain the technical terms in the text and the relationship among them to the class.

Caveats and Options

1. If the text you use in the first stage of this activity is outside of your general subject-area knowledge, consult a subject-area specialist to check on the relationships among the vocabulary items that you highlight in the text you use at the beginning of the activity.
2. Ask the students to examine their texts for vocabulary items that require the reader to understand both kinds of relationship (see Appendix C for an example of how to present such a relationship).
3. Ask the students to write a short, original text using the technical terms they have examined.

References and Further Reading

Du Bay, D. (1989). Direct effects of simulated acid rain on sexual reproduction in corn. *Journal of Environmental Quality, 18,* 217-221.

Halliday, M. A. K. (1993). Some grammatical problems in scientific English. In M. A. K. Halliday & J. R. Martin (Eds.), *Writing science: Literacy and discursive power* (pp. 69-85). London: Falmer Press.

Wignall, P., Martin, J. R., & Eggins, S. (1990). The discourse of geography: Ordering and explaining the experiential world. *Linguistics and Education, 1,* 359-392.

Appendix A: Sample Worksheet

This worksheet is based on DuBay (1989).

The following terms occur in the text you have just read.

apply	dry pollen	pollen tube
apricot	flowers	stigma
cherry	grape	stigmatic surface
crops	herbaceous species	

1. Read the text again and underline every occurrence of these terms.
2. Complete the chart below in a way that illustrates the relationship among these terms.

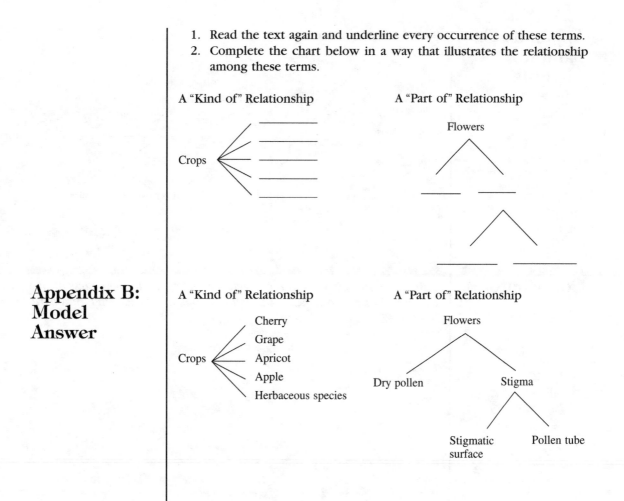

A "Kind of" Relationship

Crops

A "Part of" Relationship

Flowers

Appendix B: Model Answer

A "Kind of" Relationship

Crops

Cherry
Grape
Apricot
Apple
Herbaceous species

A "Part of" Relationship

Flowers

Dry pollen   Stigma

Stigmatic   Pollen tube
surface

Appendix C: Sample Analysis

Both Kinds of Relationship

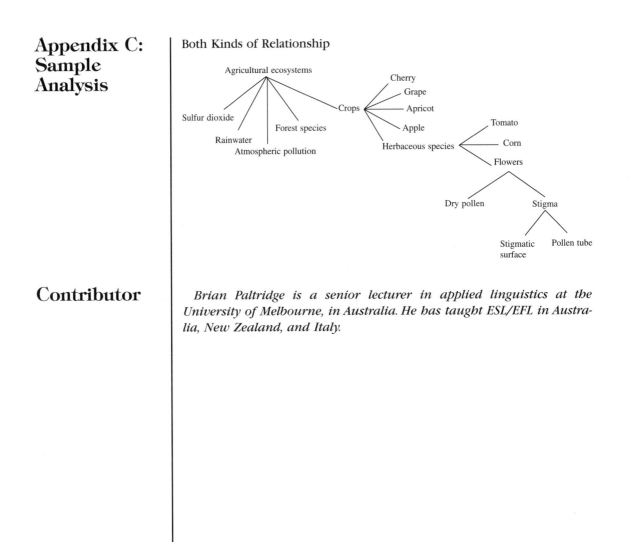

Contributor

Brian Paltridge is a senior lecturer in applied linguistics at the University of Melbourne, in Australia. He has taught ESL/EFL in Australia, New Zealand, and Italy.

Catching on to AIDS

Levels
Intermediate +

Aims
Brainstorm to build a
base of existing
knowledge
Do library research for a
collaborative project
Learn about AIDS

Class Time
2-3 hours +
(preparation)
2-3 hours +
(presentations)

Preparation Time
Variable

Resources
Material on AIDS

Through this activity, students reach an understanding of AIDS by building on their existing knowledge and clearing up misunderstandings and prejudices. Beyond this, they learn how to cooperate with others by planning, organizing, and working on a group research project. The students' reaction is often "Hey, I can do this," as they come to realize that learning can be both valuable and enjoyable.

Procedure

1. Have the students individually write down everything they know about AIDS. Then ask them to write down questions they have about AIDS or aspects of the AIDS issue they are interested in finding out more about.
2. Have the students form pairs and exchange the information they have written down. If time allows, have two pairs join to form groups of four and, once again, exchange information and ideas.
3. After allowing suitable time for discussion, have the groups first report on what they know about AIDS. Do not comment on the accuracy of their knowledge at this time. Any misunderstandings and inaccuracies will be cleared up during the subsequent investigations.
4. Go through the questions they have about AIDS, and write them on the blackboard, or have one member from each group write the group's questions on the blackboard. Once all the ideas are written down, group them into general categories, such as *medical, history, prevention, prejudice,* and *statistics.*
5. Tell the students to choose the topic that most interests them and join classmates with the same interest in a research investigation.
   - Let the groups form naturally; do not force the students into groups (although it may sometimes be necessary to balance the groups).

- Keep the size of each group between three and six members. If more than six students choose the same topic, split them into two groups.
- If you wish, have the students write their names on the blackboard under the topic they are interested in, or designate various areas of the room as topic areas in order to expedite group formation.

6. Outline the group investigation process. Explain that the students are to
   - plan how they will investigate their topic
   - carry out the investigation
   - plan how they will present the information to the class
   - make their presentation

   Ensure that all the groups understand the process, especially if it is their first investigation. (For more information on the stages in the group investigation process, see Sharan & Sharan, 1992.)

7. Have each group summarize the planned investigation on paper, including who will do what and when, and hand it in to you. Use the summaries to make sure groups stay on target and to anticipate possible problems.

8. In the following lessons, bring to class books, pamphlets, movies or videos, and other material on AIDS appropriate for the students' level. Have the students conduct their research and organize their presentations.
   - Encourage the students to be as creative as possible with their presentations so that the information has the greatest impact on the audience. Possible forms of presentation are an interactive speech, a self-published book, a play, or a video.
   - Because of the serious nature of the topic, be careful at this stage that the students' information is as accurate as possible.

9. Once all the groups have finished their presentations, lead a class discussion on what they have learned and, perhaps as important, how it was learned. Point out that the investigation process is applicable not only to the classroom but in daily life as well, and illustrate with some simple examples, such as investigating airline ticket prices or finding suitable entertainment for an upcoming party.

Caveats and Options

1. This type of studying and learning might be new, and therefore difficult, for many students. If you feel that your students might have trouble working with the topic of AIDS, do a group investigation with a less complex topic or with one that is more familiar to the students. Once they are comfortable with the process, move on to the investigation of AIDS.

2. Another aspect of this activity that often causes problems is the sudden change in the teacher's role. The students may find it difficult to adjust to self-directed learning, especially if they are used to treating the teacher as a fount of wisdom. Resist the temptation to do more than guide the students to find answers themselves. Instead of providing answers to the students' questions, respond by suggesting where or how they can find the answer.

3. To shorten the process, eliminate Steps 1-3 of the Procedure. Instead, give the students some general background material on AIDS and then give them the general categories. The groups' first step would be to list several questions that will help them investigate their assigned topic.

References and Further Reading

Kagan, S. (1992). *Cooperative learning*. San Juan Capistrano, CA: Kagan Cooperative Learning.

Sharan, Y. (1994). Group investigation and second language learners. *The Language Teacher, 18*(10), 18-19.

Sharan, Y., & Sharan, S. (1992). *Expanding cooperative learning through group investigation*. New York: Teachers College Press.

Sharan, Y., & Sharan, S. (1994). Group investigation in the cooperative classroom. In S. Sharan (Ed.), *Handbook of cooperative learning methods* (pp. 97-114). Westport, CT: Greenwood Press.

Slavin, R. E. (1990). *Cooperative learning: Theory, research, and practice*. Englewood Cliffs, NJ: Prentice Hall.

Contributor

Christopher Jon Poel, associate professor of English at Musashi Institute of Technology, in Yokohama, Japan, is interested in testing, cooperative learning, and task-based materials development.

Question Authority

Levels
Intermediate +

Aims
Learn interactive reading
strategies
Understand computer
science terminology and
textbooks

Class Time
30 minutes

Preparation Time
Minimal

Resources
Introductory computer
science textbook with
chapter overview
containing topic
headings
Role cards
Overhead projector,
transparencies, and pen
(optional)
Timer (optional)

M̲any ESP students need to develop skills in reading interactively. This is especially true of students in computer fields, in which the ability to postulate and test one's understanding and expectations of concepts, procedures, and operations is essential. This activity helps students who have learned to read English using the grammar-translation method develop interactive reading skills by generating and answering their own questions about the text, in this case *Essentials of Computing* (Capron, 1995).

Procedure

1. Ask the students to open the textbook to the chapter overview at the beginning of the next chapter to be studied.
2. On the blackboard, list the main headings and corresponding subheadings from the chapter overview.
3. Next to one of the subheadings, write one or two questions one might expect to be answered in that section. For example,
   Subheading: The Complete Hardware System
   Questions: What is a hardware system? What are the parts of a hardware system?
4. Ask the students (as a class) to come up with another question for any one of the subheadings.
5. Place the students in small groups, and assign or have them choose the following roles: (a) a leader to keep the group on task and using English, (b) a writer to record the group's ideas, and (c) a reporter to share the group's ideas with the class.
6. Have each group come up with at least three additional questions they expect to be answered in the chapter, using any subheadings they choose. Circulate to help and to explain the assignment to groups that are having trouble.

7. Ask each group's reporter to tell the class one of the group's questions, giving the appropriate subheading. Write the questions on the blackboard next to the subheadings.

8. After all the groups have had an opportunity to report at least one question (preferably one that no other group has reported), ask the reporters for more questions.

9. Write the following instructions on the blackboard or on an overhead transparency:
   - In your groups, find the answers to as many questions as you can in the next 10 minutes. Try to answer at least three.
   - Write down each answer, the page number, and the location on the page (top, middle, or bottom).
   - For questions that are not answered in the chapter (or answers you can't find), write *NA* (no answer) and the numbers of the pages on which you looked for the answer.

10. Tell the students to begin. After a set time, stop the groups (with a timer, by flashing the lights, or both) and get their attention. Ask each group to answer at least one question orally for the class.

Caveats and Options

1. In Step 5, adapt the assignment and choice of group roles as you please; for example, combine the roles of leader and reporter if the students are working in pairs, or add a grammar judge for groups of four.

2. To choose roles quickly, have each group choose letters a–c or numbers 1–3 for their members. Have the members of one group blindly pick cards with the designated roles printed on them, and assign the corresponding letters or numbers from each group to the same roles. If you wish, be more deliberate in your assignments or take the time to allow the students to choose the roles they are most comfortable with.

3. Allow about 5 minutes for Step 6 (possibly extended by 2 minutes if the students are not finished). Ask faster groups to generate additional questions, or allow some groups to report only one question. It is important to keep the activities moving and to keep all the students engaged and active.

4. In Step 7, have the students write the answers on the blackboard.

5. The first time you do this activity, avoid steps that take explanation or that may be more distracting than helpful. However, add more student facilitation if you use a similar activity sequence again; this can increase students' investment in the activity and provide additional practice in related skills.

6. For Step 9, allow 10 minutes (possibly extended to 15) the first time, and ask for a minimum of three answers. However, the time and number of questions will vary with the general ability and motivation of your group as well as your time constraints.

7. To shorten the activity,
   ● In Step 10, simply collect the students' work as an in-class assignment without sharing answers as a class.
   ● Omit Step 7, 8, or 10, or all three.
   ● Have the students find answers only to their own group's questions (and the sample questions).
   ● Assign Step 9 as written homework.

8. To extend the activity, in Step 10 have the students answer as many of the questions as they can.

References and Further Reading

Brinton, D. M., Snow, M. A., & Wesche, M. B. (1989). *Content-based second language instruction*. Boston: Heinle & Heinle.

Capron, H. L. (1995). *Essentials of computing* (2nd ed.). Redwood City, CA: Benjamin/Cummings.

Kasper, L. F. (1994). Improved reading performance for ESL students through academic course pairing. *Journal of Reading, 37*, 376-384.

Contributor

Doug Sawyer is an assistant professor at the University of Aizu's Center for Language Research, in Aizu-Wakamatsu City, Japan.

A Tree for Posterity

Levels
Advanced

Aims
Extract information
from an English text
Use that information on
an exam in the L1

Class Time
1 hour

Preparation Time
Minimal

Resources
Field-specific English
language textbook
Field-specific dictionary
Overhead projector,
transparencies, and pen
(optional)

Although many EFL students at universities have to read field-specific articles in English, they most likely attended high schools that emphasized everyday English, not ESP. Therefore, the students have little knowledge of the specialized vocabulary of their own field and must consciously study it. Even after 10 years of English in junior high and high school, many students experience fear or at least confusion when they start studying field-specific textbooks in English on their own. The following exercise uses materials taken directly from a textbook to show that a rather limited core vocabulary is repeated. Once the students know this core vocabulary, they can extract information with relative ease.

Procedure

1. Ask the students to turn to a new chapter in their field-specific textbooks.
2. Make sure that every student understands all the words in the title and all the subtitles. If some students hesitate, have them translate all the subtitles.
3. Have the students read the abstract individually. Explain any words they do not know.
4. Divide the class into two groups and the chapter into two parts. Assign one part of the chapter to the students in each group, and have the students individually generate written summaries of their halves. (With a long text, this may take 30 minutes.)
5. After the summaries are ready, pair up the students and have them compare their summaries for about 5 minutes.
6. In a teacher-led question session, elicit the main information from the students, and write it on the blackboard or an overhead transparency.

7. Discuss the summary as a whole. Ask the students if they had any special difficulties with the text. Pay very careful attention to those passages that are structurally difficult, and if the students did not understand some part of the text, go over that part with them.
8. If there is any time left, ask the students to compare the information given in the tables with the information in their summaries to see how much of the crucial data can be obtained directly from the tables.
9. Have the students learn all the vocabulary as homework for the next lesson, and give them a quiz on the vocabulary the next time you meet with them.

Caveats and Options

1. Encourage university students to make their own field-specific dictionaries. Many fields advance so fast that bilingual dictionaries are constantly in need of updating.
2. If necessary, supply a terminology list. If the students are really weak in vocabulary, give the list to the students in the lesson before you do this activity, and have the students study the list as homework. Alternatively, elicit from the students unfamiliar words from the list, and ask them to group them into those used in everyday life and those that occur primarily in the discipline. In connection with Lowery and Gjerstad's (1991) "Chemical and Mechanical Site Preparation," for example, a group of students generated the following list of unknown words:

apex	conifer	gain layer
appearance	crack	meristematic
bark	divide	moisture
branch	dormancy	nutrient
bud	elongation	occur
cambrium	epidermal	phloem photosynthesis
carbohydrate	epidermis	pith
carbon dioxide	expansion	precursor
cell	flake	procambium
chlorophyll	formation	respiration

root system	significance	twig
sap	swell	vascular
sheath	tissue	widthwood ray
shoot	trunk	xylem
stem		

3. If the students' level of English is not very high, divide a long text into paragraphs, and have the students summarize the paragraphs in pairs. This will leave more time to discuss the text, and you will be able to spot difficulties more easily and address more problems. However, the longer the authentic texts the students can read on their own, the better they are prepared to tackle entire books.

References and Further Reading

Ahlsved, K. J., Mandeville, H., & von Weissenberg, K. (Eds.). (1979). *Lexicon forestale* [Forestry lexicon]. Seura, Finland: Suomen Metsätieteellinen.

Koskinen, L., Mauranen, A., & Virkkunen, A. (1987). Teaching English abbreviated clauses for Finnish readers. *Reading in a Foreign Language* 4(1), 9–19.

Lowery, R. F., & Gjerstad, D. H. (1991). Chemical and mechanical site preparation. In M. L. Duryea & P. M. Dougherty (Eds.), *Forest regeneration manual* (pp. 251–261).

McDonough, J. (1984). *ESP in perspective: A practical guide*. London: Collins ELT.

Nuttall, C. (1982). *Teaching reading skills in a foreign language*. London: Heinemann.

Saario, H. (1975). *Timber trade terminology*. Helsinki, Finland: Gaudeamus.

Sveriges Skogsvårdsförbund, Tekniska nomenklaturcentralen. (1994). *Skogsordlista forestry vocabulary*. Ekblads, Västervik, Sweden: Author.

Virkkunen, A. (1986). *English reading comprehension material for the students of agriculture, ecology and forestry*. Helsinki, Finland: Gaudeamus.

Contributor

Anu Virkkunen-Fullenwider is a lecturer at the University of Helsinki Language Centre, in Finland.

Fixing Your Roots

Levels
Intermediate +

Aims
Learn prefixes and
suffixes commonly used
in chemistry
Understand scientific
vocabulary

Class Time
1 hour over two
sessions

Preparation Time
None

Resources
Handouts on prefixes
and suffixes

Scientific vocabulary is derived mainly from Latin and Greek. Unfortunately, because very few science students learn Latin or Greek in high school, when they learn science-specific vocabulary they are often not aware of the meaning of each part of the word. Generally, scientific words are composed of a root with a prefix and a suffix. If the students know the meaning of these word parts, it is much easier for them to understand the meaning of new scientific concepts. This activity presents the prefixes and suffixes commonly found in scientific textbooks.

Procedure

Prefixes

1. Ask the students to study the table of prefixes denoting numbers or quantities (see Appendix A). This will give them insight into the origin and meaning of some prefixes they already know from their general technical vocabulary.

2. Distribute the handout in Appendix B. Have the students work in small groups of three or four to match each definition in Box A, B, or C with a corresponding prefix and report its findings.

3. Distribute the handout in Appendix C. Ask the students to think of and write down words formed with the prefixes they studied in Step 1.

4. Distribute the handout in Appendix D. Ask the students fill in the blanks in Boxes A, B, and C with words containing prefixes, using the prefixes in the corresponding boxes in Appendix B and the definitions. If necessary, help by giving clues.

5. Distribute the handout in Appendix E. Ask the students to match the word parts with their meanings and then to use the word parts to make as many words as possible.

Suffixes

1. Distribute the handout in Appendix F. Have the students work in small groups of three or four to match each definition in Box A, B, or C with a corresponding suffix and to report their findings.
2. Ask the students to use prefixes and suffixes to explain new words (see Appendix G).

Caveats and Options

1. This activity requires that the students be familiar with basic terms in chemistry.
2. To help the students understand prefixes, give clues when necessary by providing other words that are not related to chemistry (e.g., *apolitical*, *antigen*, *coordination*, *inferior*).
3. An answer key to all exercises is provided in Appendix H.

References and Further Reading

Godman, A. (1982). *Chemistry handbook.* Harlow, England: Longman.
Sharma, J. L., & Robinson, W. S. (1985). *A dictionary of science.* Delhi, India: CBS.

Appendix A: Prefixes for Number and Quantity

Directions: Study the following Latin and Greek prefixes that describe numbers or quantities.

Prefixes Denoting
Specific Numbers

Origin		Meaning
Greek	Latin	
mono-	uni-	1
di-	bi-	2
tri-	ter-	3
tetra-	quad-	4
penta-	quinq-	5
hexa-	sex-	6
hepta-	sept-	7
octo-	oct-	8
nona-	novem-	9
deca-	deci-	10
hecta-	centi-	100
kilo-	milli-	1000

Prefixes Denoting Quantities

Prefix	Origin	Meaning
hemi-	Greek	half
semi-	Latin	half
poly-	Greek	many
multi-	Latin	many
omni-	Latin	all
dupli-	Latin	twice
tripli-	Greek	three times
hypo-	Greek	less, under
hyper-	Greek	more, over
sub-	Latin	under
super-	Latin	over
iso-	Greek	same, equal, identical

Appendix B: Matching Prefixes and Meanings

Directions: Match the prefixes with their definitions. In some cases, a definition refers to more than one prefix.

Box A

Prefixes	Definitions
a- allo- amphi-, ampho- an- anti- auto- cis- co- counter-	1. acting against 2. on the same side 3. acting together 4. caused by itself 5. without, lacking in 6. different, or different kinds 7. on both sides 8. opposite in direction or in position

Box B

Prefixes	Definitions
de- dia- dis- equi- im- in- infra- inter- macro- micro-	1. through, across 2. opposite action 3. having the same number 4. small 5. between, among 6. great, large 7. below 8. the opposite

Box C

Prefixes	Definitions
non-	1. straight, right-angled, upright
ortho-	2. not
pan-	3. not, the opposite
para-	4. beyond, more than
pseudo-	5. across, on the opposite side
re-	6. joined together
syn-, sym-	7. again
trans-	8. has the same appearance but is false
ultra-	9. all, complete
un-	10. at the side of

Appendix C: Making Words With Prefixes, Part I

Directions: Work in pairs or small groups. Using the prefixes you have studied in class, make as many words as possible. An example has been done for you.

Prefix	Words
mono-	*monosaccharide, monopoly, monogamy, monotone*

Appendix D: Making Words With Prefixes, Part 2

Directions: Read the description and fill in the blank with a word, using the prefixes you have learned in class.

Box A

1. the direction opposite to the hands of a clock: _____

2. without symmetry: _____
3. the force holding two or more objects together: _____

4. the existence of an element in two or more different forms: _____

5. an isomer in which two like groups are on the same side of the double bond in the compound: _____
6. the reaction in which a substance oxidizes itself: _____

7. being without or lacking water in a crystal: _____

8. having the nature of both an acid and the base: _____

9. a catalyst that works in the direction opposite to that of a catalyst: _____

Box B

1. a common surface between two liquids or two solids: _____

2. a large molecule composed of many smaller molecules: _____

3. analysis using very small amounts of substances: _____

4. make less active: _____
5. the opposite of connect: _____
6. the line going through the center of a circle:_____

7. the opposite of active: _____
8. the condition of two rates of reaction being equal or opposite so that there is no further change in a reversible reaction:

    _____
9. not permeable: _____
10. a particle that is smaller than a molecule _____

Box C

1. not saturated: _____
2. a filter with very small holes (for filtering colloids):

    _____
3. a substance that is not an electrolyte: _____
4. a crystal system with three unequal axes at right angles:

    _____
5. a substance that has the appearance of an alum but is not an alum: _____
6. covering all wavelengths in the spectrum:

    _____
7. activate something again: _____
8. the act of combining elements or compounds to make new compounds: _____

Appendix E: What Do These Word Parts Mean?

Directions: Match the two columns.

Word Part	Meaning
aqua	1. great heat
chrom	2. air or gas
gen	3. heat
hydr	4. light
hygro	5. shape or form
morph	6. damp or humid
photo	7. water, to do with water
pneumo	8. color, to do with color
pyro	9. to produce
therm	10. water or liquids

Now try to make as many words as possible using the word parts from the box above. An example has been done for you.

Word Part	Words
aqua	*aquaculture, aqualung, aquamarine, aquarium*

Appendix F: Common Suffixes and Their Meanings

Directions: Match the suffixes with their meanings.

Box A

Suffix	This suffix denotes:
-able	1. a verb that is causative in action (to cause, to become)
-al	2. an instrument or device that records variation in a quantity
-ed	3. a general adjective, derived from verbs
-er(-or)	4. a record that is written or drawn
-gram	5. an adjective that shows an action that can possibly take place
-graph	6. a noun or a verb that describes an agent
-ic	7. a general adjective (*of*, or *to do with*)
-ify	8. an adjective showing an action under the control of an experimenter

Box B

Suffix	This suffix denotes:
-ing	1. a particulate science of accurate measurement
-ity	2. an instrument that measures quantitatively
-ive	3. a verb that is causative in the formation of something
-ize	4. a noun describing the action of breaking down into simpler parts
-lysis	5. an adjective showing an action not under the control of an experimenter
-meter	6. a noun of a state or quality
-metry	7. an adjective by replacing *-ion* in nouns

Box C

Suffix	This suffix denotes:
-ness	1. abstract noun
-ous	2. noun describing the use of instruments for observation in science
-philic	3. device that keeps a quantity constant
-phobic	4. adjective describing a liking for something
-scope	5. adjective describing a dislike of something
-scopy	6. instrument that measures qualitatively
-stat	7. noun of state or quality
-tion	8. adjective showing possession or describing a state

Appendix G: Identifying Word Class and Meaning

Directions: Fill in the chart below.

Word	Class	Meaning
equimolar	*adjective*	*having the same concentration*
hydrolysis		
pyrolysis		
dehydrate		
anhydrous		
thermometry		
chromotography		
polymorphism		

Appendix H: Key to the Exercises

Matching Prefixes and Meanings (Appendix B)

Box A		Example
a-	5	apolitical
allo-	6	allotrope
amphi-, ampho-	7	amphiprotic
an-	5	anisometric
anti-	1	antigen
auto-	4	autoreduction
cis-	2	cis-compound
co-	3	coordination
counter-	8	counteract

Box B		Example
de-	2	detoxify
dia-	1	diazo
dis-	2	disinfect
equi-	3	equilateral
im-	8	impossible
in-	8	inferior
infra-	7	infrared
inter-	5	intermediary
macro-	6	macroscopic
micro-	4	microanalysis

Box C		Example
non-	2	nonferrous
ortho-	1	orthohydrogen
pan-	9	pantheism
para-	10	parasymbiosis
pseudo-	8	pseudoaromatic
re-	7	rearrange
syn-, sym-	6	symbiosis
trans-	5	transition
ultra-	4	ultrasonic
un-	3	uncertain

Making Words With Prefixes (Appendix D)

Box A	Box B	Box C
counterclockwise	interface	unsaturated
asymmetric	macromolecule	ultrafilter
cohesion	microanalysis	nonelectrolyte
allotropy	deactivate	orthorhombic
cis-compound	disconnect	pseudoalum
antioxidation	diameter	panchromatic
anhydrous	inactive	reactivate
amphoteric	equilibrium	synthesis
anticatalyst	impermeable	
	micromolecule	

What Do These Word Parts Mean? (Appendix E)

aqua	10
chrom	8
gen	9
hydr	7
hygro	6
morph	5
photo	4
pneumo	2
pyro	1
therm	3

Common Suffixes and Their Meanings (Appendix F)

Box A		Box B		Box C	
-able	5	-ing	5	-ness	7
-al	7	-ity	6	-ous	8
-ed	3	-ive	7	-philic	4
-er(-or)	6	-ize	3	-phobic	5
-gram	2	-lysis	4	-scope	6
-graph	4	-meter	2	-scopy	2
-ic	8	-metry	1	-stat	3
-ify	1			-tion	1

Identifying Word Class and Meaning (Appendix G)

Word	Class	Meaning
equimolar	adjective	having the same concentration
hydrolysis	noun	decomposition caused by water
pyrolysis	noun	decomposition by heat
dehydrate	verb	remove water
anhydrous	adjective	without water
thermometry	noun	science of measuring temperature
chromotography	noun	analysis in which a colored record is produced
polymorphism	noun	existing in different forms

Contributor

Nada Vukadinovic is an ESP lecturer in the Faculty of Science and Engineering (Department of Chemical Education and Informatics) at the University of Ljubljana, in Slovenia.

Part VII: English for Vocational Purposes

Editors' Note

The activities in Part VII involve English for vocational purposes (EVP). EVP focuses on English taught within the workplace, factory, adult school, or other vocational setting. Its primary concerns are job search and retention, training procedures, tools and equipment, quality control, safety and health concerns, workers' rights, advancement, and getting along with coworkers, employers, and customers. It is most commonly associated with adult school and vocational training centers.

Affirmations

Levels
Beginning +

Aims
Present oneself in a
positive light to
prospective employers
Discuss job-related
personal characteristics
and experience

Class Time
30 minutes
(presentation)
30 minutes (round-robin
activity)

Preparation Time
Minimal

Resources
Black- or whiteboard
Handouts
Flexible seating
configuration
(preferred)

ESL learners (especially those with limited literacy skills or little prior education) often have difficulty finding jobs in the English-speaking job world. One impediment to getting a job is the learners' inability to "sell" themselves to prospective employers. This activity (adapted from Brinton, 1989a, p. 32) exposes learners to useful phrases that can help highlight their positive characteristics and inform employers of their job-related skills. It allows them to practice these "affirmations" with their classmates in a round-robin configuration.

Procedure

1. Begin the activity by asking the students what types of jobs they currently have and how long they have held these jobs. List the jobs on the blackboard.
2. Ask the students if any of them are currently job searching, and encourage them to relate their job-hunting and interviewing experiences.
3. Explain the goal of the activity: to learn how to highlight personal qualifications and job skills for a prospective employer.
4. Distribute a list of affirmation gambits (see Appendix A) to the students, and explain any unknown vocabulary or phrases. Allow adequate time for guided practice.
5. To provide more communicative practice, arrange the students in a round-robin configuration (either seated or standing).
6. Explain the procedures for the round-robin activity: The group will establish a rhythmic pattern by clapping (e.g., clap once on knees, then three times in the air), and each student in turn will have to make a spontaneous positive statement about himself or herself,

keeping pace with the pattern. Practice the clapping pattern with the students.

7. Begin the round robin by clapping and then modeling a job-related affirmation, such as "I'm hardworking." Then, motioning to the student to your right, elicit a similar job-related affirmation, such as "I'm reliable."

8. Continue the activity in a similar vein until all the students have had a chance to contribute an affirmation.

9. If the students are still interested, begin the activity again, with the caveat that the students must use a different affirmation each time.

10. Review any affirmations that caused special difficulty (e.g., errors in grammar or pronunciation).

Caveats and Options

1. Clapping or snapping fingers helps keep the pace of the activity lively and lends an element of authenticity in the sense that the students gain practice in spontaneously highlighting their positive characteristics.

2. Because in an actual interview the students will be "under fire," they need to have fluent command of the affirmation gambits and be able to pronounce them intelligibly. Allow for choral and individual repetition of the phrases, and pay attention to problematic segmental contrasts and cluster configurations. Rising-falling intonation patterns in statements and in series lists can also serve as a useful lesson focus.

3. To further set the scene, after Step 3 present a sample job interview dialogue (see Appendix B), and have the students practice it by alternating the roles of interviewer and applicant.

4. After Step 3, distribute a handout of useful patterns for describing job skills (see Appendix C), and explain any unknown vocabulary or phrases.

References and Further Reading

Brinton, D. (1989a). *No problem! Aprenda inglés práctico sin problema.* Santa Monica, CA: Media Education.

Brinton, D. (1989b). *No problem! Aprenda inglés práctico sin problema: Teacher's manual.* Santa Monica, CA: Media Education.

Appendix A: Affirmation Gambits

Presenting Yourself in a Positive Light

Here are some phrases you can use to tell an employer about your positive qualities.

I'm hardworking and dedicated.
I'm reliable.
I'm very flexible.
I'm confident that I can do the job.
I like responsibility.
I like a challenge.
I've had a lot of experience.
I'm a dependable worker.
I'm hardworking, trustworthy, and energetic.
I'm energetic.
I'm very trustworthy.
I'm willing to work hard.
I get along well with people.
I learn extremely quickly.
I catch on very fast.
I pick things up really easily.

Write your own positive phrases below:

_____
_____
_____
_____
_____

Appendix B: Sample Dialogue

Interviewer: So, tell me a little about your qualifications.

Applicant: Well, I have lots of experience working as a _____.
I'm confident that I can do the job.

Interviewer: What kind of worker are you?

Applicant: I'm hardworking and reliable. I'm also very trustworthy.

Interviewer: When can you start?

Applicant: I can start next week.

Interviewer: We'll call you tomorrow and let you know our decision.

Appendix C: Stating Your Job Skills

I know how to	type and file. do inventory. use the cash register.
I have done	painting and wallpapering. data processing and programming. facials and manicures.
I'm good at	using a computer. organizing and filing papers. interacting with customers.
I've had a lot of experience	repairing automobiles. operating heavy equipment. fixing plumbing.

Contributor

Donna M. Brinton is the academic coordinator of ESL Service Courses and a lecturer in the Department of Applied Linguistics & TESL at the University of California, Los Angeles, in the United States.

Name That Job

Levels
High beginning-intermediate

Aims
Learn job-related vocabulary
Focus on blue- versus white-collar jobs

Class Time
15–20 minutes (explanation)
30 minutes (game)

Preparation Time
Minimal

Resources
Magazine pictures or line drawings of various occupations
Index cards with names of occupations
Timer
Post-it notes (optional)
Vocabulary handout (optional)

The format of the game Pictionary or the TV game show *Password* can be easily adapted to provide practice with job-related vocabulary. These formats allow for communicative practice with new vocabulary items and related concepts. This activity is adapted from Brinton (1989a, p. 31).

Procedure

1. Begin the activity by asking the students what types of jobs they currently have and how long they have held these jobs. List these jobs on the blackboard.
2. Ask the students if they know the difference between blue-collar and white-collar jobs (e.g., what types of job skills are required for each category). Explain the difference, if necessary, and elicit some examples of each type of job. Write these jobs on the blackboard under the appropriate headings.
3. Select one of the games below to provide further practice, and follow the steps outlined.

Pictionary

1. Divide the class into two teams, and appoint a student scorekeeper.
2. Explain the rules of the game:
   - One member of the team will pick a vocabulary card with the name of an occupation written on it.
   - This member has 1 minute to draw a representation of the word on the blackboard while his or her team members guess the word.
   - Correct guesses are worth 5 points each.

- If the time elapses without a correct identification of the word, this member is replaced by another member of the team, and no points are awarded.

3. Begin Round 1 of the game by asking a volunteer from each team to go to the blackboard and select a card. Continue the round as above until either the job is correctly named or the time elapses without a correct guess. Award points accordingly.

4. Continue with subsequent rounds of the game until all members of each team have had a chance to go to the blackboard.

5. Have the student scorekeeper tally up the points and announce the winning team.

Password

1. Begin by creating a game show atmosphere, ideally appointing a game show host or hostess.
2. Explain the rules of the game:
   - One of the two contestants is the clue giver, and the other guesses the words (in this case, names of occupations).
   - The clue giver draws a card from the stack and proceeds to give a clue to the guesser.
   - If the partner guesses correctly, 1 point is given. Contestants attempt to get as many items correct within the set time limit (3-5 minutes, depending on the students' proficiency level).
   - No word in the word family of the target item can be used as a clue. If such a violation occurs, the host intervenes to disqualify the clue, and the contestants draw another word. For example, if the word to be guessed is *beautician*, the clue "This person makes you beautiful" would be disqualified. On the other hand, "This person does your hair and your nails" would be a valid clue.
   - Contestants do not have to give a clue for all the cards they draw. As in the TV game, the clue giver can choose not to give a clue for a particular word, or the pair of contestants can abandon an aborted communication attempt midstream and select another card. The goal, as in the actual *Password* show, is for contestants to get as many points as possible.

3. Introduce the first two contestants. Establish their roles, and have the clue giver begin the game by drawing an index card.
4. Set the timer, and allow the round to continue until the time has elapsed, awarding points for the number of items correctly guessed.
5. Continue with the next round of the game by introducing new contestants and having them perform their roles as above.
6. Once the second round is finished, pit the "defending champions" against the next pair of contestants for Round 3 and any subsequent rounds. In this way, all members of the class can alternate roles as either contestants or members of the studio audience.
7. Continue until all the words have been guessed (or interest in the activity wanes).
8. Allow the class to vote on which pair should be invited back to the show as the "grand champions."
9. Review any items that the students had particular difficulty with.

Caveats and Options

1. It is highly desirable to have a picture file that depicts various occupations, because many job names will be unfamiliar to the students. As a preparatory activity for both games, hang selected pictures around the room. Ask the students to match the names of these occupations with the pictures by affixing to each picture a Post-it note "occupation label" that you have prepared in advance. (This activity is especially recommended with learners who are still developing literacy skills.) The pictures can also be used to elaborate on the distinction between blue- and white-collar jobs.
2. For more advanced students, distribute a handout of occupation-related vocabulary (see the Appendix), and go over any unknown words.
3. With less advanced learners or learners with developing literacy skills, present a list of jobs that is shorter than the one in the Appendix. Tailor the list of jobs so that it matches those actually held by the students (or those that are within the realm of possibility for them to apply for).

References and Further Reading

Brinton, D. (1989a). *No problem! Aprenda inglés práctico sin problema.* Santa Monica, CA: Media Education.

Brinton, D. (1989b). *No problem! Aprenda inglés práctico sin problema: Teacher's manual.* Santa Monica, CA: Media Education.

Appendix: Vocabulary List

Blue-Collar Jobs	White-Collar Jobs
assembler	accountant
beautician	bank teller
busboy	bookkeeper
butcher	cashier
construction worker	clerk typist
cook	data processor
custodian	dental hygienist
dispatcher	dental technician
driver	dentist
electrician	lawyer
grocery clerk	librarian
host(ess)	nurse
housekeeper	nurse's aide
machinist	pharmacist
maid	programmer
mechanic	real estate agent
painter	receptionist
parking lot attendant	salesperson
plumber	secretary
policeman	social worker
seamstress	teacher
security guard	teacher's aide
waiter	travel agent
welder	writer

Acknowledgments

Thanks to Juan Sanchez for the idea of using Pictionary to practice occupation-related vocabulary.

Contributor

Donna M. Brinton is the academic coordinator of ESL Service Courses and a lecturer in the Department of Applied Linguistics & TESL at the University of California, Los Angeles, in the United States.

A Perfect Match

Levels
High beginning–
intermediate

Aims
Understand job ads in
the newspaper
Activate job-related
vocabulary

Class Time
1–1½ hours

Preparation Time
Minimal

Resources
Handout with
abbreviations used in
classified ads
Index cards

This icebreaker activity supplements a unit on getting a job (e.g., in an EVP or workplace literacy program). It promotes conversation in the target language while reinforcing job-related vocabulary and allowing the students to practice reading and interpreting classified ads. This activity is adapted from Brinton (1989a, pp. 33–34).

Procedure

1. Before class, prepare photocopies of a handout containing abbreviations commonly used in the job section of the classified ads (see Appendix A for an example). Also prepare the materials for the "Find Your Partner" activity outlined in Steps 8–9 below (see Appendix B for sample materials) by mounting each boxed item on an index card.
2. Begin by writing several sample classified job ads on the blackboard. For example,
   - Mgmt. Corp. Expndg. No Exp. Nec. Will Train. Mgrs. Earn $4000/mo. Call 327-3667.
   - COOK, min. 2 yrs. exp. cooking Italian dishes incl. Calamari Fritti. Snd ltr. of qual. to PO Box 7959, LA CA 90095.
   - DRIVERS/MESSENGERS M/F. Over 18. Must have own veh/liab. ins. & know LA area. Full or P/T. Co. bnfts. Call M-F, 8–4pm 747-3049.
3. Ask for volunteers to read these job ads aloud, assisting the students when necessary.
4. Ask the students what makes the ads difficult to read. Elicit from them the meanings of the various abbreviations in the ads.
5. Discuss common ways in which words are abbreviated (e.g., only the beginning of the word is written, as in *exp., veh.*; the vowels are omitted, as in *ltr., bnfts.*; the first letter only is used, as in *P/T, PO*).

Have the students search for other examples of each of these ways from the information written on the blackboard in Step 2 above.

6. Distribute a list of abbreviations commonly used in the job sections of the classified ads (see Appendix A), and go over these with the students, providing explanations for any unknown vocabulary.

7. Ask the students if they know other abbreviations that are not on the list. Write these on the blackboard.

8. Shuffle the prepared index cards, and distribute them to the students. Explain that each student should find his or her "perfect match" without looking at the other students' cards (and by speaking only English). Ask the students to stand up and walk around the room, asking pertinent questions of each other.

9. As a follow-up, have the matched pairs read their cards and explain why they are a perfect match.

Caveats and Options

1. Mounting the "Find Your Partner" information on index cards (with rubber cement or a glue stick) allows you to easily file the materials for future use.

2. Because of the nature of the activity, there may be some initial confusion or chaos. Modeling the activity first (with a stronger student) will help clarify for the students what they need to do.

3. For larger classes, prepare additional cards by looking in the classified section of the local newspaper. (The activity is more enjoyable for the students if they know the locations mentioned.)

4. Also in larger classes, split the students into smaller groups, distributing separate sets of the matching cards to each group. For this to work, you need enough classroom space to keep the groups separated.

5. Pair or group the students to write their own classified job ads using the abbreviations. Have volunteers share their ads by writing them on the blackboard and testing their classmates' knowledge of abbreviations.

6. Local newspapers are often willing to provide class sets of newspapers (especially overstocks of outdated copies). These are an excellent classroom resource and source of authentic English.

References and Further Reading

Brinton, D. (1989a). *No problem! Aprenda inglés práctico sin problema.* Santa Monica, CA: Media Education.

Brinton, D. (1989b). *No problem! Aprenda inglés práctico sin problema: Teacher's manual.* Santa Monica, CA: Media Education.

Appendix A: Abbreviations Commonly Found in Classified Ads

Abbreviation	Meaning	Example
#	number	Send telephone #.
appt.	appointment	Telephone for appt.
bnfts.	benefits	Good bnfts.
co.	company	Growing co.
conds.	conditions	Great working conds.
exp., exp'd.	experience(d)	1–2 years exp.
F/PT	full/part-time	F/PT jobs available.
F/T	full-time	F/T cook needed.
flex.	flexible	Flex. hours.
gd.	good	Gd. starting salary.
hrs.	hours	4 hrs./day.
lic.	license	California lic. required
min.	minimum	Min. 2 years experience.
nec.	necessary	Experience nec.
qual.	qualified	Qual. applicants only need apply.
req'd., req.	required	Class 1 license req.
tel.	telephone	Send tel. #.
veh.	vehicle	Must have own veh.
w/	with	Gd. job w/top salary.
xlnt.	excellent	Xlnt. bnfts. package.
yrs.	years	Must have 2 yrs. exp.

Appendix B: "Find Your Partner" Cards

WANTED babysitter exp. w/ children $8/hr. 651-0987	experienced with children
NEW COMPANY looking for drivers, Class 1 license. Bnfts.	benefits
Asst. CHEF needed. Apply in person. Hollywood area. 650-1534.	Hollywood
Dental asst. w/ exp. needed. Telephone for appt. 909-8000.	dental assistant
P/T bookkeeper needed in small Beverly Hills co. 937-7064.	part-time
Maid. Room/board. Cooking. Good English. Non smoker req'd. 856-6260.	nonsmoker
Auto mechanic. 5 yrs. exp. Top pay. 276-7712.	5 years' experience
Clerk typist. Manhattan Beach. Word processing exp. req'd. 545-5612.	word processing
Real estate AGENT. Sales license a must. Join our team. 828-2106.	sales license

Teachers, exp. in ESL. F/T. Adult students. Call 988-9919.	ESL instructor
Travel agent. Bilingual in English/Spanish. Exc. working cond. 640-2983.	bilingual
Electrician. $18.41/hr. Must have own truck. Contact 537-5250.	own truck

Contributor

Donna M. Brinton is the academic coordinator of ESL Service Courses and a lecturer in the Department of Applied Linguistics & TESL at the University of California, Los Angeles, in the United States.

One Step at a Time

Levels
Any

Aims
Review the sequence of
steps in a job task
Read and understand
the imperative verb
form and telegraphic
speech
Practice task-specific
conversation

Class Time
10–40 minutes

Preparation Time
5–30 minutes

Resources
Detailed list of steps in a
task
Large blank cards (about
5 in. × 8 in.)
Felt-tip marker

This interactive, communicative activity supports limited English profi-
cient/ESL students who are concurrently enrolled in a vocational
education program. It focuses on sequencing the steps of a task and, in
doing so, provides practice in grammar and vocation-specific vocabulary.
The activity may be practiced in English in the ESL class or bilingually and
multilingually in the vocational class.

Procedure

1. Show the class all the steps in a task (see Appendix A for an example
   from the field of cosmetology).
2. Depending on the number of students, their level of English, and the
   level of detail needed to support their vocational classes, select a
   number of tasks from the list of steps. For example, for a small class of
   beginning students, you may wish to choose task Steps 3, 4, 7, 8, 18,
   19, and 21 in Appendix A. With this modification, the activity takes
   about 10 minutes. On the other hand, using all the steps might take an
   entire class period.
3. Write each of the steps selected clearly on a card (see Appendix B).
4. Distribute the cards to various students, and have them stand in front
   of the room and begin arranging themselves in the correct order.
5. When they are ready, have them read and show their cards to you
   (and any students observing).
6. Facilitate a discussion among all the students as to the accuracy of the
   group's sequencing.

Caveats and Options

1. A task analysis in vocational education consists of a list of tasks for a given job and the detailing of each of the tasks. The task list is normally written in the third-person singular, and the task detailing is written in the imperative. A task analysis should be available from a vocational instructor and from vocational education materials. Be sure to consult a vocational instructor and appropriate written vocational materials to identify an accurate detailing of tasks. Vocational Technical Education Consortium of States (V-TECS) catalogues contain task analyses and glossary lists for almost all existing jobs. These are available from a number of distributors, including Curriculum Publications Clearinghouse, Western Illinois University, Horrabin Hall 46, Macomb, IL 61455, (309) 298-1917.

2. When eliminating task steps to simplify or shorten the activity, check with an appropriate vocational instructor to be sure that your adaptation will not compromise safety or accuracy.

3. To maintain a full level of detail while shortening the activity (or adapting it for a small class), simply choose tasks in clusters (e.g., Tasks 1–7 or 18–21).

4. Suggest bilingual or multilingual forms of this activity (see Appendix B) to vocational teachers in order to help limited English proficient vocational students learn the task steps. In addition, suggest color coding bilingual and multilingual cards (e.g., English steps written in black, Spanish translations in blue, and Vietnamese in green).

Appendix A: Examining the Steps in a Task

A Plain Manicure for Women

1. Prepare manicure table.
2. Select and arrange required sanitized materials.
3. Greet and seat patron.
4. Wash your hands.
5. Examine patron's hands.
6. Remove old polish.
7. Shape nails.
8. Soften cuticles.
9. Dry fingertips.
10. Apply cuticle remover around cuticles.
11. Loosen cuticles.
12. Clean under free edge.
13. Trim cuticles.
14. Apply cuticle oil or cream.
15. Cleanse nails.
16. Dry hands and nails thoroughly.
17. Bevel nails.
18. Apply base coat.
19. Apply liquid polish.
20. Remove excess polish.
21. Apply top or seal coat.
22. Dry nails completely.
23. Apply hand lotion.

Appendix B: Sample Sequence Cards

English

> Wash your hands.

Bilingual

> Wash your hands.
> *Lávese las manos.*

Contributor

Joan Friedenberg is a professor in the Linguistics Department at Southern Illinois University at Carbondale, in the United States, and former chair of TESOL's ESP Interest Section.

Climbs and Dives

Levels
High intermediate +

Aims
Define field-related
vocabulary
Ask questions to elicit
meaning, description, or
location
Practice reading skills

Class Time
Variable

Preparation Time
1 hour +

Resources
Game boards
Dice
Place holders (e.g.,
coins)
Colored index cards

Playing well-known games such as Snakes and Ladders that have been adapted to the technical or academic field of the language learners helps them relax, focus, and enjoy the language learning process, especially if they are experienced in the field. These games can also be used as a nonthreatening assessment of the students' speaking abilities.

Procedure

1. Write different types of questions or statements based on your students' field on cards of different colors (e.g., on red cards, questions requesting a definition of a term; on yellow cards, questions requesting a description of an instrument or tool; on blue cards, requests for a correct inference or paraphrase of a statement; on green cards, descriptions of a situation from which a plan of action must be inferred). Laminate the cards so other groups of students in the same field can reuse them.
2. Divide the class into groups of four, and give each group a game board, a die, and a stack of cards of each color. Have each student choose a place holder.
3. Explain that the aim of the game is to get from START to FINISH. Explain and demonstrate how to respond to cards of different colors and how to play the game:
   - The first player throws the die and advances the number of squares indicated by the number on the die.
   - A player who lands on a colored square picks up a card from the stack of that color and responds as indicated on the card. The other students in the group decide whether the answer given by the player is correct or incorrect. If all three, or two out of three, players agree that the answer is correct, the student who is playing

309

moves to the next white square. If they disagree with the answer chosen, the player moves back to the previous white square.

● A player who lands on a white square remains there until his or her next turn, and the next player takes a turn.

● A player who lands on a square with an aircraft (helicopter) in the climbing position must "fly" up to the next level, where the nose of the aircraft (helicopter) is located. If the square where the tail of the aircraft (helicopter) starts is in a colored square, the player picks up a card from the stack of that color and flies up only if he or she responds to the card correctly.

● A player who lands on a square with an aircraft (helicopter) in the diving position must "plunge" down to the previous level where the nose of the aircraft (helicopter) is located. If the square where the nose of the aircraft (helicopter) starts is in a colored square, the player picks up a card from the stack of that color and has to "plunge" only if he or she does not respond to the card correctly; if he or she responds correctly, the player remains in that position until the next turn.

● The winner is the first player to reach or go beyond the FINISH point.

4. Ask the groups to start playing, and answer any remaining questions about how to play the game.

5. Once the students understand how to play, walk around the room from one group to another, making notes of statements or questions that the majority of the students have agreed upon as correct but are not correct. Do not interrupt the games; just make a note of the statement or question.

6. If the students ask for your input because they can't agree on the correct answer, tell them you will deal with that point after the game. Ask them to play on according to the rules. It is important for you not to give any input during the game to avoid interrupting the flow.

7. When most groups have finished, stop everybody and ask them if there are any disagreements that were not resolved. If one group had a disagreement over a particular answer, refer it to another group for an opinion. If none of the groups agree or come up with the correct response, give the correct answer and explain why it is correct.

8. With the class, review any questions or statements that students consistently missed but thought were correct.

Caveats and Options

1. The sample game in the Appendix was created for a group of heterogeneous L1 students in the aviation field. Similar games can be created for students in other fields.
2. Putting the information on the cards in a multiple-choice format is an enjoyable way of reviewing for a test without making the students nervous about what the test is going to be about or how the questions will be asked.
3. Instead of using the board to review vocabulary, question formation, and reading skills, use it to review various grammar structures (e.g., verb tenses).
4. For more advanced student pilots, have one color represent "Radio Calls: After," and the other color, "Radio Calls: Before." The students have to give the correct radio call that would be made either before or after the one on the card that they picked up.

References and Further Reading

Dörnyei, Z., & Thurrell, S. (1992). *Conversation and dialogues in action.* Englewood Cliffs, NJ: Prentice Hall.

Klippel, F. (1984). *Keep talking: Communicative fluency activities for language teaching.* Cambridge: Cambridge University Press.

Rinvolucri, M. (1984). *Grammar games: Cognitive, affective and drama activities for EFL students.* Cambridge: Cambridge University Press.

Appendix: Sample Game

"Climbs and Dives" Game Boards

On the actual boards, the squares would be white, red, blue, yellow, and green.

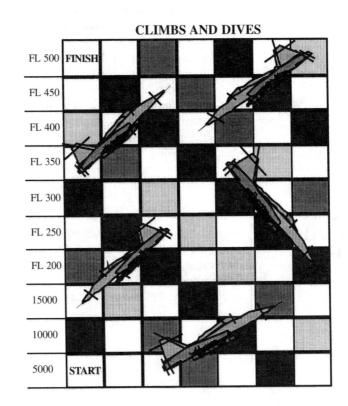

CLIMBS AND DIVES

CLIMBS AND DIVES

Index Cards

- Red cards contain vocabulary terms being studied in an aircraft systems class.
- Blue cards contain statements that the students have to paraphrase.
- Yellow cards contain terms denoting instruments or tools that the students must describe.
- Green cards contain descriptions of situations from which a plan of action must be inferred.

Contributor

Lisa A. Hima is an ESP curriculum project officer at the Defense Language Institute English Language Center, San Antonio, Texas, in the United States. She has been an adult education ESL teacher for 20 years in the United States, Mexico, and Japan.

Mythic Perspectives

Levels
Intermediate +

Aims
Identify areas of
possible interpersonal
conflict in the
workplace
Express concerns about
possible workplace
conflicts

Class Time
2–3 hours

Preparation Time
Minimal

Resources
"The Myth of Laurel"
Bay leaves
Organizational chart
Overhead projector and
transparencies
(optional)

G reek myths are wonderful ways to start lessons on human interaction: Greek gods and heroes display the full range of human frailties. As the stories are removed from religion or ideology, criticizing gods or heroes does not hurt anybody's feelings, so the students can express their opinions freely. As the common strategies for resolving conflicts in myths (turning someone into a plant, flower, or animal) no longer constitute an option, looking for realistic alternatives flows naturally from the material. This activity uses a story from Greek mythology as a springboard for a discussion of personal experiences. In the second phase of the activity, the students extrapolate from this personal experience to workplace-related issues and discuss the implications of the myth for their occupational lives.

Procedure

1. Bring bay leaves to class. Pass the leaves around, explaining that they are dried laurel leaves. Have the students rub and smell them, and ask for comments. Get the students to talk about scents and tastes.
2. Elicit any knowledge the students have about laurels (they may know about laurel wreaths for heroes and the use of bay leaves in cooking).
3. Tell the story of the laurel (see Appendix A).
4. If necessary, teach expressions for agreeing and disagreeing in discussions and meetings.
5. Divide the students into groups of four or five. Ask them to discuss the story and relate it to modern-day life.
6. Have one person serve as the speaker for the group and present the results of the group discussion in one sentence. To keep the students on track, do not allow a discussion of the various results.

7. Introduce the concept of work culture versus private culture or of company business versus private business. If the students have U.S. work experience, they can probably support your information about the strict divisions between the two.

8. Introduce an organizational chart. As an example, use your own institution and its hierarchy. Explain the channels of authority.

9. Discuss employees' rights and responsibilities.

10. To wrap up, get the students to write in their journal (or wherever they do their regular writing) any questions they have about the content of the lesson. This will let you know if any follow-up activities are necessary.

Caveats and Options

1. It is absolutely essential to give the students time to discuss their opinions without interfering. Indicate that you are willing to help with language, but approach the groups only if they signal that they want your assistance with some expressions. Do not volunteer your own feelings and opinions.

2. Like other myths, this story is very dense. It is best used at the beginning of a group of lessons on workplace interaction among colleagues and employer-employee relations. Use it in conjunction with any of the business communication books listed in References and Further Reading.

3. Using bay leaves appeals to the students' sense of touch and smell, making the activity a multisensory experience.

4. Stress the fantasy element in the myth. Make an overhead transparency of one of the numerous paintings that have been made of the story (see also Gordon, 1977). Get the students to imagine that they witnessed the event and to write a letter to a U.S. friend, analyzing their reaction to it. The aim is for the students to express their feelings.

5. Use the activity with other myths (see Appendix B for some that work well in the EVP classroom).

6. Show the short segment from the film *Working Girl* in which the heroine, Tess, loses her job because of the way she reacts to a provocation at work.

References and Further Reading

Gordon, L. (1977). *Green magic*. New York: Viking Press.

Grant, M., & Hazel, J. (1973). *Gods and mortals in classical mythology*. Springfield, MA: Merriam-Webster.

Books on various areas of conflict at work:

Hemphill, D., Pfaffenberger, B., & Hockman, B. (1989). *The working culture book 1*. Englewood Cliffs, NJ: Regents Prentice Hall.

Lougheed, L. (1993). *Business communication: Ten steps to success*. Reading, MA: Addison-Wesley.

Wiley, T. G., & Wrigley, H. S. (1987). *Communicating in the real world*. Englewood Cliffs, NJ: Prentice Hall.

Wiser, F. A. (1991). *Work-wise tactics for job success*. Chicago, IL: Contemporary Books.

Appendix A: The Story of the Laurel

Cupid, the fat little god of love, was mad at Apollo for some reason that has been forgotten. So he pierced Apollo's heart with a golden arrow, which resulted in Apollo falling in love with Daphne, daughter of a river god. As she was not attracted to Apollo, she did not respond to his advances and ran away. Apollo didn't take no for an answer and chased her, trying to rape her. In this emergency, Daphne appealed to the gods for help. As Apollo was a god himself, they did not interfere with him; instead, they helped Daphne by changing her into a tree, the laurel tree. However, even as a tree, Daphne was not safe from Apollo. He kept desiring her, broke off branches, made them into a wreath with which to adorn himself, and made the laurel tree his holy tree.

Appendix B: Myths That Work in the EVP Classroom

Greek mythology deals with the big questions of good and evil, love and jealousy, hatred and loyalty. Such myths are not useful in tackling vexing, difficult situations at work (e.g., "Colleague X always leaves at 5:00 p.m.; therefore Y has to finish the tasks"). However, myths can help explicate other fundamental, work-related issues.

Some guidelines for selecting and using myths for the EVP context follow.

- Choose myths that are short and simple enough to use as a springboard for discussion.

- Use no more than three myths per course.
- When possible, select a myth for which you can also locate a visual representation. Use the artist's version of the myth as a point of departure.
- Keep in mind that the gods and heroes of Greek mythology are not known for political correctness, admirable values, or even plain decency. Sex and power, acquired by murder, treachery, or any means, seem to have been their main preoccupation and the driving force behind most events. Select myths carefully according to the cultural backgrounds and interests of your students.

Here are some myths that work well in EVP classes.

- *Zephyr and Hyacinthus:* Hyacinthus was a beautiful young Greek who was loved by Apollo as well as Zephyr, the west wind. In his jealousy, Zephyr killed Hyacinthus. From his blood hyacinths grew.

  Application to EVP: The students will have no difficulty seeing the benefits of the company policy of leaving one's passions and problems outside the workplace. You can keep your students intrigued with more flowers (hyacinths are readily available), particularly if you want to deal with the romantic or sexual dimension.

- *Laocoon and his sons:* A famous sculpture, which stands today in the Vatican museum, depicts Laocoon and his sons being killed by sea serpents. Laocoon warned his compatriots not to bring the Trojan horse into the city and threw a spear at it. While his compatriots were still standing on the beach talking and arguing with him, sea serpents appeared and killed Laocoon and his sons. The Trojans were convinced that Laocoon did not have his people's best interests at heart and that as a result he was punished in this cruel way.

  Application to EVP: This myth lends itself to discussions of social interaction in teams and the way teams react to members who see problems and difficulties, particularly when everybody else has already agreed on a simple course of action. Class participants will have no difficulty coming up with parallels from their own experience. Marketing campaigns, for example, are often devised without a full exploration of potential difficulties because the desire for success is stronger than the desire to explore all potentialities. The team member who sees the problems is often stopped from contributing and is discouraged, usually having only the satisfaction of being able to say in retrospect, "I told you so." Note that this myth can be stretched a bit to raise the issue of the role of the whistle blower.

- *Jason, Medea, and the Argonauts:* This long and complicated myth has numerous subplots. The bare-bones version that follows is more appropriate for the EVP context. Jason was sent by his boss to bring back the Golden Fleece—a mission that was everybody's dream at the time. The king who guarded this treasure agreed to give it to Jason if the hero could accomplish several tasks for him: (a) plow a field with a team of fire breathing bulls, (b) sow dragon teeth, and (c) kill the army that would spring up from these teeth. Jason won with the assistance of the king's daughter, Medea, who knew magic. Jason and Medea together betrayed the king, killed Medea's brother, escaped, and subsequently had three sons in 10 years of marriage. Then Jason tired of Medea and divorced her for a rich young woman, but Medea killed the new bride and her sons, leaving Jason to regret his behavior. The king, in the meantime, seemed to have lost interest in the Fleece and had established other priorities. Jason could never decide whether all his heroic deeds and all the killings had been worth it.

  Application to EVP: This myth can serve as inspiration for goal setting, whole life planning, and a discussion of loyalty.

- *Pyramus and Thisbe:* Pyramus found his love Thisbe's blood-stained scarf and concluded that she had been killed by a lion. He therefore killed himself. In fact, all that Thisbe had done was to run away and hide in a cave, losing her scarf along the way.

Application to EVP: This myth leads to a discussion of what happens when people jump to conclusions. The students will no doubt note how often people despair at work, feel threatened, or even feel betrayed based on very scanty evidence, when in fact there is no real cause for these feelings.

● *Daedalus:* Daedalus was exiled because he had killed his apprentice, Perdix (who is credited with having invented the saw and the wheel), in a jealous rage.

Application to EVP: This story illustrates the jealousy of senior employees toward their junior competitors. It also hints at the fear associated with technological change and the risk of a supervisor trying to take credit for an employee's work.

Contributor

Barbara Huppauf has taught ESL for many years, specializing in vocational English and workplace literacy. She worked for the Adult Migrant Education Services and the College of Technical and Further Education, in Sydney, Australia, and now teaches in New York for the American Language Institute at New York University and at the Fashion Institute, in the United States.

Get That Job

Levels
Intermediate +

Aims
Understand norms in
U.S. employment
interviewing
Respond to difficult
interview questions
Improve verbal and
nonverbal responses to
interview questions

Class Time
2 hours over several
class sessions

Preparation Time
30 minutes

Resources
Lecture on U.S.
employment
interviewing practices
Frequently asked
interview questions

Employment interviewing is a dynamic interchange between an employer, who is looking for the best candidate to fill a position, and an applicant, who wants to find a good job. Because the interviewer controls the information flow and the decision-making process, it is important for applicants to utilize interview etiquette to their advantage. By reviewing the types of questions employers frequently ask and practicing the kinds of responses they are seeking, candidates increase their confidence, which, in turn, has a positive impact on their job search.

Procedure

1. Give a short lecture on the cultural and business expectations of employment interviewing in the United States. Topics could include the similarities and differences between employment interviewing in the United States and in the students' countries, the stages in an employment interview, or the importance in the United States of an applicant's using certain verbal and nonverbal cues during an employment interview. (Verbal cues include volume, tone, rate, and emphasis; nonverbal cues include body language, eye contact, and handshaking.)

2. Ask the students about their employment-interviewing experiences. Ask them what questions they were asked, and write these questions on the blackboard. Also ask them what aspects of their interviews were successful and how they could have improved the experience.

3. Give the class a list of frequently asked interview questions (see Appendix A). Model appropriate responses to a few of the questions on the list (see Allen, 1988).

4. Ask for volunteers to answer the questions you wrote on the blackboard in Step 2. Note which aspects of the answers are appropriate and in what ways the responses could be enhanced; model appropriate delivery.

5. Ask the students to write three interview questions on a sheet of paper. If they need help, suggest that they refer to the list of frequently asked questions provided in Step 3.

6. Ask for six volunteers to participate in an interview question-and-answer role play. Have the volunteers bring their questions to the front of the room.

7. Put the volunteers' chairs in two lines (three people to a line) facing one another (see Appendix B). Tell the students on the left that they will be interviewers and the students on the right that they will be applicants.

8. Have each applicant tell the class the kind of job he or she is interested in to help the interviewer tailor the questions.

9. Tell Interviewer 1 to select a question from his or her list and ask Applicant 1 to answer it. After Applicant 1 responds, ask the class to evaluate the response. Facilitate the evaluation.

10. Tell Interviewer 2 to ask a question of Applicant 2, and so on. Have the students continue the procedure until each interviewer has asked each applicant three questions or until you believe adequate modeling and critiquing have been done.

11. Put into two lines enough chairs to accommodate everyone in the class (see Appendix B). Make sure that each of the students is sitting directly opposite someone else and has a copy of the three interview questions they wrote in Step 5.

12. Assign one row the interviewer's role and the other row the applicant's role. Have the interviewers in turn ask the applicant sitting opposite a question from their list. With the group, evaluate the response's verbal and nonverbal strengths and suggest ways to improve the response.

13. After everyone in the applicant row has answered a question, have the interviewers and applicants switch roles. Repeat Step 12.

Caveats and Options

1. The activity works best in a group that has built up a level of mutual trust so the students feel comfortable offering and receiving constructive criticism.
2. If your students' cultural training discourages peer evaluation, expect to be involved in the facilitation process for a longer period of time and to supply the majority of suggestions for improvement.
3. Tailor the introductory discussion and question handout for specific employment situations (e.g., hotel, retail, restaurant).
4. If time allows, add a component in which the students work in groups of three and participate in 15-minute interviews. Each person role plays an interviewer, applicant, and an observer (see Appendix C).

References and Further Reading

Allen, J. G. (1988). *The complete question and answer interview book.* New York: Wiley.

Eyler, D. R. (1992). *Job interviews that mean business.* New York: Random House.

Lathrop, R. (1989). *Who's hiring who: How to find that job fast.* Berkeley, CA: Ten Speed Press.

McCabe, D. B. (1995). *Business communication: A practical career guide.* Dubuque, IA: Kendall-Hunt.

Yate, M. (1988). *Knock 'em dead: With great answers to tough interview questions.* Boston: B. Adams.

Yate, M. (1995). *Knock 'em dead: The ultimate job seeker's handbook.* Boston: B. Adams.

Appendix A: Frequently Asked Interview Questions

Are you looking for full or part-time work?
Are you looking for permanent or temporary work?
Are you willing to relocate?
Can I get recommendations from your previous employers?
Can you give an example that shows initiative and your willingness to work?

Can you work under pressure?
Describe a difficult problem you had to deal with.
Do you have a degree?

Do you have any questions?
Do you like regular hours?

Do you like routine work?
Do you prefer working by yourself or with others?
Do you think grades should be considered by first-rate employers?
Have you done the best work you are capable of doing?
Have you ever had difficulty getting along with others?

How do you feel about overtime work?
How did you get your last job?
How did you get your summer jobs?
How did your previous employers treat you?
How do you feel about your progress to date?

How do you handle rejection?
How long did you stay at your last job?
How long would you stay with our company?
How much experience do you have?
I would like to hear about a time that you experienced pressure on the job.
In hindsight, what have you done that you wish you had done differently?

In what areas do you believe your supervisor could have done a better job?
In what type of position are you most interested?
In what ways has your job prepared you to take on greater responsibilities?
Is there someone we can contact who is familiar with your experience?
See this pen I'm holding? Sell it to me.

Tell me a story.
Tell me about a time you put your foot in your mouth.
Tell me about yourself.
Tell me how you moved up in your last job.
To give a balanced view, tell me about a situation that didn't work out too
    well.

What are the disadvantages of working in this field?

What are you most proud of?

What are some of the things about your supervisor you disliked?

What are some of the things about which you and your supervisor disagreed?

What are you looking for in your next job?

What are your biggest accomplishments?

What are your future educational goals?

What are your future vocational plans?

What are your hobbies and interests outside work?

What are your ideas about salary?

What are your qualifications?

What are your short- and long-term goals?

What aspects of your job do you consider most important?

What can you do for us that someone else cannot do?

What courses did you like best? Why? What courses did you like least? Why?

What do you expect to gain from this position in our company?

What do you feel is a satisfactory attendance record?

What do you know about opportunities in this field?

What do you know about our company?

What do you think determines a person's progress in a company?

What do you want to be remembered for?

What have you learned from your previous jobs?

What is the most difficult situation you have ever faced?

What is your major strength?

What is your major weakness?

What is your most memorable moment?

What job in our company would you choose if you were free to do so?

What jobs have you held? Why did you leave?

What kind of boss do you prefer?
What kind of compensation are you looking for?

What kind of decision is difficult for you?
What kinds of things do you worry about?
What personal characteristics are necessary for success in this field?
What qualifications do you believe will make you successful in this job?
Where do you see yourself five years from now?

Which of your years in school was the most difficult?
Which jobs did you enjoy most? Why?
Why do you think you want to work for our company?
Why do you think you would like this particular type of job?
Why do you want to leave your current job? Why did you leave your last job?

Why have you changed jobs so frequently?
Why isn't your grade point average listed on your résumé?
Why should I consider an outsider when I could fill the job with someone from inside the organization?
Why should I hire you?

Why were you fired?
Why were you out of work for so long?

Appendix B: Positions for the Role Plays

Positioning the Six Role-Play Volunteers

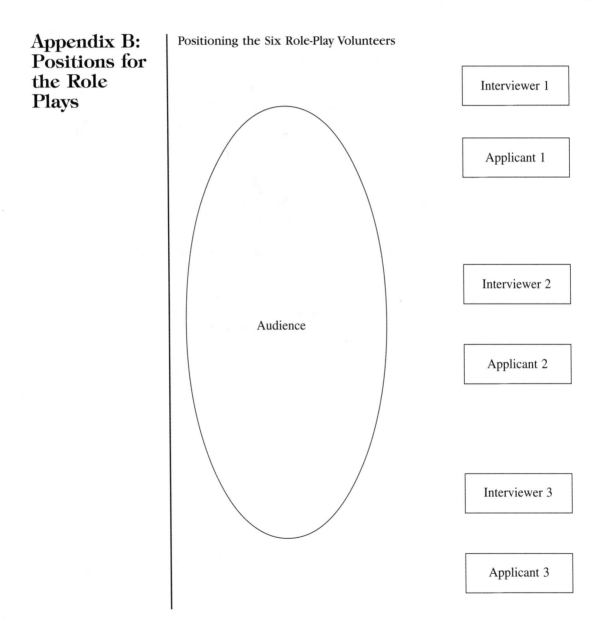

Appendix C: Mock Interview Procedures

Positioning the Entire Class for Interviewing

Interviewers

Applicants

1. Before the role play, assign the students to groups of three. Try to combine individuals whose job interests are similar. Have the three members of each group sit together.
2. Tell the group members that they will alternate the roles of interviewer, applicant, and observer. Tell each group to decide on roles for the following role plays:
   - Round 1: A interviews B; C observes.
   - Round 2: B interviews C; A observes.
   - Round 3: C interviews A; B observes.
3. Simultaneously, have the As in each group discuss with their partners the type of work they are interested in, the position they will be applying for in the mock interview, and any academic or practical experience they have in this field. (If the students are required to complete résumés for the class, have the students give their partners a copy of their résumé.)
4. For homework, ask the group members to prepare a minimum of 15 questions for their applicant. The questions should be based on the in-class discussion and interview practice as well as on the information learned about the partner in Step 3.
5. Tell the students to dress appropriately the day of the interview. Remind them that the applicant's "looking the part" affects an interviewer's perceptions.
6. On the day of the interview, have the groups of three assemble themselves around the classroom.
7. Ask the groups to decide who will be the interviewer first. When they have decided, ask each of the pairs of interviewers and applicants to stand.
8. Tell the groups that they have 15 minutes to complete the interview and that you will give them a reminder at 13 minutes by saying "13"

aloud, as well as saying "15" when the time has ended. Tell them that they must keep asking questions for the entire 15 minutes.

9. At the end of Round 1, encourage the interviewer and observer in every group to make comments to the applicant on aspects of the responses that were effective and ways the responses could be improved.

10. Repeat Steps 8 and 9 for Rounds 2 and 3.

11. Bring the entire group together and debrief the exercise. Ask questions like the following:

- Was this type of interview easier or harder than a real one? Why?
- What was the most difficult question you were asked?
- What did you think was the best response you heard in your group? Why?
- What did you witness a group member do or say that you would like to incorporate in your future interviews?

Contributor

Deborah Brown McCabe is a professor in the Marketing Department at California State University, Hayward, in the United States, where she developed and teaches a business communication course for nonnative English speakers.

When All Else Fails, Read the Directions

Levels
Intermediate

Aims
Understand and give
directions for a complex
procedure

Class Time
2 hours on two separate
days

Preparation Time
1 hour

Resources
Multistep procedures
common to students'
professions
Vocational manual

Vocational students are often required to learn complex procedures in their fields from oral or written explanations. This problem-solving activity practices the language and cognitive skills necessary to understand and communicate detailed sequencing.

Procedure

Day 1

1. Introduce the procedure to be discussed (e.g., its context, its purpose, the materials needed).
2. Hand out a scrambled version of the procedure (see the Appendix for two examples).
3. Ask the students to individually order the procedure by writing numbers next to each step.
4. Have the students compare their answers with those of another student and discuss the logic behind their sequencing.
5. Elicit the order of the steps from two or three students, and write their sequences on the blackboard in vertical columns.
6. Write the correct sequence on the blackboard next to the students' answers, and discuss the logic of the standard procedure.

Day 2

1. Demonstrate another procedure related to the students' vocation (e.g., taking blood pressure). Elicit help from students who are familiar with the procedure.
2. Ask the students to demonstrate their understanding of the procedure for the class, following your verbal instructions or those of another student.

3. Ask each student to write out instructions for the procedure, including at least eight steps.
4. Have the students compare their sequencing of the instructions with that of other students.
5. Write three of the students' procedures on the blackboard, discuss the differences among them, and compare the students' instructions with a standard example from a vocational manual.

Caveats and Options

1. In preparing students for nursing assistant training, we use this activity with procedures found in nursing assistant texts—such as weighing a patient, changing a patient's dressing, taking temperature, and taking blood pressure—that are common in the students' chosen occupations.
2. Be sure the selected procedure is readily identifiable as important for the students' field. This will permit you to use more difficult activities because the high face validity motivates the students to invest more thought and effort in the activity.
3. Choose a procedure that has some steps whose order can be debated as well as some steps that must be in a certain order. This promotes discussion and facilitates an explicit comparison of the students' assumptions with those of the text or other source material.

References and Further Reading

Gillogly, B. (1991). *The new nursing assistant.* Sacramento, CA: The Quality Care Health Foundation.

Appendix: Sample Procedures

Scrambled Instructions

Directions: Put a number in each blank to indicate the correct order.

Dressings

Dressings come in several different sizes. The size used depends on the size of the area to be covered. *Gauze* is the most common type of dressing material. Rayon strips, absorbent cotton pads, and Telfa pads are also used. Different types of tape are available to hold the dressing on the resident's skin. When applying a dressing to an elderly resident, choose the type of tape which is most easily removed to prevent damaging the fragile skin. When applying a clean, dry dressing, the following procedure should be used:

_____ Explain to the resident what you are going to do.

_____ Dispose of the bag in the infectious waste can and replace equipment.

_____ Open the dressing package, being careful not to touch the dressing.

_____ Wash your hands.

_____ Apply the new dressing, being careful not to touch the portion which will be in contact with the residents' sore skin.

_____ Assemble the necessary equipment: clean dressing, tape, scissors, plastic bag for infectious waste.

_____ Wash your hands.

_____ Thoroughly cleanse and dry the affected area.

_____ Cut strips of tape.

_____ Apply tape, covering the ends of the dressing. If tape is applied over a joint, place it across the joint, not parallel to it.

_____ Remove the old dressing and place in infectious waste bag for disposal.

Unscrambled Instructions

Dressings[1]

Dressings come in several different sizes. The size used depends on the size of the area to be covered. *Gauze* is the most common type of dressing material. Rayon strips, absorbent cotton pads, and Telfa pads are also used. Different types of tape are available to hold the dressing on the resident's skin. When applying a dressing to an elderly resident, choose the type of tape which is most easily removed to prevent damaging the fragile skin. When applying a clean, dry dressing, the following procedure should be used:

1. Assemble the necessary equipment: clean dressing, tape, scissors, plastic bag for infectious waste.
2. Explain to the resident what you are going to do.
3. Wash your hands.
4. Open the dressing package, being careful not to touch the dressing.
5. Cut strips of tape.
6. Remove the old dressing and place in infectious waste bag for disposal.
7. Thoroughly cleanse and dry the affected area.

[1]From *The New Nursing Assistant* (3rd ed., p. 192), by B. Gillogly, 1991, Sacramento, CA: The Quality Care Health Foundation. Copyright © 1991 by the Quality Care Health Foundation. Reprinted with permission.

8. Apply the new dressing, being careful not to touch the portion which will be in contact with the resident's sore skin.

9. Apply tape, covering the ends of the dressing. If tape is applied over a joint, place it across the joint, not parallel to it.

10. Dispose of the bag in the infectious waste can and replace equipment.

11. Wash your hands.

Scrambled Instructions

Directions: Put a number in each blank to indicate the correct order.

Oral Temperature

The proper procedure for measuring an oral temperature is as follows:

_____ Explain to the resident what you are going to do.

_____ With glass thermometer, shake mercury down by holding thermometer between your thumb and forefinger and shaking with a snapping motion of the wrist, away from furniture and equipment.

_____ Inspect glass thermometer. Never use a chipped or cracked thermometer.

_____ If using a digital thermometer, place disposable sleeve over thermometer.

_____ For glass thermometer, remove and observe the tip of the column of mercury. It will be easier to read if you stand with your back to the light source.

_____ Wash your hands.

_____ If glass thermometer has been soaking in disinfectant, rinse with cool water and dry with paper towel.

_____ If using a digital thermometer, read the digital display. Then remove thermometer and dispose of sleeve.

_____ For glass thermometer, leave in place for at least 5 minutes. The temperature is more accurate if left in place for 8 minutes. For digital thermometer, leave in place until beep or buzzer sounds. *Never* leave the resident with a thermometer in place.

_____ Place bulb end of thermometer under resident's tongue and ask resident to keep mouth closed.

Unscrambled Instructions

Oral Temperature[2]

The proper procedure for measuring an oral temperature is as follows:

1. Wash your hands.
2. Explain to the resident what you are going to do.
3. If glass thermometer has been soaking in disinfectant, rinse with cool water and dry with paper towel.
4. Inspect glass thermometer. Never use a chipped or cracked thermometer.
5. With glass thermometer, shake mercury down by holding thermometer between your thumb and forefinger and

---

[2]From *The New Nursing Assistant* (3rd ed., p. 217), by B. Gillogly, 1991, Sacramento, CA: The Quality Care Health Foundation. Copyright © 1991 by the Quality Care Health Foundation. Reprinted with permission.

shaking with a snapping motion of the wrist, away from furniture and equipment. If using a digital thermometer, place disposable sleeve over thermometer.

6. Place bulb end of thermometer under resident's tongue and ask resident to keep mouth closed.

7. For glass thermometer, leave in place for at least 5 minutes. The temperature is more accurate if left in place for 8 minutes. For digital thermometer, leave in place until beep or buzzer sounds. *Never* leave the resident with a thermometer in place.

8. For glass thermometer, remove and observe the tip of the column of mercury. It will be easier to read if you stand with your back to the light source. If using a digital thermometer, read the digital display. Then remove thermometer and dispose of sleeve.

Contributors

Kristi Webster McGhee coordinated a vocational ESL bridge program in Hollywood, California, for 4 years. She currently teaches EFL at George Washington University, Washington, DC, in the United States. Steve Rothkrug works part-time in the Los Angeles Community College District, California, in the United States, teaching both ESL and machine technology. His interests include transitioning students from ESL to post-ESL classes and programs.

Parachute Debate

Levels
Any

Aims
Develop fluency
through role play
Identify characteristics
of an ideal job
Practice language of
persuasion

Class Time
35-45 minutes

Preparation Time
None

Resources
None

This activity adapts a popular values clarification activity to the EVP classroom. Individuals choose their roles in the initial stage of the activity. They are given time to prepare reasons to support their choice of the ideal job before the debating stage.

Procedure

1. Ask the students to write down their ideal job. At advanced levels, encourage the students to be specific about their role in a particular institution, company, or organization.
2. Ask the students to write down five reasons why their choice is ideal.
3. Form groups of seven or eight students. Set the following scene: They are members of a corporation who are traveling together on a small company plane when it develops engine trouble. There is nowhere to make an emergency landing. The pilot tells them they must evacuate the plane before it crashes. He takes one parachute, and only five parachutes are left. Only five members of the group can possibly survive.
4. Give each student 3 minutes to persuade the others in the group that he or she should have a parachute because of his or her role in the company.
5. Have the groups reach a consensus on who survives. Have them report back to the class on the outcome of the group discussions.

Caveats and Options

1. Asking the students to choose their ideal job before knowing the scenario encourages them to make real personal choices rather than those shaped by the task.
2. Follow up with a list of 10 characteristics of the ideal job. Have the students discuss the list in groups, choose five characteristics, rank them in order of importance, and report back. The outcome of this task is often influenced by cultural factors and is particularly effective with multicultural groups.

Contributor

Teresa Thiel is a lecturer in the BEd TESL program in the Faculty of Education, University of Malaya, Kuala Lumpur, in Malaysia.